WONDER WOMAN AND PHILOSOPHY

THE AMAZONIAN MYSTIQUE

Edited by Jacob M. Held

University of Central Arkansas, AR, US

WILEY Blackwell

Registered Offices
John Wiley & Sons, Inc., 111 River Street, Hoboken, NJ 07030, USA
John Wiley & Sons Ltd, The Atrium, Southern Gate, Chichester, West Sussex, PO19 8SQ, UK

Editorial Office
9600 Garsington Road, Oxford, OX4 2DQ, UK

For details of our global editorial offices, customer services, and more information about Wiley products visit us at www.wiley.com.

Wiley also publishes its books in a variety of electronic formats and by print-on-demand. Some content that appears in standard print versions of this book may not be available in other formats.

Library of Congress Cataloging-in-Publication Data applied for

Paperback ISBN: 9781119280750

Cover image: STARS © TRACEY QUIRK / EYEEM / GETTY IMAGES; GOLD PAPER © KATSUMI MUROUCHI / GETTY IMAGES; METAL © MFTO / GETTY IMAGES

Set in 10.5/13pt SabonLTStd by Aptara Inc., New Delhi, India

Printed in Singapore by C.O.S. Printers Pte Ltd

10 9 8 7 6 5 4 3 2 1

Dedicated to my wife, Jennifer, who truly is Wonder Woman, even if she refuses to wear the outfit.

Contents

Contributors: The Myndi Mayer Foundation

Mónica Cano Abadía is an Associate Professor of Philosophy at the University of Zaragoza (Spain). Her doctoral dissertation focused on the philosophy of Judith Butler and the possibilities for social transformation. She is a feminist activist who has loved Wonder Woman ever since she read All Star Comics #8. Already being a fan of superheroes, this issue opened a whole new perspective: there were superheroines out there, fighting villains and heteropatriarchy at the same time! It's no wonder that she has also become a teacher of feminist self-defense. Her recent research interests include global justice and migrations, intersectional theory, new materialisms and posthumanisms.

Adam Barkman is a philosopher and author of five books, including *Making Sense of Islamic Art and Architecture* (Thames and Hudson, 2015), and the co-editor of four books on philosophy, film, and pop culture, most recently *Downton Abbey and Philosophy* (Open Court, 2015). Although Adam's wife doesn't claim to be a superhero, she is remarkably efficient at washing their daughter Katie's favorite Wonder Woman shirt every day so it's ready for another day of heroics.

Steve Bein is Assistant Professor of Philosophy at the University of Dayton, where he is a specialist in Asian thought, primarily Japanese and Chinese philosophy. He is a contributor to *The Ultimate Star Trek and Philosophy* and *LEGO and Philosophy*, and he is also an award-winning author of science fiction and fantasy. Despite his repeated attempts, no matter how often he spins in place he has never once managed to transmogrify himself into a scantily clad Lynda Carter.

Matthew William Brake graduated from Regent University with a Master's of Divinity in 2009. Currently, he is going to George Mason University in Fairfax, VA to pursue an MA in interdisciplinary studies with an emphasis on religion, cultures, and values and an MA in philosophy. In the past, his research has focused on the relationship between Søren Kierkegaard and mysticism, and he has written numerous articles for the series *Kierkegaard Research: Sources, Reception, Resources*. He gets terrified whenever he thinks about going for a PhD and could use some of Wonder Woman's courage!

Like Elizabeth Holloway Marston, the real-life inspiration for Wonder Woman, **Maria Chavez** is a graduate of Mount Holyoke College. She's also happy to see Grant Morrison's Wonder Woman returning back to her feminist and kinky roots. When Wonder Woman asks, "Isn't it more fun to make the man obey?" Maria would respond, "Yes it is, Wonder Woman. Yes it is!"

Roy T. Cook is CLA Scholar of the College and Professor of Philosophy at the University of Minnesota—Twin Cities. He is the author of *The Yablo Paradox: An Essay on Circularity* (Oxford, 2014) and *Key Concept in Philosophy: Paradoxes* (Polity, 2013) and the co-editor of *The Art of Comics: A Philosophical Approach* (with Aaron Meskin, Wiley-Blackwell, 2012), the *Routledge Companion to Comics* (with Aaron Meskin and Frank Bramlett, Routledge, 2016), and *LEGO and Philosophy* (with Sondra Bacharach, Wiley-Blackwell, forthcoming).

Sarah K. Donovan is an Associate Professor of Philosophy at Wagner College. Her teaching and research interests include community-based, feminist, social, moral, and Continental philosophy. While she is not known for her keen fashion sense, she still thinks a twenty-first-century Wonder Woman really should ask, while looking at her outfit in the mirror, "Would Tim Gunn say 'make it work'?"

Chris Gavaler is an Assistant Professor of English at Washington and Lee University. His book *On the Origin of Superheroes* was published by the University of Iowa Press in 2015, and he has collaborated with

Nathaniel Goldberg on essays in the *Journal of Pop Culture*; *Foundation: The International Review of Science Fiction*; *Batman, Superman, and Philosophy*; and *The X-Files and Philosophy*. His sense of humor was accidentally erased during the last reboot.

Nathaniel Goldberg teaches philosophy at Washington and Lee University. He's written an academic book called *Kantian Conceptual Geography*, and with Chris Gavaler is writing a popular book called *With Great Power: How Superhero Comics Channel and Challenge Philosophy*. Like Wonder Woman, he was originally named "Suprema."

Jacob M. Held is Associate Professor of Philosophy and Director of the UCA Core at the University of Central Arkansas in Conway, AR. He is also the general editor of the "Great Authors and Philosophy" series with Rowman and Littlefield, and editor of *Stephen King and Philosophy*, the inaugural volume in that series. And although psychotherapy could probably adequately explain his fascination with Wonder Woman, that's one area where he's happy living an unexamined life.

Allie Hernandez is a sophomore at Health Careers High School in San Antonio, TX. She is an avid reader, writer, and illustrator of graphic novels and the superhero genre. Allie has even created her own female superhero, Domino. When she isn't drawing or reading, she is probably engaging in her other loves: music, food, and sleep.

Jill Hernandez is an Associate Professor of Philosophy at the University of Texas at San Antonio, and specializes in topics at the intersection of ethics, early modern philosophy, and philosophy of religion. She is the author of *Early Modern Women and the Problem of Evil: Atrocity and Theodicy* (2016), *Gabriel Marcel's Ethics of Hope: Evil, God, and Virtue* (2013), and the editor of *The New Intuitionism* (2012). Mostly, though, she fights evil with her Super Crew—Gustavo, Allie, and Sofie … and Sofie's wonderbunny, Puff-n-Fluff.

Matthew A. Hoffman is a PhD student at the University of Edinburgh, having previously been at Florida State University and King's College London. His research interests are in ethics and the social side of moral philosophy. Lately, however, most of his time has been spent reading comics, which turns out to be a more expensive hobby than buying philosophy books.

Melanie Johnson-Moxley teaches philosophy at Columbia College and the University of Missouri. Her research interests include comparative philosophy, the history of women in philosophy, and the work of A.N. Whitehead. She is a member of the Society for the Study of Women Philosophers and the International Institute for Field-Being. She has revered Wonder Woman above all other superheroes since she could first twirl a lasso and will unabashedly give the Amazon salute in public.

Nathan Kellen is a PhD candidate in philosophy at the University of Connecticut. His research is primarily on the nature of truth and logic and their connection to other areas of philosophy. He has contributed papers to *More Doctor Who and Philosophy* (Open Court, 2015) and (co-written with Roy T. Cook) to *The Ultimate Star Wars and Philosophy* (Wiley-Blackwell, 2015). Unfortunately for him, Wonder Woman's golden lasso cannot be used to figure out how to finish a dissertation, even if that dissertation is on truth.

Dennis Knepp teaches philosophy, religious studies, and Greek mythology at Big Bend Community College in Moses Lake, WA. He has chapters in the Blackwell Philosophy and PopCulture books on *Twilight, Alice in Wonderland, The Girl with the Dragon Tattoo, The Hobbit, Avatar, Superman, Black Sabbath*, and *Star Wars*. Dennis often exclaims "Suffering Socrates!" or "Great Heraclitus!" when he uses a lasso of truth-tables.

Sara Kolmes is a PhD student in philosophy at Georgetown University, and holds Master's degrees in history and philosophy of science, and philosophy from Florida State University. Her main areas of interest are bioethics and environmental ethics, although if working on aesthetics would mean she could justify going to concerts as work, she'd start working in that area in a heartbeat.

James Edwin Mahon is Professor and Chair of the Philosophy Department at CUNY-Lehman College. His research interests include the philosophy of deception, the history of moral philosophy, and applied ethics. From childhood, he has been a Marvel Comics person, and not a DC Comics person. But he has made an exception in this instance, because it's Wonder Woman. As she says, "If it means interfering in an ensconced, outdated system, to help just one woman, man or child ... I'm willing to accept the consequences."

Trip McCrossin teaches in the Philosophy Department at Rutgers University, where he works on, among other things, the nature, history, and legacy of the Enlightenment. Hearing Diana tell Bruce Wayne recently, "You've never met a woman like me," he can't help but think he's heard this somewhere before, and maybe more than once.

Francis Tobienne, Jr. is Professor of Literature, Writing, and Humanities at South University, Tampa and Senior Dali Research Fellow at The Salvador Dali Museum, St. Petersburg, FL. He is the author of *Mandeville's Travails: Merging Travel, Theory and Commentary* (2016), *The Position of Magic in Selected Medieval Spanish Texts* (2008), as well as editor of *Occultus: the Hidden and Macabre in Literature and Film* (2016). Although he wears bowties to work, he is still hoping to get into The Justice League where his 4-year-old daughter Marisol is Wonder Woman and 2-year-old son Xavier is Batman.

Sabina Tokbergenova is a philosopher interested in ethics and social philosophy. Her most recent publication is a chapter in *Aliens and Philosophy*. Like Diana Prince, Sabina wears glasses, but unlike Wonder Woman, Sabina is no good without hers.

Mark D. White is chair and professor in the Department of Philosophy at the College of Staten Island/CUNY, where he teaches courses in philosophy, economics, and law. He is the author of five books and 60 journal articles and book chapters, and the editor of six books in the Blackwell Philosophy and PopCulture series, including *Batman and Philosophy* (with Robert Arp) and *Superman and Philosophy*. He is adamant that until Wonder Woman has to wear pants again, neither does he.

J. Lenore Wright is the Director of the Academy for Teaching and Learning and Associate Professor of Interdisciplinary Studies and

Philosophy at Baylor University. Her scholarly interests include theories and representations of the self and feminist philosophy. In 2006, she published *The Philosopher's "I": Autobiography and the Search for the Self*. Other publications include "From 'I' to 'We': Acts of Agency in Simone de Beauvoir's Philosophical Autobiography" in *Philosophy of Autobiography* and "Who's Afraid of Naomi Wolf: Feminism in Post-feminist Culture" in *Feminism and Popular Culture*. She has also published in *Teaching Philosophy* and the *Journal of Interactive Instruction Development* and is an academic consultant for the International Organization for Student Success. In her spare time, she enjoys running and rearing her reluctant but willing sons as future feminists.

Andrea Zanin is the author of the pop-culture blog Rantchick.com. She currently lives in London, where she spends her time writing, ranting, being a journalist, and pretending she's Amazonian. Unfortunately, she's not very good at it—lacking in the required height, speed, and breast size. Plus, as it turns out, Zeus is not really her dad (bummer) nor does she have a cool tiara. Talk about feminist faux pas! Andrea has contributed chapters to various pop-culture and philosophy books, including *Sons of Anarchy*, *Hannibal Lecter*, and *X-Files*.

Acknowledgments

First and foremost, thanks to Bill Irwin. Since the beginning of my career—with my earliest publication in *Buffy the Vampire Slayer and Philosophy* (edited by James B. South)—he has been a constant in my academic life and I have benefited immensely from his presence. Thanks also for the helpful comments on my own work in this book, and for being an ideal editorial partner. I'd also like to thank all the contributors. Writing for an editor can be difficult, and they have all been gracious in accepting editorial suggestions and have written some wonderful essays. A book like this is only as good as its contributors, and we made a great book.

Editor's Note

Over the more than 75 years in which Wonder Woman has entertained us, there have been variations in certain names. For example, her mother is referred to as both Queen Hippolyta and Queen Hippolyte. Likewise, the Amazons suffer at the hands of both Hercules and Heracles. Marston used the god of war's Roman name, Mars, not Ares. Thankfully, the change in names is mostly superficial. However, standardizing the use of these names in this volume, although it would simplify matters, would lead to inaccuracies since alternate versions were, in fact, used throughout Wonder Woman's history. Therefore, I have deferred to the authors and allowed the use of the name that is most accurate given the context of the author's essay.

Introduction
In and For a World of Ordinary Mortals

Jacob M. Held

I've been waiting for Wonder Woman. But as anxious as I've been, I've also been a bit wary. The Amazonian princess is complex, and complexity doesn't translate well on the big screen—the small screen fares only slightly better.

Wonder Woman is problematic. She's a sexy woman. That can't be denied. But she's also a superhero, a fully empowered woman, even at times a god. The masculinity of Batman and Superman befits them as heroes, as strong, powerful, and righteous. By contrast, the femininity of Wonder Woman complicates matters. Objectification is a threat for Wonder Woman. Does her sex appeal diminish her gravitas? Is she less of a heroine and more of a sexual fantasy? And often, resisting her objectification, Wonder Woman can look more like a feminist cause than a hero. Maybe that's okay, though, considering her origins as feminist propaganda. Any way we look at it, we confront the ambiguity of Wonder Woman. She is not just a superhero, nor is she defined by her gender. However, a focus on either overshadows and seemingly diminishes the other.

Echoing the existentialist philosopher Simone de Beauvoir (1908–1986), I've used the term "ambiguity" to describe Wonder Woman.[1] Beauvoir uses the term to describe woman's place in the world. As she sees it, women are caught in a bind. Acquiesce to gender norms and lose oneself, or become oneself and lose one's place in the world.

Wonder Woman and Philosophy: The Amazonian Mystique, First Edition.
Edited by Jacob M. Held.
© 2017 John Wiley & Sons, Ltd. Published 2017 by John Wiley & Sons, Ltd.

So women are in an ambiguous place, and Wonder Woman emphasizes this time and time again. Is she in love with Steve Trevor? Will she marry? Is she a lesbian, straight, or bi? Do these categories even apply to her? Is she mortal or a god? Is she human or Amazon? Is she American or cosmopolitan? She is always torn between two, or more, worlds and is forced to navigate these worlds, thereby creating an identity for herself by defining herself over and against various standards and expectations. She can only become Wonder Woman in opposition, creating a place for herself by continually rejecting previous spaces. Where does she belong? On Paradise Island, or in Boston. On Mount Olympus, or back on Earth. With a partner, or alone.

This ambiguity is not unique to Wonder Woman. We all must wonder where we belong. Although Wonder Woman's challenges are hers by virtue of her being female, and although they are more obvious given the way in which society deals with gender, we are all torn between what we are and what we want to become. We are all limited beings who have to deal with our unique situations and circumstances, our race, gender, class, capabilities, and social position.

We need to embrace Wonder Woman in all of her contradictions. She is a reflection of, and challenge to, our norms, our values, our society. She exemplifies our ideals, while posing serious questions about the place of those ideals in modern society. She speaks to our better selves while recognizing our frailty. She speaks to excellence in an imperfect world. She speaks to meaning and order in a chaotic world. She speaks to integrity in ambiguity. Like Wonder Woman, we live in ambiguity, but we have to live. So we stake our commitments and move forward doing the best that we can.

The aim of this book is appropriately ambiguous. Considering Wonder Woman philosophically is both fun and serious. So, read for pleasure and pause for contemplation.

Note

1. For her classic presentation of these issues, see Simone de Beauvoir, *The Second Sex*.

Part I

YOU ARE A WONDER WOMAN

Becoming a (Wonder) Woman
Feminism, Nationalism, and the Ambiguity of Female Identity

J. Lenore Wright

More than 70 years have passed since the debut of Wonder Woman in *All Star Comics*. To the wonder of many, Wonder Woman remains one of the most popular comic-book superheroes of all time. As Jill Lepore aptly observes in *The Secret History of Wonder Woman*, "Aside from Superman and Batman, no other comic-book character has lasted as long."[1] What, precisely, gives Wonder Woman her wondrous staying power in the American popular consciousness?

Her overt femininity (need I mention the bustier, boots, and bracelets?) coupled with her Amazonian strength and speed ("she was both stronger than Hercules and swifter than Mercury") crosses gender and generational divides.[2] The raven-haired beauty emboldened a generation of men reared on pin-ups and promises to fight fascism in World War II. The lasso-wielding freedom fighter empowered women to leave the domestic sphere for the public sphere and take control of their lives and livelihood.[3] The lone female founder of the Justice League of America (formerly known as the Justice Society of America) inspired countercultural Americans to voice stories of struggle and alienation. Today, the tiara-wearing heroine's combined fierceness and frivolity appeals to readers' fluid understanding of gender norms and identities.[4] Ironically, it is Wonder Woman's ambiguity that makes her appeal so enduring.

Wonder Woman and Philosophy: The Amazonian Mystique, First Edition.
Edited by Jacob M. Held.
© 2017 John Wiley & Sons, Ltd. Published 2017 by John Wiley & Sons, Ltd.

Wonder Woman is a walking—and sometimes flying—paradox of attributions and images. She is, at once, a female sex symbol and feminist icon: physically enchanting, psychically vulnerable, morally virtuous, financially independent, self-determining, and, in tune with her womanly ways, self-sacrificing. "She was meant to be the strongest, smartest, bravest woman the world had ever seen," writes Lepore.[5] In short, Wonder Woman represents a robust modern conception of American womanhood.

This chapter explores the complexities of Wonder Woman's identity, as she navigates male and female spheres of existence to embody a modern American ideal.[6] The French philosopher Simone de Beauvoir (1908–1986) maintains, in the *Ethics of Ambiguity* (1947) and *The Second Sex* (1949), that sexual differences shape human existence insofar as society offers men and women different possibilities for expressing who they are and what they desire. Whereas man actively creates his destiny, woman passively accepts her uncertain existence. The critical feminist task is for women to transcend barriers to freedom so they can begin to forge their identities and enjoy self-fulfillment. Wonder Woman exemplifies this "woman of tomorrow."[7] "Wiser and stronger than men," she gives up her right to eternal life and commitment to remain "aloof from men" to join her love interest, Captain Steve Trevor, an army intelligence officer, in America and defend democracy "and equal rights for women."[8] Wonder Woman challenges established social roles and the assumed facticity of life by creating her identity in the world, an identity born out of sacrifice and pain. In becoming who she is—in making a new life in a new country under a new name—Wonder Woman gives new meaning to Beauvoir's claim that "One is not born, but rather becomes, a woman."[9]

What is a Woman?

On the cusp of her 40th birthday, Simone de Beauvoir became preoccupied with the question, "What has it meant to me to be a woman?" Previously, she had insisted that women's lives were no different from men's lives. Beauvoir initially rejected the term "feminist" to describe herself and distanced herself from feminist thought. Yet, as she considered the condition of women further, she realized that being a woman had shaped her experiences in profound ways. Beauvoir writes, "I looked and it was a revelation: the world was a masculine world, my childhood had been nourished by myths formed by men, and I hadn't reacted to them in the same way I should have done if I had been a boy."[10]

Beauvoir adopts the question "What is a Woman?" as the guiding question of her pivotal feminist text, *The Second Sex* (1949), in which she observes that despite significant social and cultural differences worldwide, women share the experience of being dependent persons. Men, by contrast, are independent; they are the creators and prime examples of absolute rules and values in a fixed patriarchal system. Man, then, defines humanity:

> Thus humanity is male and man defines woman not in herself but relative to him; she is not regarded as an autonomous being... And she is simply what man decrees; thus she is called 'the sex,' by which is meant that she appears essentially to the male as a sexual being... She is the incidental, the inessential as opposed to the essential. He is the Subject, he is the Absolute—she is the Other.[11]

In defining humanity, man pursues a freely chosen future. He invents tools and creates values that allow him to transcend the repetition of life. Woman, bound by her body—bound by what Beauvoir characterizes as her immanence in reproduction—is imprisoned in the repetition of life. She is unable to subdue her body or control her future. (Historically speaking, pregnancy and childbirth reduce women's capacity for work and make them dependent upon men for protection and food. This was particularly true before the advent of reliable birth control. Of course, Amazons don't have this worry.) Woman is thus immanent rather than transcendent, dependent rather than independent, and, therefore, denied her very humanity. Beauvoir embraces the philosophical leanings of her romantic partner and intellectual companion, Jean-Paul Sartre (1905–1980), who advances the existentialist idea that individuals are responsible for determining who they are and what meaning their lives bear. Similarly, Beauvoir maintains that women, like men, must look reality squarely in the face and assume a responsibility for changing it by engaging in a struggle for freedom. Marston anticipates and aides Beauvoir's call in the figure of Wonder Woman.

Wonder Woman's feminist spirit originates in her ancestry. We learn in the introductory issue (*All Star Comics* #8, December 1941–January 1942) that Wonder Woman is the daughter of Hippolyte, Queen of Amazonia, an ancient Greek nation ruled for centuries by women. Threatened by the Amazons' autonomy and power, Hercules attempts to defeat the Amazons through combat. He loses. But through deceit and trickery, he manages to secure the magic girdle created by Aphrodite to ensure Hippolyte's success. The Amazons are enslaved until their degradation becomes unbearable. Aphrodite takes pity upon Amazonia and returns the magic girdle to Hippolyte, who overcomes the male captors, flees Amazonia with her female subjects, and establishes a new world on an uncharted island they name Paradise Island.[12] Like the historic path of liberation for modern women, the Amazons' liberation is not without conditions. "Aphrodite also decreed that we must always wear these bracelets fashioned by our captors, as a reminder that we must always keep aloof from men."[13] Wonder Woman, who later acquires the name Diana after her godmother, the goddess of the moon, threatens this newly established order when Wonder Woman falls in love with an American captain who crash lands his airplane on Paradise Island. Her mother warns, "So long as we do not permit ourselves to be again beguiled by men! We are indeed a race of Wonder Women! That was the promise of Aphrodite—and we must keep our promise to her if we are to remain here safe and in peace! That is why this American must go and as soon as possible!"[14]

Despite Wonder Woman's respect for her mother's authority and commitment to women's independence, romantic love prevails. Wonder Woman gives up eternal life (that's right, *eternal* life) and her beloved home on Paradise Island for Captain Trevor. Like modern women everywhere, Wonder Woman sacrifices her self-interest for the sake of womanhood: devotion and service to men above fidelity to oneself. Patriarchy assigns women this familiar, secondary role. Yet, like the modern women Marston envisions and seeks to inspire, Wonder Woman does not relinquish her independent identity entirely. She transfers her nationalist commitments to her new homeland of America, "the land she learns to love and protect."[15] She both embraces and subverts traditional female roles, thereby challenging prevailing notions of womanhood. Lepore observes that Wonder

Woman's shifting identity and iconographic representation from the 1940s to the present mirrors ongoing and often inconsistent constructions of womanhood:

> Wonder Woman isn't only an Amazonian princess with badass boots. She's the missing link in a chain of events that begins with the woman suffrage campaign of the 1910s and ends with the troubled place of feminism fully a century later. Feminism made Wonder Woman. And then Wonder Woman remade feminism, which hasn't been altogether good for feminism. Superheroes, who are supposed to be better than everyone else, are excellent at clobbering people; they're lousy at fighting for equality.[16]

In 1911, the terms "Amazon" and "New Women" were applied to women who rebelled against social norms, left home, and attended college.[17] "Feminism," a term rarely used before 1910, was common by 1913. "Feminism meant advocacy of women's rights and freedoms and a vision of equality markedly different from that embraced by the "woman movement" of the nineteenth century, which had been founded less on a principle of equality than a set of ideas about women's moral superiority."[18]

Marston tethered the feminist philosophy of *Wonder Woman* to the progressive views of early feminists, views he inherited from his beloved professor of philosophy, George Herbert Palmer. Palmer supported women's suffrage and women's education on the grounds that "girls are also human beings, a point often overlooked."[19] But Marston also understood and at times empathized with the social and political forces that vie against women's equality, real as well as symbolic forces that keep women dependent on men. It is fitting, then, that the singular weakness he gives to Wonder Woman, loss of strength, occurs whenever a man binds her in chains. Equality in theory is well and good. In practice, however, even Wonder Woman is subject to male power.

The fantasy of American women throughout the early twentieth century is realized again and again in the adventures of Wonder Woman: *to escape*.[20] In the words of Annie Lucasta ("Lou") Rogers, a feminist cartoonist and colleague of Wonder Woman cartoonist Harry G. Peter, she and other women wanted to know "how to arrange the world so that women can be human beings, with a chance to exercise their infinitely varied gifts in infinitely varied ways, instead of being destined by the accident of their sex to one field of activity—housework and child-raising."[21] Embedded in Roger's claim is an idea fleshed out by Marston and Peter in the character of Wonder Woman and theorized by Beauvoir: the ambiguity of existence should enrich women's lives and expand their capacity for self-definition, not confine them to a less significant and/or diverse existence. Self-identity, then, is a philosophical and political endeavor. Unless women resist the prescribed identity and artificial essence assigned to them—women are the weaker sex, women are objects, women are inherently feminine, and, therefore, submissive—and claim the freedom to define for themselves who and what they are, women will never be fully human. In Linda Stein's words, the Wonder Woman stories express Marston's belief that "individuals free of gender stereotypes are also free to develop to their full potential."[22]

Wonder Woman realizes the critical link between personal emancipation and collective liberation. "I'll rely on myself and not a man," she tells Prudence, a rescuee. The defender of democracy develops her abilities, pursues economic opportunities, and addresses world problems. Moreover, she illustrates the existential and political value of freedom from male oppression: "What a sweet sound! My man-made bonds have snapped! My woman's power returns again" (*Wonder Woman* #4, April–May 1943). Wonder Woman's self-empowerment is a productive model of female transcendence.

The Ambiguously Feminist Superhero

For Wonder Woman and her early readers, the personal *is* political, as the feminist slogan goes. Mitra C. Emad argues that Peter's iconographic blending of politics and personhood—star-spangled tights on a sensuous female form—invited women of the war generation to see themselves in Wonder Woman's narrative of American exceptionalism and achievement:

> Until his death in 1947, Marston, in collaboration with artist Harry G. Peter, produced a comic in which the hero, while often saving Capt. Trevor, primarily saved helpless women from imminent death and destruction, attempting also to empower women to look after

themselves and discover their own physical and economic strengths. Girls are taught that if they "feel [they] can do things, so [they] can do them," and women are exhorted to "get strong and earn your own living."[23]

The overlaying of politics on Wonder Woman's ageless yet ever-changing body, however, creates a philosophical quandary.[24] The nation is a man's domain, and nationalism a man's game. The body is a woman's domain, and embodiment a woman's game. Hence, appending national identity to woman's identity creates "oppositional encounters" between masculine, public ideals and feminine, private ideals.[25] It also creates a tension between purported sources of power: political authority or political influence. The super-powerful warrior, free from traditional gender norms, fights monsters and men, flaunting the unlimited power of the state. The super-feminine woman, bound by traditional gender norms, enacts an attractive, heteronormative identity, surreptitiously creating her own furtive field of influence among uber-powerful men.[26] How is one to understand the conflicting ideals Wonder Woman embraces? She is a modern (super-) woman who must make hard choices about which spheres of society to enter, and, thus, which elements of identity to surrender or proclaim. In short, she must relinquish some freedom to become a woman; i.e., to be subdued, sexualized, and made safe for a man's world. Women are in an ambiguous position. A woman can pursue her freedom by rejecting societal norms and expectations and consequently be outcast, thus subverting her attempt at freedom, or she can adopt these norms and standards and thereby subvert her subjectivity. A woman must navigate between two worlds, treading a fine line between transcendence and immanence, subject and object, freedom and servitude. The feminist philosophy of *Wonder Woman* is ambiguous indeed.

Marston and his collaborators exploit Wonder Woman's ambiguity by invoking distinct male and female spheres of activity. They then judiciously elevate one sphere (and one correlative identity) above the other. Which sphere gets privileged varies according to the cultural context in which the comic is produced. In a wartime edition of *Wonder Woman* comics (*Wonder Woman* #5, June–July 1943), a period in which women assumed vacated male positions to facilitate military success, George Washington appears as a symbol not of patriotism but patriarchy, poised to undermine women's emerging equality. "Women will lose the war for America!" he declares, "Women will betray their country through weakness if not treachery."[27] Marston "places gender above nationalism in rendering George Washington in such unpatriotic tones," Emad explains. "In other words, Marston seems to say, nationalism at the expense of women's power remains a conventional nationalism that must be subject to critique."[28]

The push for social change throughout the Marston era of *Wonder Woman* comics is a boon to first and second-wave feminists. Marston develops themes and images empowering to women and affirming of their intellectual and economic interests: "normal human females successfully acting as presidents, professors, and police officers."[29] This progressive trend falters, however, under the economic and social pressures of World War II and the postwar era. Men re-enter the workforce, reassert their authority, and reclaim their privileged economic positions. Women return to the domestic sphere and resume household and childcare duties, duties they do not necessarily enjoy or find fulfilling, as Betty Friedan documents in *The Feminine Mystique* (1963). *Wonder Woman* writers and artists follow suit. Steve Trevor reminds Wonder Woman that "she is only a woman, after all," in the Fall 1944 issue of *Comic Cavalcade* #8. He then persuades her to marry him—she needs a man to protect her, he avers. She responds in kind: "Steve, dear, now that we're going to be married, won't you please let me be your secretary?" Her first assignment is to type the following memo: "Every woman's place is in the home and girls should not try to do the work of men. They should be busy keeping house for their husbands." Between the 1960s and 2000s, Wonder Woman's power is steadily realigned with femininity and sexuality, expressions of women's inescapable embodiment. Wonder Woman's battle with the creature Decay in May 1987 illustrates this regressive shift. "By successfully vanquishing Decay, a symbol of social and environmental degradation, Wonder Woman demonstrates that the separate spheres can remain intact, femininity will not be corrupted by too much power, and gender—as long as it is feminine and beautiful—can coexist with nation."[30] *Wonder Woman* further perpetuates the ideology of separate (and unequal) spheres by rendering femininity as "heroic, self-sacrificing, and good," meanings that also "render the separate spheres of femininity and nationalism as sacrosanct."[31] Battle is undertaken in service to the nation, not out of duty to self. "Only a sudden call for help could prevent Wonder Woman from marrying Steve Trevor" (*Sensation Comics* #94, November–December 1949).

Marston's vision of the modern American woman, embodied in the figure of Wonder Woman, is a woman who must exercise power covertly:

> Wonder Woman emerges to call attention to the price wartime women had to pay for admission to the man-made world: a fractured sense of self and the duplicitous social practices necessary to negotiate the maintenance of submissive femininity while participating in the public sphere of wartime society. Wonder Woman accomplishes this feat not with her considerable Amazon powers, but with female female [sic] impersonation, disguise, and deception—the tactics of female trickery.[32]

Wonder Woman's strength and endurance are admirable symbols of American power. Her masculine attributes, however, must be "lassoed into submission, sometimes by her own power" to bolster feminine ideals.[33] Because female power threatens the entire apparatus of a male-dominant world—money, position, and control—it must be suppressed.

The ambiguous feminism of *Wonder Woman* is seen in Wonder Woman's subjugation. Who (or what) is poised to subdue her? Suffering Sappho! It is femininity, of course. Wonder Woman must subdue herself by feigning feminine weakness and submission. She is praised in the meaningfully titled "The Battle of Desires" for teaching a young boy named Don to control his dominance (*Comic Cavalcade* #16, August–September 1946). Although Wonder Woman, like Beauvoir, boldly proclaims her womanhood, she never fully escapes a woman's fate: woman is the *Other* (object) to a man's Self (subject). "This is the fundamental characteristic of woman," Beauvoir writes; "she is the *Other* at the heart of a whole whose two components are necessary to each other."[34] She explains the process by which women assume their alterity, their Otherness, in the following passage from *The Second Sex*:

> At the moment that women are beginning to share in the making of this world, this world still belongs to men: men have no doubt about this, and women barely doubt it. Refusing to be the *Other*, refusing complicity with man, would mean renouncing all the advantages an alliance with the superior caste confers on them.[35]

So long as male and female spheres exist, women must make difficult choices about which sphere to engage, and, thus, which capacities, interests, and elements of identity to sacrifice. Wonder Woman's life mirrors this two-sphere model of society: she leaves the woman's world of Amazonia for the Man's World of America. *Wonder Woman* writers attempt to resolve the ambiguous identity of Wonder Woman in the person of Diana Prince, a person who "resorts to trickery and covert action to protect the discrete realms of national interests and feminine submissiveness."[36] Unfortunately, this resolution undermines Wonder Woman's power and reinforces female inferiority generally, further relegating women to the status of *Other*. The response of Wonder Woman's enemies to her assertion that "no bullet can hurt me while I wear my moonstone" says it all: "She ain't human" (*Moon Girl* #3, Spring 1948). Beauvoir concludes that women's equality is contingent upon women's abilities to free themselves from the status of *Other*. Women must, like the classic-era Wonder Woman, become active agents in the political sphere. They must invest themselves in projects in the world, including the project of their own identity formation. It is noteworthy that Gloria Steinem not only featured Wonder Woman on the cover of the inaugural issue of *Ms.* magazine (1972), she also included as a feature article "New Feminist: Simone de Beauvoir."

The contemporary focus on Wonder Woman's femininity and beauty at the expense of her brains and brawn undermines the progress Marston helped facilitate in the 1940s. Stephanie Cawley and Ann Matsuuchi characterize the post-Marston period of *Wonder Woman* comics as a period of heightened sexism and superficiality.[37] Writers trot out one hypersexualized image and retrograde storyline after another. Attention is paid almost exclusively to Wonder Woman's stereotypical feminine interests—romance, marriage, and domestic virtues: "Wonder Woman, Romance Editor" (*Wonder Woman* #97, March 1950). Rather than occupying the male sphere to push for transcendence and liberation, Wonder Woman's main occupation appears to be satisfying the male gaze. Cawley rightly observes that the sexualized representation of Wonder Woman from the 1990s to the present "certainly problematizes the suggestion of her status as a feminist icon."[38] We face a frustrating conclusion: Wonder Woman, ambiguously feminist superhero. Must women (still!) sacrifice economic independence for personal freedom? Is ambiguity the best we can hope for nearly 70 years after *The Second Sex*? The transition from Wonder Woman as active agent with her own independent identity to Wonder Woman as subdued and sexualized female illustrates the ambiguous feminist philosophy of *Wonder Woman* comics. It also exemplifies the ambiguity of human existence in general; an ambiguity that all too often binds rather than frees women. Wonder Woman teaches us that freedom from the assumed facticity of life is hard won.

To Become a (Wonder) Woman

One of the historical obstacles to the achievement of a broad feminist program is that more than campaigns for racial or (male) political equality, feminism impacts every aspect of life and identity—mental, physical, moral, legal, familial, political. Thus, a comprehensive feminism seems to threaten everything in a male-dominated society. It is probably also the reason that major steps forward (women's suffrage, for example) never amount to a sweeping change. Diana Prince's disruption of masculine and feminine norms offers promising possibilities for transcending a two-sphere (male–female) model of social existence. "With Marston's advocacy for strong, independent women," claims Stein, "Wonder Woman begins to change the doctrine that "male" means aggression and "female" means submission."[39]

Marston's vision lives on. The New 52 Wonder Woman (DC Comics, 2011) and recent relaunch with Earth One realign Wonder Woman with modern feminist sensibilities. These sensibilities— "I have given (Wonder Woman) the dominant force but have kept her loving," Marston writes—both resist and reinscribe gender stereotypes.[40] Wonder Woman is powerful, but her power is soft. This is not perfect progress (one wishes for something a little more linear), but it is a vast improvement over the "bullet-breasted sex object" that emerged after Marston's death.[41]

Women continue to see their efforts to navigate barriers to success— underemployment, unequal pay, discrimination, and implicit bias— mirrored in Wonder Woman's struggles to live in Man's World while remaining true to her own self-interests. They bear the weight of oppressive messages about their feminine obligations. They feel the chains of their stagnant situations. Should women accept Wonder Woman's advice to young Olive in "The Bog Trap": "you'll do better next time" (*Sensation Comics* #58, October 1946)? Or should women follow Wonder Woman's example and "make bad men good and weak women strong"?[42]

The incrementalism of change in women's lives is exasperating. Individual achievement rarely translates into broad, structural change. Collective progress is scattered and slow. Nonetheless, the work of real and mythic female figures like Beauvoir and Wonder Woman charts a promising path forward. "As far as being a superhero role model for women's freedom," Stein asserts, "I still believe she's the best."[43] The real job for Wonder Woman and her fans is to bring Amazonia to America by breaking down the barriers that impede women's advancement in the public sphere.

The return to a less-objectified Wonder Woman is a sign that society is once again contesting women's inferiority. "Wonder Woman symbolizes many of the values that feminists hold dear today," Stein explains. "Strength, self-reliance, mutual support, peace, respect for human life, and trust in soft power rather than violence and aggression to solve the world's conflicts."[44] Now a new generation of readers can ponder the feminist concerns that *Wonder Woman* raises: biological sex and gender identity, racial and ethnic bias, social and economic inequality, and the value of human liberty. It remains to be seen whether our favorite female superhero can save the world from itself. Suffering Sappho indeed.

Notes

1. Jill Lepore, *The Secret History of Wonder Woman* (New York: Vintage Books, 2015), xi.
2. Roy Thomas, *Wonder Woman: The War Years 1941–1945* (New York: Chartwell Books, 2015), 10.
3. Mitra C. Emad, "Reading Wonder Woman's Body: Mythologies of Gender and Nation," *The Journal of Popular Culture*, 39(6) (2006) 954–984, 962. Emad writes that "an estimated 4.7 million women responded to the labor shortage call" created by the entry of men into the armed forces. She adds that "for most women, this was their first opportunity to move into high-paying industrial jobs, and for black women it marked a preliminary movement out of domestic service."
4. For a description of Millennials, see Rachel Slaymaker and Kerri Fisher's "Striving for Cultural Competence While Preparing Millennials as

Emerging Professionals," in the *Journal of Social Work Values and Ethics*, 12(2) (2015).

5. Lepore, *The Secret History of Wonder Woman*, xi.
6. We cannot escape the ambiguity of our age: identity politics, including LGBTQ considerations; debates regarding bathroom usage and assigned or adopted gender identity; etc.
7. Wonder Woman's creator, William M. Marston, envisioned a "woman of tomorrow," a woman who would "take over the rule of the country, politically and economically." *Wonder Woman: The War Years 1941–1945*, 8–9.
8. Thomas, *Wonder Woman: The War Years 1941–1945*, 19–21, copied from "Introducing Wonder Woman," *All Star Comics* #8 (December 1941–January 1942); script William Moulton Marston; art H.G. Peter.
9. Simone de Beauvoir, *The Second Sex*, translated by Constance Borde and Sheila Malovany-Chevallier (2009), 283. Originally published in French in 1949.
10. Deirdre Bair, *Simone de Beauvoir, A Biography* (New York: Touchstone, 1990), 86.
11. Beauvoir, *The Second Sex*, 5–6.
12. *Wonder Woman: The War Years 1941–1945*, 15–16. It should be noted that Wonder Woman's origin myth has been written multiple times. For an analysis of Wonder Woman's origin myths, please see Mitra C. Emad, "Reading Wonder Woman's Body: Mythologies of Gender and Nation," cited above.
13. Ibid., 15.
14. Ibid., 16.
15. Ibid., 21.
16. Lepore, *The Secret History of Wonder Woman*, xiii.
17. Ibid., 17.
18. Ibid., 18–19.
19. Ibid., 8.
20. Professor Hugo Münsterberg, a German professor of psychology at Harvard, attempted to denigrate the aspirations of American women in the early 1900s by stating that "the aim of the German woman is to further the interests of the household, but the aim of the American woman is to escape." See Jill Lepore, *The Secret History of Wonder Woman*, 32.
21. Quoted by Lepore in *The Secret History of Wonder Woman*, 84.
22. Linda Stein, Winter 2010, "Wonder Woman: A Comic Book Character Shows the Way," *Online Issues* magazine, http://www.ontheissuesmagazine.com/2010winter/2010winter_Stein.php.

23. Emad, "Reading Wonder Woman's Body: Mythologies of Gender and Nation," 959.
24. Ibid., 955.
25. Ibid., 956.
26. Carolyn Cocca, "Negotiating the Third Wave of Feminism in Wonder Woman," *American Political Science Association Political Symposium* (2014), 98–103, 98.
27. Thomas, *Wonder Woman: The War Years 1941–1945*, 243.
28. Emad, "Reading Wonder Woman's Body: Mythologies of Gender and Nation," 963.
29. Ann Matsuuchi, "Wonder Woman Wears Pants: Wonder Woman, Feminism, and the 1972 'Women's Lib' Issue," *Colloquy: Text Theory Critique* 24 (2012) 118–142, 122.
30. Emad, "Reading Wonder Woman's Body: Mythologies of Gender and Nation," 972.
31. This argument is made by historian Lori Landay and quoted in "Reading Wonder Woman's Body: Mythologies of Gender and Nation," 964.
32. Ibid., 965.
33. Ibid., 956.
34. Beauvoir, *The Second Sex*, 9.
35. Ibid., 10.
36. Emad, "Reading Wonder Woman's Body: Mythologies of Gender and Nation," 965.
37. Stephanie Cawley, December 30, 2012, "Comics and American Feminism: Wonder Woman." The Stockton Postcolonial Project and Ann Matsuuchi, "Wonder Woman Wears Pants: Wonder Woman, Feminism, and the 1972 'Women's Lib' Issue," *Colloquy: Text Theory Critique* 24 (2012) 118–142, 122–124.
38. Ibid.
39. Stein, "Wonder Woman: A Comic Book Character Shows the Way," *Online Issues* magazine, http://www.ontheissuesmagazine.com/2010winter/2010winter_Stein.php.
40. Ibid.
41. Ibid.
42. Ibid.
43. Ibid.
44. Ibid.

The God of War is Wearing What?

Gender in the New 52

Sarah K. Donovan

With attractive and scantily clad female characters, Zeus as a philandering womanizer, the First Born as a hyper-masculine war monger, and Hera as a jealous wife blaming other women for her husband's infidelities, *Wonder Woman* (the New 52 series) confirms some age-old stereotypes about men and women.[1] But, if you look in the right places, *Wonder Woman* (the New 52) also challenges some traditional gender stereotypes.

Hell Hath No Fury

The end of the twentieth and beginning of the twenty-first century have witnessed great strides in gender equality for, among others, heterosexual women and members of the LGBTQ community.[2] However, many people are still most comfortable with a binary understanding of sex and gender. This binary says that you are male or female, and masculine or feminine. *Wonder Woman* (the New 52) helps illustrate the history of this binary understanding and its stereotypical thinking. Historically, masculine social behavior is coded as rational (emotionless), autonomous (self-sufficient), and authoritative (leader). Typical feminine social behavior is coded as emotional (intuitive), interconnected (dependent), and nurturing (caregiver).

Wonder Woman and Philosophy: The Amazonian Mystique, First Edition.
Edited by Jacob M. Held.
© 2017 John Wiley & Sons, Ltd. Published 2017 by John Wiley & Sons, Ltd.

At first blush, *Wonder Woman* (the New 52) confirms these stereotypes. Just look at Hera and Apollo. Hera, the scorned woman, hunts
down young Zola, who is pregnant with Zeus's child. When Wonder
Woman brings Zola and a wounded Hermes to the Amazons' home
on Paradise Island, Queen Hippolyta warns her that "Hera's jealousy
is not just legend, but fact."[3]

We hear more about this jealousy when Wonder Woman and Hera
both learn that Zeus is also Wonder Woman's father. Wonder Woman
demands that Hippolyta defend her decision to conceal the truth. Hippolyta says, "... if Hera learned you were her husband's daughter, she
would have murdered you in your crib."[4] As Hera comes to confront
Hippolyta, a storm rages on Paradise Island. Hippolyta says that the
storm's fury "... is of a woman scorned."[5]

Hera is not only jealous of Zeus's mistresses, but also in danger of
losing all her power now that Zeus is gone. Like a character out of
a Jane Austen novel, Hera learns that her entire worth depends upon
her husband. In *Blood*, Poseidon tells Wonder Woman that now that
his brother, Zeus, is dead, he will claim the heavens as his own. He
says of Hera, "Without a king, the queen has nothing." To make matters worse, Poseidon and Hades contemplate the possibility of sharing Hera and the throne. In what is ultimately a ploy to make Hera
appear, Lennox and Wonder Woman propose to Poseidon and Hades:
"What if heaven were ruled by day by the sea... And by night by
shadow. Sharing a queen?"[6] Hera rages at the thought of being shared
by Zeus's brothers (who, by the way, thought it was a great idea).

Hera is not the only one who starts out with some heavy gender
baggage. *Blood* opens with Apollo serving champagne to three pretty
and flirty young women in a penthouse suite in Singapore. He uses the
women as his oracles, which we can call objectifying them because
he has no interest in them besides their use value. After inducing a
prophetic trance in them so he can gather information, Apollo transforms into his true form as the god of the sun. The women are incinerated and their ashes scattered.

Apollo, like his older brother, the First Born, represents a hyper-
masculine, alpha male who wishes to depose his father, Zeus, from
the throne and who will use people to do this. Unlike Hera, who is
dominated by emotion, Apollo is calm and cool in his quest for dominance. After his oracles report that Zeus does not exist, Apollo seeks
out his brother Ares. Apollo is not trying to destroy his rivals, but

politicking to replace Zeus. Unlike Hera, Apollo doesn't act off the cuff—he gathers information. His oracles are a consistent source, as we see when he once again uses young women in *Flesh* to find out who the First Born is (and, yes, they once again burn when he is done).[7] While he realizes that the First Born is a threat, Apollo opts to keep him prisoner (which doesn't end well for Apollo!). In sum, Apollo is a domineering and calculating male god.

While Hera and Apollo provide us with straightforward examples of binary and stereotypical representations of gender behavior, the philosophical history of these representations adds nuance. In the classic text *Man of Reason*, Genevieve Lloyd provides an exemplary challenge to the stereotype in the history of philosophy that men are rational and women are emotional.[8]

Lloyd shows us how great intellectuals—from the Pre-Socratics, to Descartes and Hegel—have looked to reason and rationality as genderless and sexless markers of intelligence, and as tools for understanding and properly organizing the world around us. Yet, since the Pre-Socratics, women have been excluded from rationality (not seen as worthy of education and viewed as dangerous to politics), and even coded as irrational. Rather than simply arguing that women are as rational as men, Lloyd argues that reason and rationality are not genderless and sexless. She does this not because she wants to claim that women and men are fundamentally different.[9] Her claim is more modest. She argues that how we experience ourselves in our social, economic, sexual, and political environment influences both how we use our reason and how we define rationality. So we could say that men and women can have the same faculty of reason (by virtue of being human), but might develop, experience, and use it differently by virtue of different experiences, which are influenced by how our societies code masculinity and femininity.

Who Are You Calling Second?

In one of the most important early books in twentieth-century feminist philosophy, *The Second Sex*,[10] philosopher and novelist Simone de Beauvoir (1908–1986) explores women's inequality to men. Whereas Lloyd discusses how this inequality, in terms of assigning rationality to men and emotion to women, is detrimental for both men and women, Beauvoir looks at it through an existential lens. Atheistic existentialists, like Beauvoir and her lifelong partner Jean-Paul Sartre (1905–1980),[11] believe that existence precedes essence. This means that humans are born without a predetermined course of action. Without a determined essence or a god to give us a blueprint for our lives, it is up to us to define ourselves.

Beauvoir recognizes how gender plays a role in women's ability to embrace and act upon their existential freedom. While men are typically trained by society to be independent and create their own meaning in the world (or, as Beauvoir calls it, to exercise transcendence), women are typically taught to play a secondary role to the men in their lives (or, according to Beauvoir, to exist in a state of immanence). In this way, women are defined by others (and, existentially, are the *Other*, or those who experience alienation as they are defined by other people), while men define themselves. Beauvoir denies that there is anything natural about this situation. Women and men are born equal and free, but social expectations and training often prevent women from actualizing this freedom.

We might interpret the transformation of Hera throughout *Wonder Woman* (the New 52) as an existential movement from immanence to transcendence. Hera begins as the wife of Zeus. Although she has power, she is defined, and defines herself, in relation to her husband. She obsesses over how much he desires her. She takes every instance of infidelity as an attack on her self-worth. Hera's dependence is so extreme that she will destroy all evidence of Zeus's unfaithfulness—even if it means murdering children (think of poor Siracca in *Iron*[12]). From an existentialist perspective, we can call Hera Zeus's *Other*—she doesn't define herself independent of his desire for her.

When Apollo makes Hera mortal in *Guts*,[13] she is initially despondent. However, she begins to bond with other people (in particular, other women) who do not care for her only because they desire her. She begins to chart an independent identity for herself as her own person and not as the wife of Zeus. In *Flesh*, Hera says about becoming mortal, "… it was as if my blood cooled down. Nows last longer. Time slows experience. There's a piece missing in me that I don't miss." As a mortal, Hera experiences time and faces death. Her existential awareness of mortality helps her to recognize how empty her life was before, and to carve out new meaning.

Further, when Apollo restores Hera's power upon his death in *Flesh*, she acts as an active agent who would lead and defend others. Rather than reverting to her project to kill any woman or child who might interfere with her relationship with Zeus, she wants to build an army to defeat the First Born—her first child with Zeus. Hera even thanks Wonder Woman for defending them, and for taking her in, when she says, "Forgiveness seems to be the order of the day... I ask the same of you."[14] But the true mark of Hera's transformation is her willingness to help baby Zeke, Zeus's last-born bastard son, to claim his birthright as King of Olympus instead of her own child, the First Born. Finally, Hera has taken some control over her own life.

Aggressive Men and the Women Who Nurture Them

Whereas Lloyd diagnoses how rationality is not immune to socialization, and Beauvoir articulates women's existential plight as the *Other* to men, Wendy W. Williams examines how stereotypes about men and women play out on a cultural level in American law. In "The Equality Crisis," Williams analyzes how cultural values unconsciously program many of us to resist true equality between men and women.[15] Deep-seated, gendered cultural values rest upon our binary thinking about gendered social behavior. Much like Lloyd and Beauvoir, Williams argues that gendered cultural values are often viewed as natural and intractable rather than created and reinforced by culture.

Williams believes we have cultural biases about men as natural aggressors in both war and sex, and women as natural mothers and care takers—and our laws about combat and maternity leave have reflected this (although this has and continues to change with regard to both women in combat and family leave). *Wonder Woman* (the New 52) provides some illustrative examples.

Ares embodies Williams's cultural value of men as aggressors in war. A young Ares presents an uncomplicated version of himself to a young Wonder Woman in *Iron*, when he says "I be blood! I be guts! I be iron! I be war!" He also diminishes Wonder Woman's training by the Amazons when he says there are "Warrior ways that only a god can teach."[16] An older, disillusioned Ares does not look the part of the aggressive, male warrior, but he upholds his values. He copes with the violence he engenders with alcohol and pessimism. As he tells Apollo in *Blood*, "Our fate, it's not up to us... The world will be ruled by war. It's inevitable."

The First Born is also a prime example of an aggressor in war. As he says when we first meet him in *Iron* (after he eats poor Duerson's head), "I am the one with no name. The crippler of souls. The First Born." In *Flesh*, Apollo's oracles tell us more about the First Born. We learn of his history of brutality when they say that, as a child, "... the **First Born** fed on something else. Like, where others would learn **fear, he** learned **hate**." Through war and murder, the First Born "... conquered it **all**. The world was a mirror image of his black **heart**." When Zeus, Poseidon, and Hades worked together to destroy the First Born's army, and banished him to the center of the Earth, it took him seven thousand years, driven by hate and aggression, to claw his way out. The First Born is exemplary of a male aggressor in war.

Zeus's sexual prowess is an example of the cultural value of the virile man who is the aggressor or instigator in sex. Zeus has multiple children by women other than his wife, Hera. Further, he is a trickster when he initiates his affairs. Hermes tells Zola in *Blood* that "When Zeus consorts with a woman other than his wife, he chooses a form that will inspire an uncontrollable lust in them." This account of Zeus's methods aligns with Williams's belief that men are often culturally portrayed as initiators of sex, and women are characterized as vulnerable to trickery and in need of protection (rather than initiators themselves).

Demeter is an example of the mother and nurturer of humanity. She is not only a goddess of fertility, but Hermes brings Zeke to her for safe keeping. Demeter holds baby Zeke within her own womb in her efforts to protect and nurture him. We witness the colliding of cultural values when Ares steals baby Zeke. Demeter tells Wonder Woman, "He ripped me open and took the baby. And I let him do it... I couldn't stop him."[17] Demeter is here a marker of deference, sacrifice, and martyrdom—all stereotypical feminine characteristics.

Williams discusses how cultural assumptions about male aggression and female maternal instincts make gender stereotypes seem like inevitable truths rather than stereotypes to be challenged, and how they undermine calls for equality between men and women. For example, Williams says that we cannot stomach women as aggressors in war because we think of "mom" going off to fight, and not a woman who is equal to a man in skill and training. Further, we are conflicted when we think about paternity leave because, while we want women to be equal, many of us have deeply held beliefs that women are the only ones qualified to take care of children. We cannot stomach equality in parental leave because we imagine "dad" completely bewildered in the face of infant care. We do not envision a man who is as capable as his female counterpart in figuring out how to bond with, nurture, and care for the needs of a child (and most first-time mothers—biological or adoptive—will confess to how big the learning curve is).

Everyone (and No One) is Watching You!

Although *Wonder Woman* (the New 52) has many examples of stereotypical gender behavior, it is also loaded with examples where the characters push back against the stereotypes and bend gender norms. For example, in *Blood*, Hippolyta describes her equality in sex with Zeus, and Zola doesn't apologize for having sex with whomever she pleases. Hera is able to shift from being a stereotypical scorned woman to a more compassionate, self-defined individual.

French philosopher Michel Foucault (1926–1984) and contemporary American philosopher Judith Butler are two important philosophers who influenced the early thinking about gender bending. And *Wonder Woman* (the New 52) helps illustrate their thinking. Foucault is central to the history of continental philosophy and is also widely cited by literary theorists, sociologists, and political theorists. Foucault is famous for interrogating the authenticity of grand narratives, or the belief systems that societies construct to describe themselves. He questions them by presenting alternate histories, or genealogies, of social norms (like sexuality and punishment) and institutions (like marriage and prisons). His genealogies underscore how focusing on a different set of facts changes a narrative. This, in turn, shows how knowledge is constructed. But this is not to suggest that history is merely the story told by the victors, and that Foucault's only goal is to give voice to the underdog. Foucault's theory is more complex, and it has to do with his understanding of power.

Foucault examines how power works when it is not consciously wielded by a person, but is hidden and self-reproducing. In *Discipline and Punish*,[18] he gives his well-known example of the Panopticon, which helps us to understand his view of power apart from the people who wield it.[19] The Panopticon is a prison design with a guard tower in the center and cells constructed in a circle around the tower. The guards in the tower can see the entire cell, but the prisoners cannot see inside the tower. The prison functions well because it trains the prisoner to internalize the rules so deeply that s/he no longer needs them externally enforced.

This is an example of how power works in western society. Foucault believes that people internalize (usually mindlessly) the norms of society, instead of genuinely reflecting on what we ought or ought not to do. In this way, long entrenched social institutions and theories of knowledge can reproduce negative social, economic, and political outcomes. In effect, no one is running the machine, but everyone thinks that someone is. Further, rules and dominant beliefs often seem "natural," and beyond question, when they are, in fact, socially constructed and supportive of some form of power of which we are not consciously aware. Foucault's Panopticon is a famous example of his belief that most of us are duped in the face of power structures; we fail to reflect on the constructed nature of knowledge and norms.

Apollo identifies and challenges an unexamined but dominant narrative in *Flesh* when he ascends to the throne on Olympus, and suggests that they exclude his sister, Wonder Woman, who refuses to claim her mantle as the god of war. Apollo says to Poseidon, "We should look at this as an opportunity." When Poseidon says indignantly, "An Olympus without war?" Apollo responds "Don't tell me it's not something **all** of you would have preferred ages ago. This is an opportunity to usher in a new, enlightened Olympian age... to bury the past." Poseidon's shock reveals a belief that war is simply a natural, inevitable, and eternal part of Olympus that must be represented by a god. Apollo dares to challenge the seemingly natural order of Olympus. In similar ways we see Zola, Hera, and Wonder Woman challenge traditional concepts of gender.

The God of War is Wearing What?

Judith Butler's ground-breaking *Gender Trouble*[20] is well known for its examination of how social conventions unconsciously construct and reinforce traditional masculinity and femininity (which she calls gender normativity), and how to subvert them. Butler examines what she calls a cultural imperative for people to be identifiably masculine or feminine, to comply with heterosexual norms, and for biological bodies to match conventional gender identity.

Butler argues that binary thinking about gender is often done in the service of maintaining gender norms and heterosexuality. Here she is influenced by Foucault's belief about the internalization of norms, and the manner in which society teaches us to police ourselves. She questions the larger, socially acceptable, cultural narrative about femininity, biology, and sexuality. She wonders if there are alternate ways to organize information so that we can see how power plays a role in cultural views about gender and sexuality.

Butler's example of the drag performance gets at the heart of her view of gender. A drag performance is successful not because a person in drag has convinced us that s/he is imitating a real man or woman. It is successful when it underscores that there is no real, or natural, man or woman to imitate. In fact, all gender is a performance.[21]

Wonder Woman (the New 52) is full of examples of people giving non-conventional performances of their gender (although certainly not as disruptive as what Butler is describing—but her view is still instructive). For example, in *War-Torn* we explore the Amazonian commitment to shunning the world of men.[22] Not only do Amazons reject the male world, but these women are also aggressors in war when they slaughter the male village on Paradise Island. In *Iron*, the god War shows compassion toward a young Wonder Woman when she challenges him to what must be a fight to the death, and he spares her life, saying, "A warrior fights to the death but not on this night, little one." In *Iron*, War also rescues Zeke from Hermes and returns him to Zola.

Wonder Woman herself is one of the more interesting examples of a non-conventional performance of gender in *Wonder Woman* (the New 52). In *Flesh*, Wonder Woman finally embraces her mantle as the god of war. Hera is newly restored as a goddess, and presents Wonder Woman with an army of Amazons to fight the First Born. In addressing them, Wonder Woman says she will lead "Not as your princess but as the god of war!" While Williams demonstrated how war is typically seen as the domain of men, Wonder Woman and her mostly female army are taking it over. They perform their gender as feminine in their style of dress, but they subvert their typical gender role with their performance as ruthless warriors.

One Big Happy Family

Wonder Woman (the New 52) demonstrates traditional, binary gender roles but also bends norms in an interesting way that is relevant to contemporary thinking about gender. We looked at how gender bending impacts individual characters, but we can now extend our thinking to one type of family structure that it leads to. As Zola says to Zeke in *War*,[23] "You're gonna learn is, you have a weird family. Or we do. A weird, wonderful family." And weird it is! Case in point: Hera tries to kill Zeke, but eventually helps Wonder Woman, Zola, Hermes (and more!) to beat the First Born (Hera's own child) and place Zeke on Zeus's throne (not knowing, of course, that Zeke is actually Zeus reborn, and Athena, Zeus's daughter, helped him as Zola). Zola refers to a non-traditional family that includes pretty much every god except the First Born, and challenges a belief that only a two-parent traditional nuclear family can be a site of love, loyalty, and honor. It also has room for the requisite craziness that goes along with family. (I mean, doesn't every family have a Strife?) Wonder Woman's family is part biological and part constructed, yet it is one that many a mere mortal would envy. And it only exists because of some gender bending.

Notes

1. All references to graphic novels in this chapter are limited to volumes 1–7 of the *Wonder Woman* New 52 series.
2. My focus here is on broad and introductory themes in feminism, and I therefore do not discuss specific kinds of feminism like women of color feminisms (or Marxist, or psychoanalytic, or radical). However, I cannot emphasize enough that no one can have a nuanced understanding of feminism if they don't seriously examine how, among other categories, race and class intersect with gender (this is called intersectionality). To help readers embark on that complex journey, I recommend starting with Rosemary Tong's *Feminist Philosophy: An Introduction*. While the entire book is worth reading, be sure to read chapter 6, "Women of Color Feminism(s)." Tong's book also provides excellent bibliographies for further reading about all types of feminism.
3. Brian Azzarello, Cliff Chiang, and Tony Akins, *Wonder Woman*, vol. 1: *Blood* (the New 52) (New York: DC Comics, 2012).

4. Ibid.
5. Ibid.
6. Ibid.
7. Brian Azzarello, Cliff Chiang, Goran Sudzuka, and Matt Wilson, *Wonder Woman*, vol. 5: *Flesh* (the New 52) (New York: DC Comics, 2015).
8. Genevieve Lloyd, The Man of Reason: "Male" and "Female" in Western Philosophy, 2nd edn (New York: Routledge, 1983; reprinted 1993).
9. Carol Gilligan famously made this argument in *In a Different Voice* when she said that male morality is dominated by reason while female morality is governed by emotion. Carol Gilligan, *In a Different Voice: Psychological Theory and Women's Development* (Boston, MA: Harvard University Press, 1982; reprinted 1998).
10. Simone de Beauvoir, *The Second Sex*, translated by C. Borde and S. Malovany-Chevallier (New York: Alfred A. Knopf, 2010). If you are just beginning to read Simone de Beauvoir, you will find a clear introduction in Debra Bergoffen's entry on Simone de Beauvoir in the *Stanford Encyclopedia of Philosophy*, http://plato.stanford.edu/entries/beauvoir/#RecBea. Bergoffen also provides an excellent bibliography for further reading.
11. If you are interested in learning more about Jean-Paul Sartre, you might begin with Thomas Flynn's entry in the online *Stanford Encyclopedia of Philosophy*, http://plato.stanford.edu/entries/sartre/. Flynn also provides an excellent bibliography for further reading.
12. Brian Azzarello and Cliff Chiang, *Wonder Woman*, vol. 3: *Iron* (the New 52) (New York: DC Comics, 2013).
13. Brian Azzarello, Cliff Chiang, and Tony Akins, *Wonder Woman*, vol. 2: *Guts* (the New 52) (New York: DC Comics, 2012).
14. *Wonder Woman*, vol. 5: *Flesh* (the New 52).
15. Williams, Wendy, "The Equality Crisis: Some Reflections on Culture, Courts and Feminism," in *Feminist Social Thought: A Reader*, edited by Diana Tietjens Meyers (New York: Routledge, 1983; reprinted 1997), 695–713.
16. *Wonder Woman*, vol. 3: *Iron* (the New 52).
17. *Wonder Woman*, vol. 3: *Iron* (the New 52).
18. Michele Foucault, *Discipline and Punish: the Birth of the Prison*, translated by Alan Sheridan (New York: Vintage, 1985). For a clear introduction to Foucault's work, and a bibliography for further reading, consult Gary Gutting's entry in the *Stanford Encyclopedia of Philosophy*, http://plato.stanford.edu/entries/foucault/.
19. See, in particular, *Discipline and Punish*, Part Three: "Panopticism," 205–208.

20. Judith Butler, *Gender Trouble: Feminism and the Subversion of Identity* (New York: Routledge, 1990).
21. See *Gender Trouble*, "From Interiority to Gender Performatives," 134–141.
22. Meridith Finch, David Finch, and Sonia Oback, *Wonder Woman*, vol. 7: *War-Torn* (the New 52) (Burbank: DC Comics, 2015).
23. Brian Azzarello, Cliff Chiang, and Goran Sudzuka, *Wonder Woman*, vol. 4: *War* (the New 52) (Burbank: DC Comics, 2014).

Wonder Woman vs. Harley Quinn
The Paradox of the Moral Hero

Jill Hernandez and Allie Hernandez

This chapter is unique for several reasons. First, it brings together two unlikely authors—a PhD ethicist and her 15-year-old high-school daughter, whose diverse interests include thinking about depictions of female characters in graphic novels. Second, it compares two unlikely DC female characters—Wonder Woman (the Amazonian princess heroine who protects innocent citizens from evil) and Harley Quinn (the ever-evolving anti-hero who vacillates between being an outright villain to being merely window dressing for her boyfriend, the Joker). The conclusion of the chapter is unlikely, too: neither Wonder Woman nor Harley Quinn can ultimately succeed in their roles as moral hero and immoral anti-hero when their popularity depends upon them being depicted as sexual objects.

It's a big year for female supers, and Wonder Woman and Harley Quinn both find their way onto the big screen. But, beyond their Hollywood resurgence, when we look at how DC has changed the way they are drawn over time, a philosophical puzzle emerges: as Wonder Woman and Harley Quinn are more provocatively drawn, their success as hero and villain plummets—and we want Wonder Woman (especially) to succeed as a *moral* hero, not just as a superhero. We will use Aristotle's ethics to show that it isn't Wonder Woman's virtue that is thwarted, but her *phronesis* (practical wisdom). Harley's anti-heroism is similarly in jeopardy, since *phronesis* helps any person set

Wonder Woman and Philosophy: The Amazonian Mystique, First Edition.
Edited by Jacob M. Held.
© 2017 John Wiley & Sons, Ltd. Published 2017 by John Wiley & Sons, Ltd.

and meet goals. The result is two drastically different characters—Wonder Woman, a superhero and moral model, and Harley Quinn, the foil to Wonder Woman's ideal—who both decline as supers when their sexuality is emphasized.

Merciful Minerva! Look at That (Costume)!

Even though Wonder Woman's history is much longer than Harley Quinn's, both characters have been through decades' worth of changes.[1] The first images of Wonder Woman in the 1940s featured a solidly built, muscular, and tall princess. Her costume, despite its changes, is iconic: each is some version of a red, white, and blue costume that becomes emblematic of American patriotism. The 1940s suit is more modest than those worn by swimsuit starlets of the period, though drawn with knee-high boots, large briefs, and tunic top that shows neither cleavage nor midriff. Variations of the suit included a blue skirt that fell to Diana's knees. Wonder Woman's signature outfit debuted in the 1960s: a body suit without the skirt, with the same knee-high boots and tiara. The leather cuffs of the 1940s become metal in the 1960s and she is drawn with a new weapon: her lasso. In spite of some short-lived changes in the costume in the 1970s, the 1960s Wonder Woman threads stay largely unchanged—and become even more identifiable as Wonder Woman's when Lynda Carter dashes onto the small screen. There are fewer stars in the blue briefs, and the eagle that adorns the top stretches its wings across Carter's bust, but apart from those minor changes, the suit became synonymous with power, capability, and beauty in women.[2] The impact of the 1960s Wonder Woman outfit lasts, really, until the 1990s. (Although the late 1980s featured a Wonder Woman with the big hair of the decade, and more defined muscles, the changes to her costume—such as integrating the "WW" into the eagle of the tunic—are relatively small.)

The sexualization of Diana's character is most obvious in the 1990s. Some people point out that virtually all female characters underwent a sexualization in the 1990s—despite this being the decade in which some (like Harley Quinn) are most conservatively dressed. But, Wonder Woman is completely transformed in the 1990s—instigated when Diana loses the title of Wonder Woman in a fight with Artemis. When Artemis takes over, Wonder Woman undergoes her most provocative changes. Artemis's hair is long, strawberry blonde, and bedraggled. Her bust is her prominent feature, thrust out, and seemingly augmented. Her briefs are no longer briefs, but an extreme French-cut near-thong that has some stars on it to highlight her extremely thin thighs. Her frequent pose is dominatrix-like, her hair whipping about her body, and a quiver of arrows suggestively dangling across her crotch (rather than on her hip). Artemis-as-Wonder-Woman also has the knee-high boots that look similar to the Lynda Carter version, with the exception of black leather laces. Interestingly, when Diana is not Wonder Woman, she undergoes a similarly sexualized transformation. Unable to give up entirely her superhero ways, she parades around in all black, except for a yellow "WW" belt affixed to biker shorts. Her bare midriff dazzles underneath a skimpy black bra (which is itself attached by a double-V strap back and front). Her stiletto boots evoke a sexy biker chic rather than superhero functionality. Sometimes she pairs the outfit with a midi-jacket and gloves. After Artemis's death, Diana literally picks up the crown, and figuratively, the Wonder Woman mantle. For a few years, the post-Artemis Wonder Woman features a sexier take on the classic Wonder Woman costume. The near-thong is replaced with a fuller French-cut brief, giving way to tremendously muscular legs. The breasts are still prominent, but a bit smaller. Her hair returns to its 1980s volume, with 1990s curl. And the boots lose their dominatrix laces. The image is startling in its ferocity.

In the 2000s, redesigns make the 1990s sexualization of Diana and Wonder Woman an important historical and philosophical artifact. The iconic costume returns in the *Justice League* cartoon, aimed at children. Adults see two versions of Wonder Woman—the first, a Sons of Anarchy-esque character with black leggings and boots, dark biker jacket, and a red and gold top (with still-prominent bust) and the second, a 2015 fully clothed Wonder Woman. Her tunic seems to be Kevlar armor, and even protects part of her neck. Her arms are fully concealed, from gold shoulder plates to gold armbands, with blue Kevlar in between. Her boots are now thigh-high, but appear to be an important defensive tool, and her already completely covered muscular legs are adorned by an additional loin skirt. The most recent version of Wonder Woman, in the 2016 *Batman v Superman*, keeps the thigh-high weapon boots, loin skirt, and armorized costume but, because it's a Zac Snyder film, the colors are muted to appear gold.

It isn't controversial to say that Wonder Woman—a comic-book heroine that has never gone out of print since her inception—has always served as the ideal woman of the time. Her pin-up girl status of the 1940s helped aid the American war effort. The classic Wonder Woman costume from the 1960s until (with some notable, and cringe-worthy, exceptions) today is drawn to reflect strong women who can independently save the day (as she has done throughout her comic book runs), work alongside the guys (as in the *Justice League*), and fight for women's rights (such as suffrage, education, equality of pay and employment, and access to birth control[3]).

Although her history is not as long—and her goal is typically to undermine the superhero—Harley Quinn has gone through a similar evolution in the way that she is drawn.

Call Me Harley! Everyone Does!

Harley Quinn debuted in *Batman: The Animated Series* in 1992 as an accomplice to the Joker and was originally supposed to be a one-time character. But fans were wild for the cutesy and funny girl partner, so she returned by popular demand and today is one of the most loved (and controversial) female characters in the DC Universe.

Similar to Wonder Woman, Harley's costume has become a classic, from her *Animated Series* debut throughout the early 2000s. That costume clads Harley in a form-defining but non-revealing red and black jumpsuit with her signature pigtail-fitting hat, which allows for her to be flexible and athletic (especially since her primary form of mobility is jumping from rooftop to alleyway of Gotham City). But with DC's relaunch of the New 52 in 2011, Harley's character took an *extreme* turn. The once playful and innocent clown turned into someone who looks, as some fans claim, like she came straight from a brothel. In addition, Harley is no longer that playful and innocent girl she once was: she is a monster—volatile, vicious, and violent. The most recent change for Harley will be in *Suicide Squad*, her first cinematic appearance. It is hard to definitively say anything about this Harley at the moment, but we can infer plenty from set pictures and screen grabs from the trailers. Harley is dressed in sparkly red and blue short shorts, a hole-filled tee with "Daddy's Little Monster" written on it, fishnets, Adidas platforms, tattoos, blue and pink dyed hair, and occasionally a jacket that reads "Property of Joker." Actors in the movie have teased Quinn as fun, violent, psychotic, and "pretty vicious," although Margot Robbie (who portrays Harley) said that she felt "self-conscious" while filming in her flimsy Harley outfit.[4]

Despite when and how Harley Quinn and Wonder Woman are depicted, their main roles as anti-hero and hero depend on them either disrupting justice (for Harley) or ensuring that justice is served (for Wonder Woman). Each of them, at their best, actually map onto Aristotle's idea for moral heroes and villains.

Athena's Shield! No Nada Zero Zip Zilch Nothin' (to Know)!

Aristotle would probably have been a fan of graphic novels. Not only was he the student of Plato (who was himself the student of real-life hero Socrates, who refused to run away to escape his death penalty sentence for corrupting the youth by teaching them philosophy), but he was enamored with the same questions that graphic novels bring up: Is it possible to be a good bad guy? Can we only call someone a "good person" after they have died and we know all that they have done? What happens when good people are part of a corrupt state? Can you want bad things and still be moral? Do your friends matter, morally? We think Aristotle would have especially been interested in Wonder Woman and Harley Quinn as graphic novel characters— Wonder Woman as an ideal moral hero, and Harley as the epitome of a moral anti-hero.

Aristotle thinks that we live the best lives possible when we strengthen what makes us human—our bodies and our minds. Iconic Wonder Woman is set apart by her strength, her power, her independence, her beauty, and how she carries herself.[5] But to be a superhero, she also has to possess self-confidence, courage, and wisdom. Each of these three are crucial to Aristotle's view of the moral hero. But virtue, physical strength, and a good reputation can't be attained without honing that part of us that sets us apart from every other species—our *reason*. Aristotle wrote a significant amount about athletes and the good habits they have to develop to succeed, but he thought even the best physical specimens will fail if they don't have wisdom to know how to become strong or to compete. The best soldier (another favorite topic of Aristotle's) could be the bravest of his company, but without wisdom to know when his courage should be used, he'll charge straight into his own death.

That kind of wisdom is called *phronesis*, or practical wisdom. *Phronesis* is not book-smarts. Rather, it helps regular people set goals and attain them, interact with a wide range of people without causing offense, resist desires that lead to impractical or immoral choices, and know how to improve personally and in relationships. In superheroes and villains, *phronesis* helps them become unstoppable.

Although Aristotle's moral goal is to help us become fulfilled, virtuous people, it's pretty easy to see why *phronesis* would benefit Wonder Woman and Harley Quinn in their efforts to be the best hero and antihero in the universe. Since *phronesis* aims to help us achieve our goals, heroes and villains both benefit by becoming practically wise. Just like the courageous soldier, we want our superheroes to be informed about the consequences their actions will bring, and the best time to use their abilities. Similarly, we disrespect villains who are so dumb—or so hasty—that they haven't thought through what they are up against and how best to be bad.

Aristotle actually says a lot about moral heroes and moral antiheroes. The moral hero (or "virtuous agent") uses *phronesis* to practice habits that silence unhealthy desires in the hero. Such a hero no longer battles temptation in her pursuit to do good. She is steadfast in her commitment to live a contented, flourishing life of virtue. Wonder Woman frequently uses practical wisdom to outsmart (rather than overpower) her enemies. A fantastic example is in *Wonder Woman* #34, when she is almost killed by the demi-god Strife. Physical strength fails Diana, and at the end of the issue Strife readies the death blow for a nearly passed out Wonder Woman. Before she can be killed though, Wonder Woman convinces Strife that if she died, there would be lasting peace—something Strife (obviously) couldn't put up with. So, Strife carries a battered, beaten, but alive Diana to safety.[6]

But Aristotle also thinks that *phronesis* is beneficial for the moral anti-hero (or "vicious agent"). The anti-hero is a master at manipulating situations to serve her self-interest, but also masters her desires so that they, too, will help her attain her goals. She is patient in her commitment to live a life where no one gets in her way. Harley Quinn, at her best, demonstrates this excellently. In an issue of *Suicide Squad*, she is forced to kill her prized pet hyenas after the Joker poisoned them and ordered them to attack her.[7] In a recent issue of *Harley Quinn*, still mentally disturbed by the loss, she encounters the Joker in a prison and they fight. Throughout the fight, Joker mocks Harley with sexual ferocity—insisting on how much she still wants him and loves him.[8] She knows that to best him she has to rise above his crude invective and use his weaknesses (including his distractability and love of his own voice) against him. Fueled by the darkest and angriest hatred within her, she leaves the Joker bloodied, tells him that he "disgusts" her, and warns him that if she ever hears from him, or if he dares threaten her friends or family, she will kill him.

Of course, Aristotle wouldn't think Harley's *phronesis* leads her to morality—although it would make her a serious villain. Wonder Woman, and heroes like her, are better heroes when they are armed with practical wisdom to defeat their opponents and seek justice. And, for those people who do not want to be moral—but only want to serve themselves, like Harley Quinn—*phronesis* can still be an important tool for getting what you want. Neither Wonder Woman nor Harley Quinn can achieve their goals as hero and anti-hero if they lack the ability to outsmart (and so outlast) their opponents. In short, the most successful hero and anti-hero have one thing in common: they have *phronesis*.

My Boss Likes Me to Wear (Just) a Smile to Work!

Unfortunately, neither Wonder Woman nor Harley Quinn always exhibit *phronesis*, and our view is that, often, what they seem to lack in practical wisdom is related to a real lack in clothing. Their altered, sexualized apparel evinces a shift in their very purpose, or function, within the graphic novel, from world-wise hero/anti-hero to objectified, sexual beings. Aristotle never actually wrote about whether we lose *phronesis* as we lose crucial body-part coverage in public, but if he could have indulged an interest in graphic novels, we think he would have. Even though Diana and Harley remain firmly on opposite sides of justice, they both suffer a lack of *phronesis* when they are drawn as sex objects.

Maybe it's true that everyone loses *phronesis* when their clothes come off, but the bigger problem facing Wonder Woman and Harley Quinn by losing *phronesis* is that their moral goals (for Wonder

Woman, to preserve peace and for Harley, to upset it) are disrupted. They actually become less heroic (less powerful, less convincing) when they are drawn provocatively. And although we won't conclude that it *must* be true that revealing costumes result in a lack of heroism or anti-heroism for any character, we think the evidence shows that the sexualization of these two does undermine how seriously we can take them as supers.

Comparing Wonder Woman and Harley Quinn as potentially flawed moral hero and anti-hero requires comparing them as women and as supers. Harley has, until recently, been known as Joker's girlfriend (so already dependent on a man for her success), whereas Diana has escaped marriage (though not its pull[9]). Harley becomes Harley only after falling under the Joker's spell at Arkham Asylum, where she was Harleen Quinzel, famed psychiatrist. Diana is sometimes a thinly veiled (slightly mousier) cover for Wonder Woman, although often Diana is not an alter-ego at all. Harley is manipulated by the Joker because of her need to be noticed, loved, or adored; Diana sometimes strings Steve along but typically love interests just get in the way of being Wonder Woman. In both women, their relationships with men are a source of significant weakness. Much has been made of Harley's abusive relationship with Joker; just as many deride Wonder Woman's original weakness: "As per Aphrodite's law, when an Amazon's bracelets are bound together by the actions of a man, she loses her powers."[10]

The differences in *phronesis* between the women are also bound—not to the actions of men—but to how they are presented to them. Harley Quinn's best-known origin story introduces her as the fully clothed imp who unsuccessfully tries to kill Commissioner Gordon and seduce the Joker. Rejected as a love object, Harley then succeeds in kidnapping Joker's archrival, Batman, and delivers him to the Joker. Harley expects him to be proud of her, but instead he is livid. The Joker knocks Harley unconscious and begins to battle Batman, and becomes more enraged when Batman admits that Harley came closer to getting rid of him than the Joker ever did.[11]

Harley's *phronesis* and role as anti-hero might be at unparalleled heights in this first issue. We learn that she has an MD, and though she has an unrequited love for the Joker, she uses her rejection to capture his worst enemy in just a few short hours. After this, Harley continues to pull off a series of capers, both with and without the Joker, relying on various melee-style weapons, from bombs disguised as pies to her famous bang-pistol. In the 19-year time period since the introduction of Harley Quinn, this is the most exposed we are to Harley's internal battles. We fall in love with her as a villain in part because she represents someone who is unhinged, powerful, uncontrolled, and yet fighting a war of her own. Issues prior to her 2011 reboot see her breaking up with the Joker,[12] taking on Bruce Wayne by herself,[13] working with Two-Face to kidnap and steal,[14] and appropriating a Batgirl persona to wreak havoc on Gotham.[15] Each of her endeavors are perfectly anti-heroic—and require *phronesis*: they take planning, inspire the independent growth of her evil and quirky character, require forethought, and help readers think of her as a standalone character worthy of our continued attention.

But the New 52 Harley Quinn series is a significant, hypersexualized reboot of a character as the 1990s Wonder Woman. While the series marks a time in which Harley Quinn is no longer solely known as Joker's girl, she is now only depicted as a character who functions at the level of the double-entendre, where sex is always possible. Harley starts to lose the playful quality that endeared many to her and becomes—well, *crazy*—and as a sexual object, the least likely to take seriously as an anti-hero. The comics include threesomes with Poison Ivy, long conversations with her pet stuffed beaver, and sexual encounters with anyone she wants something from. An exchange with Green Arrow is a great example. In the first panel, we see someone holding a smoking gun that looks to be stoppered with something. Next, Harley waves the gun around and says, "No. Way." Harley tells Green Arrow, in the last panel, "Do it again!" When he asks, "What...?" she replies, "Shoot another arrow into my gun barrel." Harley trades in her ability to know how to be a bad guy— she becomes outrageously violent (corresponding to her imaginative weapons), but loses focus on who and what she is fighting against or for. (Gone already are the *Suicide Squad* graphic novel days of being part of a team of black-ops villains.) DC is now marketing Harley as the "Clown Princess of Crime." The result is one that reviewers describe thusly: "*Harley Quinn* is an antidote to the far too serious super hero operas that it shares its universe with." Harley has devolved into a character that isn't meant to be taken seriously, except as a sexual fantasy.

This isn't to say that female characters can't be successful and sexualized to a degree. Rather, when the sole emphasis of Harley as a character is as a sexual conquest (or conquistador), then her ability to be a powerful villain or anti-hero evaporates. What has been lost? Knowledge of who is the opponent, why they are to be opposed, and what counts as success. In making her a singularly focused character, we as readers are unable to value her for anything else. And *that* is a loss of self—of who she has been for two decades. By sexualizing the character, the writers/illustrators have diminished the impact and the gravitas of the character. As a sexual object, presented only, or nearly exclusively, in this light, she can only be seen as one-dimensional. Perhaps this is also a commentary on the readers, on the way we process or internalize sexual norms and expectations. But even so, that would simply reinforce the point. *Phronesis*, or practical wisdom, one's efficacy in the world, is coded through one's image, and a hyper-sexualized image diminishes one's capacity to be maximally effective in the world. These supers don't function as well when their functionality is tied to sexualization. Being presented as, and received as, a sexualized being does affect one's ability to function well in the world.[16]

Great Hera! Wonder Wowsa!

It's really too bad that Harley has lost her hold on practical wisdom along with her clothing, because she would be a better, more successful anti-hero if we could buy into what she cares about, and could predict (even if her character is meant to be unpredictable) ways she can emerge as a villain to cheer for. We almost lost Wonder Woman to the same fate.

Recall Artemis's takeover of Wonder Woman in the 1990s. Diana is relegated to subcontract work. Among requests asked of her are to star in strip clubs, sell her used underwear, and kill errant spouses[17]—a far cry from saving Earth from the god of war! She does take payment for security detail, and gets so hard up for cash (apparently the Wonder Woman gig was well paying!) that she tries to kill Paulie Longo for the bounty (a million large).[18] When Diana is kidnapped by the Joker and inundated with his perverse jokes, she asks the god Pan for help, and he provides her with witty repartee, rather than the ability to escape.[19] During this time, Artemis is seen by some as an efficient Wonder Woman, but seems to be overwhelmed at the ... *phronesis* ... it takes to be Wonder Woman. She travels to the Amazon to take on poachers but concludes that it is too difficult for one person to solve, and when she uses the lasso (she's been practicing), its power makes "Involute the Conqueror" have a guilt trip about the wrongs he had done in his life and he shoots himself.[20] Artemis also doesn't have the quality Aristotle expects heroes with *phronesis* to have: the ability to set goals and relate to various people well. She talks tough, of course, but she crows to Diana, "You are incapable of real action! Your weakness has cost you your home, your name, and your legend,"[21] and later in the same issue, she clucks at Diana for being jealous. The Artemis-as-Wonder-Woman debacle ends (for both Artemis and Diana) in the 100th issue, in which Artemis (having been torn to pieces with her own lasso by the Magician) tells Diana, "Take back your uniform, Diana. I have ... dishonored it. My ambition and arrogance nearly got us both killed. YOU are Wonder Woman."[22]

Artemis is right about one thing—the uniform was dishonored in the 1990s reboot. And, though it took a few years for Wonder Woman and Diana to get back on track to an intelligent, strong, fierce character with *phronesis*, the 2000s and recent reboots may have gotten us there. For whatever damage the New 52 has done to Harley Quinn's character, the New 52's Wonder Woman is indeed a moral hero.[23] Her causes are about what *ought* to be done—she is after justice. And she is once again guided by *phronesis*. In each of the current iterations, whether she fights gods, aliens, monsters, or men, Diana starts by arming herself with facts (e.g., she goes into the underworld alone to rescue Zola, but prepares by conversing with Hephaestus first[24]), warns others about the integrity of the enemy ("these soldiers are devoid of mercy"[25]), aims toward her own improvement ("truth is best shared by example"[26]), stops the bad guys justly ("she grabs the man, threatens him, chokes him, and throws him *through* the door to the front lawn, where he begs for the police to arrest him"[27]), and even shows her opponents alternatives to evil action ("A life of endless murder?" Wonder Woman tells Astarte when she wants to enslave Earth, "I offer you a way out"[28]). Perhaps the most endearing quality of Wonder Woman's *phronesis* is that it isn't perfect. She sometimes doesn't know what to do or doesn't quite make the right calculation. (She tells Pele, for example, that she didn't know that Zeus—the patron god of the Amazons—had killed Pele's father despite being a peaceful man. Pele then throws Wonder Woman into a volcano and Diana must denounce Zeus's actions in order to make amends.[29])

What continues to draw us to Wonder Woman is that she is enough of everything we want (physically, intellectually, emotionally, and morally) from a superhero. Not a *female* superhero, but a superhero. As readers (or viewers), we like a sexy superhero. Part of the allure of a costume can be, after all, what is costumed. But the question for us is, *what is the main function of this character?* Just as with the current rendering of Harley, Wonder Woman historically is at her least effective as a hero when her primary role is as a sex object. When she's designed to be titillating, then her character suffers, and her ability to be an effective, ideal super suffers. In the 1990s, she suffered. But Wonder Woman today is an excellent moral hero: relatable because she isn't perfect, powerful because she's evolving, admirable because of her ability and beauty, and imitable because of her *phronesis*. And as her current getup lets her go full out after the bad guys without being hampered by being drawn solely as a sex idol, we (daughter and mother, young and not-as-young) see a Diana we want to continue on for the next 100 years—mostly as the muscular, graceful Amazonian princess wielding a lasso, cuffs, and a classically colored, functional armor that covers a little more than the bare essentials.

Notes

1. http://www.techtimes.com/articles/57607/20150615/evolution-woman-wonder-costumes-throughout-years.htm has a great visual on Wonder Woman's evolution in dress since her inception, and was helpful to us when we were writing this chapter. Accessed May 28, 2016.

2. We should say here that Lynda Carter felt that the show's costume was too revealing.

3. *Wonder Woman* retells the story of "wonder women" in the suffrage movement; graduates women with higher education degrees from "Wonder Woman College"; pushes for equal pay and pay for domestic work; and Wonder Woman herself became an icon for the feminist movement by being featured on the cover of the inaugural issue of *US* magazine in 1972. Jill Lepore, *The Secret History of Wonder Woman* (New York: Vintage Books, 2015).

4. *Movie Pilot*, "Quinn and Bare It: Margot Robbie Admits She Was Self-Conscious in Harley Quinn's Revealing Outfit," http://moviepilot.com/posts/3889457. Accessed May 28, 2016.

5. Lepore (2015) discusses these aspects as part of William Marston's desire to create a character who would embody "a great movement not under way—the growth in the power of women" (196, 191–198).

6. *Outer Places*, "9 Things You Might Not Know About Wonder Woman," http://www.outerplaces.com/science-fiction/item/10310-9-things-you-might-not-know-about-wonder-woman. Accessed May 28, 2016.

7. *Suicide Squad*, Issue 15, December 12, 2012.

8. *Harley Quinn*, Issue 25, February 17, 2016. This encounter was (to date) the last meeting between the two in print.

9. Lepore (2015, 227–230) includes "The Amazon Bride", *Comic Cavalcade* #8 (Fall 1944) as an example of Wonder Woman's feminist leanings. In it, Diana wakes from a nightmare in which she married Capt. Steve Trevor.

10. *Wonder Woman*, #229 (March 1977).

11. "Mad Love," episode of "The New Batman Adventures," January 16, 1999.

12. *Harley Quinn*, 1:1.

13. *Harley Quinn*, 1:6.

14. *Harley Quinn*, 1:2.

15. *Harley Quinn*, 1:10.

16. See American Psychological Association, "Task Force on the Sexualization of Girls." Report of the APA Task Force on the Sexualization of Girls (Washington, DC: American Psychological Association, 2007). Retrieved from http://www.apa.org/pi/wpo/sexualization.html (accessed July 18, 2016).

17. *Wonder Woman*, 2:91, November 1994.

18. *Wonder Woman*, 2:94, February 1995.

19. Ibid.

20. *Wonder Woman*, 2:93, January 1995.

21. *Wonder Woman*, 2:98, June 1995.

22. *Wonder Woman*, 2:100, August 1995.

23. It's too early to tell with Rebirth, but Earth One seems promising.

24. New 52 *Wonder Woman*, 4:8.

25. New 52 *Wonder Woman*, 4:27.

26. New 52 *Wonder Woman*, 4:34.

27. New 52 *Wonder Woman*, 3:5.

28. New 52 *Wonder Woman*, 3:43.

29. New 52 *Wonder Woman*, 3:35.

Great Hera!
Considering Wonder Woman's Super Heroism

Trip McCrossin

It seems reasonable enough to assume that superheroes are heroes. On the face of it, they share at least some characteristics conventionally associated with heroism. Consider the following four-part tentative definition of heroism.

First, heroes act to safeguard others. Batman and Superman, for example, have kept mostly to safeguarding the citizens of Metropolis and Gotham City, respectively. Even during World War II, Batman's mandate extended only modestly to the war effort, unlike Superman's, which extended a bit more broadly. Wonder Woman, in contrast, has had a broader mandate from the start.

Not only does she leave Paradise Island to return home the injured Trevor, but her mandate ranges over no less than the "world torn by the hatreds and wars of men."[1] Her purpose is no less than to "wage battle for freedom, democracy, and womankind thru-out the world!"[2] And in the *Wonder Woman* film franchise, she's involved in World War I. However local or global the safeguarding, one's not much of a hero if one's not doing the basic safekeeping thing.

Second, heroes safeguard those around them, near or far, in a manner that's *moral*. "She appears as though from nowhere," Wonder Woman does, "to avenge an injustice or right a wrong!"[3]

Third, heroes safeguard those around them in an *altruistic* manner; they selflessly help others. Think about how often Wonder Woman has

Wonder Woman and Philosophy: The Amazonian Mystique, First Edition.
Edited by Jacob M. Held.
© 2017 John Wiley & Sons, Ltd. Published 2017 by John Wiley & Sons, Ltd.

neglected her own wants, desires, or welfare to safeguard others. She leaves her home to return Steve Trevor—even if curiosity motivated this just a tinge—and stays to assist in the war effort, protect humanity from Ares, and continually sacrifices for others.

Fourth, heroes safeguard those around them in a manner that is *atypical*—in ways that the unheroic are unwilling or unprepared to act. If a hero's actions weren't atypical, that is, then heroism would be a widespread phenomenon, void of meaning.[4]

So, what makes heroes "super"? What makes them so is the conventional exaggeration of the first and fourth characteristics. On the one hand, superheroes act to safeguard others *systematically*. Wonder Woman's "battle for freedom, democracy, and womankind thru-out the world!" has been with us for over 75 years.[5] On the other hand, they act in a manner not just atypical, but *radically* so. Wonder Woman performs her daring feats, that is, with "the agility of Mercury and the steel sinews of a Hercules!"[6]

While Superman, Batman, and Wonder Woman are similar in these respects, there are also differences, two in particular, that help to clarify their heroism. So, let's consider a fifth and sixth part of our definition of heroism.

(Super)Heroes as (Super)Samaritans

In addition to the systematic, generally moral, specifically altruistic, radically atypical safekeeping of others, we also want heroism to be *supererogatory*—performed without obligation.[7] A Good Samaritan is someone who acts to promote another's welfare, *on purpose*, but *not out of obligation*. We can think of a hero in the same spirit, and not as just a *Good* Samaritan, but as an *Extraordinary* Samaritan. Heroism is a property not only of acts, but also of actors. To get at this idea, let's compare the following two cases.

Consider first the case of Wesley Autrey. On January 2, 2007, Mr. Autrey jumped onto the subway tracks at the 137th Street station in Harlem to save a young man, Cameron Hollopeter. Mr. Hollopeter had fallen in as a result of a seizure, and Autrey laid himself over Hollopeter in between the tracks as the oncoming subway train rolled over them. For this, Autrey was dubbed the "Hero of Harlem." When asked what motivated him to act as he did, however, Autrey resisted the language of heroism. "I don't feel like I did something spectacular," he said, "I just saw someone who needed help. I did what I felt was right."

Consider also the case of Captain Chesley "Sully" Sullenberger. On January 15, 2009, Captain Sullenberger piloted US Airways flight 1549 to an emergency water landing on the Hudson River. His actions saved the lives of all aboard and those who would have been injured or killed if the plane had crashed anywhere else in the vicinity. For this, Sullenberger was dubbed the "Hero of the Hudson." Mayor Bloomberg commented that Sullenberger had done "a masterful job of landing the plane in the river and then making sure everybody got out." Why didn't Bloomberg call him a hero? Presumably, for the same reason Sullenberger himself admits; his actions were simply "what we're trained to do."

It's hard to imagine Sullenberger turning to his co-pilot, saying "I'm sitting this one out," and not being judged negligent. Autrey, however, if he'd turned to someone on the subway platform and spoken similarly, might well be excused. To sit in a captain's chair is to accept certain obligations toward one's passengers, but to stand on a subway platform is to accept few, if any, such obligations toward one's fellow commuters. Autrey was not obligated to act as Sullenberger was. Autrey acted as a Samaritan, an *extraordinary* one. It's not for nothing that he's more widely known as the "Subway Samaritan," and for precisely this reason he's also the "Hero of Harlem."

But isn't there a worry here, if Samaritanism as a characteristic of heroism leads us to find Autrey more heroic than Sullenberger? Worse, might the idea undermine the latter's heroism altogether? Let's consider police officers and fire fighters, for example, in the twin cities of *Batman v Superman*, or military personnel, such as Steve Trevor. Would they take issue with the idea that doing what they're "trained to do," and paid for, is not heroic?[8]

One way we might respond would be to distinguish *becoming* a police officer, fire fighter, or military personnel, in which case we accept the corresponding general duty to serve the public, from *continuing* to *be* one, in which case we fulfill more routinely the various particular duties expected of us as police officers, fire fighters, or military personnel. Along these lines, we might be reluctant to attribute heroism to the relatively routine business of rescuing the Joneses from a fire, burglary, or the ravages of war. But we might want to call it heroic when actions are likely to cause significant injury or worse. So what does this tell us about the heroism of Superman, Batman, and Wonder Woman?

Consider the phenomenon of superhero retirement, as reflected, for example, in the storylines of *The Dark Knight Rises* and *Batman v Superman*. We're meant to enjoy the idea of Batman's happy retirement at the end of *The Dark Knight Rises*, even while we imagine Batman is still needed, as turns out to be the case in *Batman v Superman*. In the same spirit, it seems that we're again meant to enjoy and find reasonable Wonder Woman's retirement in the beginning of *Batman v Superman*, even while she comes out of retirement before too long.

We relate differently, however, to the idea of Superman's retirement. We find it harder to imagine. It seems that the only way to depict it is as either voluntary but disastrous, as in the 1980 *Superman II*, or as compelled and unhappy, as for example in the 1996 *Kingdom Come* storyline. In this sense, Superman's role as hero seems to be compulsory whereas Batman's and Wonder Woman's roles are voluntary and supererogatory. Thus, according to this interpretation, Wonder Woman and Batman are, in a sense, more heroic. Wonder Woman isn't obliged to come to Man's World to bring justice and equality. Rather, she goes out of her way, winning a contest, in order to have the right to do so. She volunteers, and she can return to Paradise Island whenever she chooses.

Making Heroes

In addition to heroic acts consisting of the systematic, generally moral, specifically altruistic, supererogatory, and radically atypical safekeeping of others, we also want them to be *replicable*—at least in principle. Let's look at Autrey again, but this time let's give him a superpower to see how this may alter our evaluation of his heroism.

What if we were to learn that prior to helping Hollopeter, Autrey had acquired one or more of the abilities possessed by three of Marvel Comics' Fantastic Four? Sue Storm, for example, as the Invisible Woman, can surround herself and others in an impregnable force field. What if Fantastic Autrey, let's call him, could do likewise, and so be immune from harm, as he lay atop Hollepeter? Or what if like Ben Grimm, as the Thing, he had petrified skin, or like Reed Richards, as Mister Fantastic, he could stretch himself out and so thin himself prudentially? The origins of Fantastic Autrey's ability, whatever it may be, might be accidental, like those acquired by the Fantastic Four, or learned, like those that gave us Aquaman, or gifted, like those that gave us Green Lantern, or inborn, like those that gave us Superman, or learned, gifted, and inborn, like those that gave us Wonder Woman. Whatever the origin, they wouldn't have made it *easy* for Fantastic Autrey to safeguard young Cameron, but they would have nonetheless shielded him from harm. So if it were Fantastic Autrey who helped Hollopeter, we would naturally understand the manner of assistance as unavailable to us, making it difficult for us to imagine that we'd have acted as he did.

No matter how *super* Fantastic Autrey would be, and no matter how grateful young Cameron would surely be, would *we* think of Fantastic Autrey as a hero? Arguably, we wouldn't. We might happily suggest that the Fantastic Four become the Fantastic Five, but at the same time, regarding the question of heroism as opposed to superheroism, we would likely learn less happily that Fantastic Autrey was in no real danger. Part of the reason we value the *real-life* Autrey as a hero, and heroes in general, is because we imagine that if *they* can do what they do, then *the rest of us* can as well. They are aspirational figures, the very best of humanity.

In this spirit, Batman's actions, while extraordinary, are the result of abilities that are refinements of ones otherwise routinely human, and so replicable by the rest of us, at least in principle. Superman's, by contrast, while also extraordinary, result from abilities that are out of the reach of the rest of us, and so not replicable, either in principle or in practice. And then there's Wonder Woman. As we conventionally picture her, Wonder Woman appears to be more like Superman than Batman in terms of the replicability of her actions. We could probably get hold of a respectable enough tiara, that is, but much less obviously a magic lasso, bullet-repelling bracelets, or an invisible plane, let alone the "agility of Mercury and the steel sinews of a Hercules!" All three superheroes work for and among us, but as we conventionally picture her, Wonder Woman appears not to be one of us. She's Amazonian. She's not simply highly skilled and trained.

Rather, she's born of gods, gifted beyond measure, and at times even divine.

Making and Remaking Wonder Woman

Let's consider again the phenomenon of superhero retirement—Wonder Woman's in particular.

In a note that Marston sent along with his first script, he described the "under-meaning" of Wonder Woman's story as follows:

> Men (Greeks) were captured by predatory love-seeking females until they got sick of it and made the women captive by force. But they were afraid (masculine inferiority complex) and kept them heavily chained lest the women put one over as they always had before. The Goddess of Love comes along and helps women break their chains by giving them the greater force of real altruism. Whereupon men turned about face and actually helped the women get away from domestic slavery—as men are doing now. The NEW WOMEN thus freed and strengthened by supporting themselves (on Paradise Island) developed enormous physical and mental power. But they have to use it for other people's benefit or they go back to chains, and weakness.[9]

This nicely summarizes Wonder Woman as she is during the Golden Age of comics, from the late 1930s through the early 1950s. During the Silver and Bronze Ages, however, through the late-1970s and then the mid-1980s, respectively, Wonder Woman's "under-meaning" was altered.

Shortly before Marston's death in 1947, Robert Kanigher took over scripting Wonder Woman, and in 1958, a little over halfway through his first stint, he revamped Wonder Woman's origin story to make her abilities more magical. For most of us, when we picture Wonder Woman, it's Kanigher's Wonder Woman we picture, in part because she's the Wonder Woman of the ever-memorable television series.

In the interim, between Kanigher's two stints, Denny O'Neil assumed scripting duties for Wonder Woman, working with artist Michael Sekowski. Both came to DC Comics from Marvel Comics with its cohort of more down-to-earth superheroes, and together they fashioned for her a four-year, some would say infamous, course change. Wonder Woman was, in effect, Marvelized. "For ten thousand years, we have lived here, performing the mission assigned to us," Queen Hippolyta tells her daughter, "helping mankind to find maturity! But now, our magic is exhausted! We must journey to another dimension, to rest and renew our powers!" Diana decides to remain earthbound, because of her devotion to Trevor, even though doing so means the loss of her powers. "I hereby relinquish all mystic skills!" she declares, "I lay upon the sacred altar the glories of the Amazons and willingly condemn myself to the travails of mortals."

Shortly after, newly installed in the Lower East Side of Manhattan, and content to lead a vapid life of romance and fashion, she happens on an old blind man being accosted. She instinctively goes to his aid, but he easily dispatches his assailants. The old man, I Ching, is the last of an ancient order of monks that Dr. Cyber has recently wiped out. Taking Diana under his wing, I Ching teaches her a variety of martial arts, to replace her former mystical skills, and together they search for Trevor, who's been kidnapped by Dr. Cyber. When Cyber kills Trevor, Diana and I Ching travel the world—paraphrasing the language Marston used to introduce Wonder Woman—to "avenge injustice [and] right [the] wrong!"

The four-year Diana Prince era, while perhaps well intentioned, is rightly criticized for being scripted in a manner painfully out of step with the development of feminism, which Wonder Woman was meant to embody.[10] Still, in the present context, striving to sort out Wonder Woman's heroism, it's nevertheless telling. In advance of creating Wonder Woman, Marston spoke of the "sound wishes" that motivate superheroes to develop and use "great power, when we get it, to protect innocent, peace-loving people from destructive, ruthless evil."[11] Faced with the evil of Dr. Cyber, and newly bereft of her mystical skills, Diana would naturally ask "What would *Bruce Wayne* do?" Faced with personal tragedy that reflects a broader evil, as Wayne was, Diana develops her natural abilities, as did he.

Diana is "freed and strengthened" by I Ching, and working with him she "developed enormous physical and mental power." Just as most of us don't have the wealth and position of Bruce Wayne, we won't happen to stumble upon monks at just the right time. Still, at least in principle, what Diana does in becoming, not the more mystical Wonder Woman, but, as the series was renamed during this era, *Diana Prince: Wonder Woman*, others can do as well.

The bracelets, lasso, and plane are helpful. But the bracelets are helpful only if we've developed serious agility and hand–eye coordination. And Marston's own Lie Detector, while it doesn't hang as nicely on one's belt, can nevertheless stand in, to an extent, for the lasso. And the plane, well, Diana could always purloin a stealth fighter from the military. The point is that as per Marston's original vision, the challenge is to create circumstances—whether those of Paradise Island or the Lower East Side in the late 1960s—that allow us to be "freed and strengthened [...] for other people's benefit." Diana Prince allows us, as Bruce Wayne did before her, to aspire to precisely this—to be *super heroes*.

Superheroes and Super Heroes

Superman, Batman, and Wonder Woman emerged out of the pages of Detective Comics in quick succession, in the summer of 1938, spring of 1939, and winter of 1941, respectively, when humanity was in need of superheroes. But if superheroes aren't equally heroic, what's important about having both superheroes, such as Superman, and also *super heroes*, such as Batman and Diana Prince, Wonder Woman?

As we get further and further from the World Wars, we're not behaving proportionally better. We are as beset as ever by the problem of evil—asking ourselves no less frequently and urgently why, to paraphrase Marston, "innocent, peace-loving people [suffer] from destructive, ruthless evil." And it seems that by commission or omission *we* are mostly, if not entirely to blame. How then are *we* going to fix this? Naturally, we turn to superheroes like Superman. But we also *want* there to be such *super heroes* as Batman and Wonder Woman, so that we may hold out hope still, however meekly, that there may remain a few brave souls, not just in our midst, but *in our ranks*, willing to help lead us out of our self-imposed peril, and in the process inspire others to do the same.

Wonder Woman was always intended to be inspirational, to be an ideal toward which we could aspire. Her roots in feminism are testimony to this. Consider the feminism that Marston reflects in Wonder Woman—"freed and strengthened by supporting" one another, women develop "enormous physical and mental power,"[12] and use it to "save the world from the hatreds and wars of men,"[13] and help humanity "to find maturity!"[14] But the project only works if Wonder Woman can inspire others to be like her, and this can happen only if she's a superhero who's a super hero. Fortunately, it seems she's exactly that.[15]

Notes

1. Roy Thomas, *Wonder Woman: The War Years 1941–1945* (New York: Chartwell Books, 2015), 13. [William Moulton Marston, "Introducing Wonder Woman," *All Star Comics* #8, December 1941–January 1942.]
2. Ibid., 25 [William Moulton Marston, "Wonder Woman," *Sensation Comics* #1, January 1942.]
3. Ibid., 13. [William Moulton Marston, "Introducing Wonder Woman," *All Star Comics* #8, December 1941–January 1942.]
4. David Rand and Ziv Epstein have recently proposed an additional part of the definition of heroism. In their 2014 study of over 50 Carnegie Hero Medal recipients, they report that when subjects "explain why they decided to help, the cognitive processes they describe are overwhelming intuitive, automatic and fast"—more unreflective, that is, than reasoned. ("Risking Your Life without a Second Thought: Intuitive Decision-Making and Extreme Altruism," *PLOS ONE*, October 15, 2014. See also Erez Yoeli and David Rand, "The Trick to Acting Heroically," *The New York Times*, August 30, 2015.)
5. Thomas, *Wonder Woman: The War Years 1941–1945*, 25. [William Moulton Marston, "Wonder Woman," *Sensation Comics* #1, January 1942.]
6. Ibid., 25 [William Moulton Marston, "Wonder Woman," *Sensation Comics* #1, January 1942.]
7. J.O. Urmson proposes this in his essay "Saints and Heroes," in A.I. Melden (ed.), *Essays in Moral Philosophy* (Seattle, WA: University of Washington Press, 1958). His essay generated enduring interest in, and substantial work on, supererogation as a key ethical concept, including David Heyd's *Supererogation: Its Status in Ethical Theory* (Cambridge: Cambridge University Press, 1982) and, more recently, Andrew Flescher's *Heroes, Saints, and Ordinary Morality* (Washington, DC: Georgetown University Press, 2003).
8. Aristotle makes a related point in Section 2 of Chapter 8 of Book III of his *Nicomachean Ethics*, regarding the role of experience in exhibiting courage, and the way in which this allows us to account for citizen-soldiers acting in circumstances in which professional soldiers refrain.

9. Jill Lepore, *The Secret History of Wonder Woman* (New York: Alfred A. Knopf, 2014) (Kindle version).
10. Ibid. See also Part III of Tim Hanley's *Wonder Woman Unbound: The Curious History of the World's Most Famous Heroine* (Chicago, IL: Chicago Review Press, 2014).
11. Ibid.
12. Ibid.
13. Thomas, *Wonder Woman: The War Years 1941–1945*, 25.
14. Lepore, *The Secret History of Wonder Woman*.
15. I'd like to dedicate this to the Wonder Women who've taught and otherwise inspired me over the years—my mom, my teachers, Susan Neiman and Carol Rovane, and, of course, friends, colleagues, and co-parents, Erin Carlston, Rachel Devlin, Deborah Greenwood, Tamara Joseph, Kathy Newman, Jayne Pagnucco, Gina Pearson, Marina Sitrin, and Sue Zemka. I'm also grateful to Susan Neiman for my interest in, and understanding of, the related problems of heroism and evil. I'm grateful as well to Erin Carlston and Carisa Showden for the case of Sully Sullenberger, and what I believe is the helpful contrast it provides to Wesley Autrey. I'm additionally grateful to the folks in my Enlightenment Philosophy class, during the summer of 2015, for raising the worry involving police officers, fire fighters, and military personnel.

Part II
DISPATCHES FROM MAN'S WORLD

Wonder Woman
Feminist Faux Pas?

Andrea Zanin

Born out of the horror of World War II, Wonder Woman, Earth's first ever female superhero, was created as an antithesis to the blood-curdling masculinity that characterized the man's world it was back then—in 1941. Champion of justice, love, peace, and gender equality, America's feisty heroine inspired women to the feminist cause—a movement and philosophy advancing the wellbeing of women politically, economically, socially, and culturally. Wonder Woman was an attempt to reshape the "feminine destiny" articulated by French philosopher and feminist Simone de Beauvoir (1908–1986). In her post-World War II book *The Second Sex*, Beauvoir argues that "One is not born, but rather becomes, a woman."[1] By this, Beauvoir meant that women are not born "feminine," but rather are constructed that way through social indoctrination. The saga of Wonder Woman sheds light on women's history in resisting this social indoctrination from the 1940s to the present day.

Who Can Match Up?

Beauvoir focuses on the notion that woman has been held in a relationship of long-standing oppression to man through her relegation to being man's "Other." Beauvoir asserts that the self needs otherness

Wonder Woman and Philosophy: The Amazonian Mystique, First Edition.
Edited by Jacob M. Held.
© 2017 John Wiley & Sons, Ltd. Published 2017 by John Wiley & Sons, Ltd.

in order to define itself as a subject. The category of the otherness, therefore, is necessary in the constitution of the self *as a self*. In her investigation into the meaning and construction of femininity, Beauvoir finds that woman is consistently defined as the *Other* of man, who takes on the role of a subject, an active, actualized human being. As Beauvoir explains, woman "is the incidental, the inessential, as opposed to the essential. He is the Subject, he is the Absolute—she is the Other."[2]

The social structure changed briefly in the 1940s. While guys were off mowing down the enemies, gals were back home keeping things together—wearing the pants and doing it well. It took the upheaval of a world war to remind society that women are as capable as men, that they are worth more than the value society had dictated for hundreds of years. Women were liberated from the shackles of "Man's World" (even if for a brief moment) that prescribed procreation, above all else, as feminine purpose.

Wonder Woman was a representation of the unconventional, emancipated woman who darkened the door of a post-war world. She was anything *but* incidental or inessential. The change in social context had the potential to redefine what it meant to be a woman. And yet, 75 years later, in an ironic twist of culture, America's heroine has become something else, something problematic. In a new millennium, "wonder woman" is an unattainable ideal. She represents a pressure to be the impossible.

Today, Wonder Woman, with her Amazonian physique, superior strength (and breasts—*can't forget those*), intelligence, generosity, and unfailing love is the bane of womankind's existence. Quite simply, who can match up? But Wonder Woman, the heroine, was intended to empower, not belittle—right? Somewhere along the way we started taking the metaphor a little too seriously. She was an ideal, an example of what women could be. Is it wrong to strive for "perfection" and to have examples that show what it can look like? Is it a cop out to say that it puts pressure on us? Don't we need the pressure? Do we not risk succumbing to mediocrity without it?

So many questions with no easy answers. Naming Wonder Woman a feminist failure, calling her a malfunctioning icon, is harsh. Not only does it imply the downfall of a hero, but also the disintegration of a social ideal. But the feminism that Wonder Woman was born into is not the feminism of the new millennium—times have *a*-changed.

Brawn and Bondage

It should come as no surprise that Wonder Woman has fizzled from feminism. After all, how reliable is a feminist icon intent on massacring the manacles of misogyny, but created by a man... *who's also "a kinky bondage enthusiast"*?[3] William Moulton Marston, the mastermind behind Wonder Woman, was thrice graduate of Harvard University with a law degree and PhD in Psychology, and also the inventor of the polygraph. So the guy was smart. He was also liberal, living (in the 1940s) in an unconventional polyamorous relationship with two accomplished, highly educated women, Elizabeth Holloway Marston and Olive Byrne. Both were involved in the Women's Rights Movement, and Byrne had close connections to the Birth Control Movement. One can only assume that these women served as inspiration for Marston's most famous words that "the future is woman's" and that "women, as a sex, are many times better equipped to assume emotional leadership than are males."[4]

Inspired by his experience with polygraphs, which showed that women were more honest, reliable, and could work more efficiently than men, Moulton hoped to create a figure that women could aspire to.[5] It sounds nice—noble even—and yet something just doesn't sit right. Gerard Jones, American author and comic book writer, describes the Wonder Woman comics penned by Marston as packed with bondage, spankings, enslavement, and punishment of both men and women. He says that every single Wonder Woman comic that Marston created depicted bondage and a myriad of other sexual fetishes.[6] Submission is introduced on the first page of *Sensational Comics* #4 (1942), written by Marston and illustrated by H.G. Peter, where a troop of scantily clad women are taught discipline with the help of a whip, and are chained and tortured for non-compliance. Even Wonder Woman is not exempt from servitude. Revealed in the comic is her one shocking weakness (which she does not have today)—that all of her powers would be lost if her hands were bound together by men.

Narrator: Wonder Woman in despair remembers all too late the Queen's warnings...

Queen: Daughter, if any man welds chains on your bracelets, you will become as weak as we Amazons were when we surrendered to Hercules and his Greeks.

And who can forget *Wonder Woman* #6 (1943), where our favorite heroine demonstrates an Amazonian training ritual known as the "Ordeal of a Thousand Links," reminiscent of Harry Houdini's underwater escape stunt. In the comic, several stage hands bind Wonder Woman from head to toe with thick, sturdy shackles. They also place a heavy hood over her head, which makes it impossible for her to see or hear anything. The next stage of the act involves submerging Wonder Woman into a large, glass tank filled with water from which she must escape. But Priscilla Rich steals the magic lasso from her hip and uses it to supplement the links of chain binding Wonder Woman's arms and legs behind her back—and Wonder Women is unable to break her bonds. Everything works out in the end, but what's intriguing about this entire scenario is Marston's visceral descriptions of the restraints used. As described by the emcee in the scene: "This is the famous 'brank'—a leather mask worn by women prisoners in St. Lazare prison, France. It covers the entire face and muffles a prisoner's voice! The wide iron collar on Wonder Woman's neck comes from Tibet—it prevents the prisoner from bending his head. The ancient Greek manacle clamps the ankles firmly together."[7] *So*, not just any old restraints; specific ones (special ones!)—the knowledge of which requires special interest and research.

Marston's fascination with women in chains manifests in the Wonder Woman mythology, wherein Hippolyta is seduced by Hercules, who steals her girdle, allowing him and his men to enslave the Amazons. Hippolyta prays to Aphrodite, begging for help. Aphrodite agrees to give her the power to break her chains, but decrees that the Amazons must always wear metal bracelets as reminders that they must never submit to men. Should a man ever weld chains to the bracelets again, the Amazons would lose their strength. So even though the Amazons are free, by wearing the bracelets they open themselves up to enslavement. Thanks to Aphrodite's mandate, the Amazons are bound to their male counterparts. The goddess, as per Marston's back story, embodies an ironic lack of faith in her own gender.

In his book *Wonder Woman Unbound: The Curious History of the World's Most Famous Heroine*, Tim Hanley writes "Marston's theories idealized women and sexualized their power. Basically stating that they were better suited to rule solely based on their ability to fulfill the desires of the men they subjugated."[8] Hanley argues that although the sexual undercurrents influenced by Marston's love of a little "whip 'n' whimsy" are buried, and although the implications are dark, unless one has an intimate knowledge of Marston's work, the subtext is unnoticeable.[9] But does that exclude servitude from unconscious infiltration—permeating the subconscious mind and thus affecting conscious thought?

At least in his intent, Marston gave feminists an icon, one who reminded women that they didn't need to be *Other*, that they could achieve equality and perhaps even superiority. Such was the hope personified by Wonder Woman.

Damn You Hitler!

In the 1943 issue of *The American Scholar*, Marston called *Wonder Woman* "psychological propaganda for the new type of woman who should [he believed] rule the world."[10] *Wonder Woman* #12 (1945) includes an image entitled "The Conquest of Venus."[11] Princess Diana of Themyscira, Amazonian princess, triumphs by turning two masculine weapons against each other in an ironic example of her mission to rid the world of the violence spawned by males by using the same violence in the process. This is an odd portrayal, coming from a man who said "there isn't enough love in the male organism to run this planet peacefully. Woman's body contains twice as many love generating organs and endocrine mechanisms as the male."[12] Perhaps Marston's Wonder Woman was saving up her love and peace for a rainy day? Whatever Marston's theory, the point of "The Conquest of Venus" is that women could do as men could—and perhaps needed to!

Wonder Woman's Amazonian ancestry emphasizes the power struggle between the sexes in World War II America. Although feminism is not about hating men, in a world where men are revered and women are suppressed, men will become an unavoidable ideological foe. Once Hippolyta has freed herself from the chains of Hercules, with the help of Aphrodite, she leads the Amazons to victory once again. This time, though, they leave Man's World, and travel to the faraway Paradise Island. Here, without the influence of men, they are able to build a utopian civilization. It's a poignant reference. Without men, women are at their best. It's also an extreme supposition, but, according to history, not necessarily incorrect. Dorothy Sue Cobbles says, "Women changed as much as the men who went to war; they had a taste of an independence they hadn't known before, which allowed them a feeling of self-confidence and self-worth ... but the freedom and independence women experienced during the war didn't last."[13] The dudes came home, impregnated their wives, and got their jobs back.

Even rambunctious Rosie lost her riveting job. The familiar face of J. Howard Miller's bicep-wielding gal, sprouting a "We Can Do It!" speech bubble from her indignant mouth, became a whole lot less familiar after 1945. Rosie the Riveter represented the rights of millions of women performing jobs previously reserved for men, rights that lost momentum when Hitler was defeated (damn you Hitler!). But she'd left her mark; what women judged as fair between the sexes had changed dramatically—during and after World War II.[14] Post-war women, more than in previous generations, combined marriage, child rearing, and employment. Stay-at-home Mom gave way to Working Mom and Working Wife, and the dual responsibilities of home and job were now long-term realities for many women. The problem was that society didn't always recognize the change.[15] But Wonder Woman did—as did her writers and creators (men and all). Rosie might've faded from familiarity but Diana of Themyscira, her compatriot, transcended the return of the recruits, hailed as an evangelistic icon for a new breed of female.

The Amazons Wept

After the war, women realized that sex-based hierarchies needed dismantling, and feminists rose to the cause. Questions like whether men and women could do the same jobs or share equally in care giving were asked but not really answered. The struggle that feminists engaged in after the war was an ideological battle for equal worth. If the women's sphere and what women did could be equally valued, then half the battle had been won. The midcentury priority was ending the unequal valuing of gender differences, not ending the difference itself. This gave rise to social justice feminism, which sought women's rights as part of a broad agenda concerned with economic fairness and civil rights.[16] While this was going on, Wonder Woman—a touchstone for feminine power and freedom during the war—was living out the comic heyday (or golden era) and transitioning into a silver era, an era that, unbeknownst to fans, heralded the undermining of Wonder Woman as icon.

In 1947, William Moulton Marston died, and with him went his weird fetishist vision of women in cuffs, ruling the world. Robert Kanigher took over writing duties and did "a terrible hatchet job."[17] According to Tim Hanley, Kanigher, although prolific, was not much of an author, and rather than intentionally replace Marston's message of freedom and independence with his own agenda (which wouldn't have been a bad thing, necessarily), he merely "sat down and typed"[18]—winging it. Marston fans would argue that Wonder Woman lost the focus that made her a feminist icon during World War II. Love, marriage, and family became a constant theme in the superhero comic books of the 1950s—normal women wanted them, and superheroes longed to give up their lives as crime fighters in favor of domestic bliss. In the 1950s, Steve Trevor (Wonder Woman's primary love interest from the very beginning) and Wonder Woman were an item. She still rebuffed his marriage proposals, as she had done in Marston's version, but minus the resolve. In *Wonder Woman* #102 (1958), when Steve proposes, Wonder Woman eagerly replies: "I'd love to Steve! You know I like to be with you!... I can't marry you – until my services are no longer needed to battle crime and injustice! Only then can I think about myself!" The implication: Wonder Woman *would've* if she *could've*. Marston's Wonder Woman just didn't want to.

That said, Wonder Woman was still a superhero—powerful and magnificent. Kanigher altered her origin, imbuing her with qualities from the Olympic deities who wrought her; beautiful as Aphrodite, wise as Athena, swifter than Hermes, and stronger than Hercules.[19] So although Wonder Woman softened in her feminist resolve—longing for quiet domesticity and giving in (somewhat) to the masculine charm of her beau—she remained supreme in her power. Marston intended "a feminine character with all the strength of Superman plus all the allure of a good and beautiful woman."[20] And Wonder Woman was still *all that*, though she cried like a baby in Kanigher's origin story when all the Amazon men were wiped out by their enemies in war... *not very Amazonian.*

Throughout the 1950s and into the 1960s, while social justice feminism was working hard to change perception, Wonder Woman battled aliens and continued to rebuff Steve. Outside the context of war and without a strong writer, Wonder Woman's cultural significance was fairly generic. And then ... she gave up her powers, left the Justice League (which *she* had founded), turned into a fashionista, married Steve Trevor (in the alternate history Earth Two), had a kid, and became a housewife.

A Freakin' Fashion Boutique?

In 1968, feminists rallied against an institution that symbolized women's enslavement to beauty, the Miss America Pageant. As many see it, this protest was the founding event of the Women's Liberation Movement, which sought a holistic transformation of society, one that would do away with male dominance in every sphere (public and private) and challenge old gender patterns.[21] Coinciding with this cultural shift was an all-new Wonder Woman, which launched in November 1968 (the Miss America protest occurred in September 1968), under the penmanship of Denny O'Neil and Mike Sekowsky.

O'Neil and Sekowsky transitioned Wonder Woman from Amazonian warrior to human being, from costumed crime fighter to mod heroine. Welcome to the bronze era!—in which Diana, previously princess of Themyscira, became better known as Diana Prince. After being told by Queen Hippolyta that the magic of the Amazons is exhausted after their 10,000-year stay on Earth, and that they must go to another dimension to rest and renew their powers, Wonder Woman renounces her costume and refuses to leave Earth, saying that Steve Trevor needs her. She doesn't stay because she is an icon for a just cause—*nope* ... her man needs her.[22] Diana Prince is then forced to perform the Amazon rite of renunciation that removes her powers. Okay—so she *is* trained in karate and other martial arts to compensate, which enables her to kick some ass while she runs a trendy fashion boutique in New York's Greenwich Village, *but seriously*. This new era of Wonder Woman was a way of trying to fit the heroine into a contemporary world of women's lib and mod fashion, but it was misguided. Feminists were fighting against enslavement to beauty ... and what does Wonder Woman do? Open a fashion boutique. That's not to say that fashion was not important to the women's lib movement. It most definitely was, but the aim was to redefine traditional concepts of beauty. It was about celebrating real women's bodies and encouraging women to "dress to express" as opposed to conforming to the gender dictates of society. Feminists encouraged women to engage with their natural physicality. In her examination of the correlation between femininity and subjectivity, Beauvoir argues "For girls and boys, the body is the first radiation of a subjectivity, the instrument that brings about the comprehension of a world."[23] She adds that "[t]he body is not a thing, it is a situation: it is our grasp on our world and our sketch of our project."[24] And from the day that this body emerges into the world, it is bound by the conditions of external norms that define subjectivity.

In the bronze era, the femininity prescribed by Wonder Woman was something that damaged her previously iconic feminism. The heroine's first gift from the gods in Kanigher's revamped origin edition is beauty from Aphrodite. She's slim, big-breasted, with a flowing mane of hair, and a face prettier than any Miss America contestant. She's clothed by men. *And then she opens a fashion boutique!* Wonder Woman seemed to represent that which the modern, independent woman was rallying against. Realistically, very few women could live up to the imposed archetype. Beauvoir comments on the fact that the imposition of extrinsic femininity dooms the female subject to immanence, denying women's individuality and trapping them inside unrealizable ideals. She writes, "To be feminine is to show oneself as weak, futile, passive, and docile. The girl is supposed not only to primp and dress herself up but also to repress her spontaneity and substitute for it the grace and charm she has been taught by her elder sisters. Any self-assertion will take away from her femininity and her seductiveness."[25]

The femininity of the Bronze Age Wonder Woman wasn't just about fashion. Steve was a big part of it too. Rather than using the "no powers Wonder Woman" storyline to portray women as strong and independent with or without supernatural influence, O'Neil and Sekowsky turned her into a swooning sap. In *Wonder Woman* #182 (1969), the narration accompanying a scene in which Diana Prince is trying on clothes in London with a new beau reads "Happiness for any healthy, red-blooded young gal, is bedecking herself in the latest fashion finery ... and our Wonder Woman just happens to be a healthy, red-blooded young gal." The new Wonder Woman got attention from men, and Steve also started to pay Diana extra attention. Subtext: It's good to be pretty because boys will like you, and will also pay for stuff—like Reginald Hyde-White did in issue #182 of 1969. After Steve's death, there was also Tim Trench, Patrick McGuire, Rangor,

Baron Anatole Karoli, and Jonny Double. *Whew*—Wonder Woman was a busy girl. Not that having partners is anti-feminist, but Diana was written in a way that made it seem as if she needed men to boost her self-esteem. The boutique storyline twisted Wonder Woman into something that contravened her natural femininity. While real-world feminists got the guys to help out around the house, fought for equal wages, and pushed themselves into professions that traditionally excluded them, Wonder Woman turned into a sad cliché.

Modern Mediocrity?

The 1980s produced a new generation of feminists—women who had been raised by feminists and cultivated through formal education, parental upbringing, and mass culture.[26] Generation X and the millennial generation were born during and after the upheavals of the 1960s and 1970s, and have thus taken for granted many of the social, political, and economic gains achieved in the decades prior to and surrounding their births.[27] For these women, feminism was initially more a mindset than a movement—something "entwined into the fabric of their lives"[28]—until they realized that some of the rights they had taken for granted were tenuous. This realization led to a revival of feminist energy in the 1990s. And Wonder Woman? Well, that sad cliché—it remained intact.

In the late 1980s George Pérez revitalized Wonder Woman with a new origin story, harkening back to the feminist undertones of the Golden and Silver Ages, and the comic did well—but not for long. Pérez moved on and Wonder Woman was thrust back into banality—forging a career as a space pirate. After the Amazons disappeared, leaving our heroine homeless, Diana got a job at a Mexican fast-food restaurant, Taco Whiz. *Enthralling*. After this defamation of Wonder Woman's character, one would assume the title "Wonder Woman" rendered innocuous—a modern-day joke? But it's not innocuous, neither is it a joke. In fact, Wonder Woman has successfully encapsulated much of the irony that enveloped her conception. The modern era left the heroine without much feminist clout, but, moving into a new millennium, Wonder Woman, in expression, has certainly not been forgotten.

As feminism flourished over the post-war decades, even with a couple of lulls, modern females have been raised to believe that they can do anything boys can do. As if to prove the point, feminism moved into a state of excess, giving birth to the notion of the modern superwoman—a wonder woman who can do it all and have it all: a healthy family, a great job, good looks, and fun in between. It was an idea celebrated for a brief period in the 1980s and Wonder Woman, in spite of her feminist decline, embodied (and still embodies) the idiomatic reference.[29] In 1975's adapted TV series, *The New Original Wonder Woman*, starring Lynda Carter, Queen Hippolyta tells her child "Go in peace my daughter. And remember that, in a world of ordinary mortals, you are a Wonder Woman." The rest of us are not. Wonder Woman makes this quite obvious. Anyone born *not* a princess is already excluded—so that's like 99.999 percent of the population demoted by social order. And that's just the start. You— woman of small breast and cellulite thigh, wispy hair, mediocre bicep, and slight belly bulge—you're OUT. So are you, one who has squandered love, who has repudiated goodness with harsh words, angry intent, or scorn-filled malice. Wonder Woman doesn't seem to leave us much hope. The condition of our existence, our humanness, the flaws in our faces and sins of our souls, prevent us from achieving the heroine's symbolic perfection, which, according to the doctrine of Wonder Woman, is what it takes to be a hero. History speaks for itself: Marston anticipated a modern world ruled by women, and there've been a couple of leader/prime minister types, some business owners, and a girls' rugby team or two. It's not bad, but clearly the world is still working on acknowledging women as beings of power and leadership. As an idiom, Wonder Woman is a whole lot of pressure. The truth is that although women's movements have expanded the opportunities and options available to women and men, these possibilities remain deeply embedded in inherited political, cultural, and economic structures that have remained largely unchanged. Astrid Henry observed that:

> [the] American workplace is still designed around the mythical male worker who can devote long hours to his job because he has no obligations in the home. Women are still expected to do the vast majority of the housework and childcare within the home, even as they work outside the home at nearly the same rates as men do.[30]

The expectation inherent in this "wonder woman" standard is not only monumental but ludicrous. And so, more and more, women of all generations are critical of the idea—"having it all" comes at a steep price of soul, sanity, and survival.

And yet, perhaps I've been a little extreme in my judgment. When Wonder Woman says to us "Please take my hand. I give it to you as a gesture of friendship and love, and of faith freely given. I give you my hand and welcome you into my dream,"[31] rather than freak out at the possibility of failure, why not accept the challenge on one's own terms? After all, Wonder Woman is a mere figment of our collective imagination. The real wonder of being a woman is living to fight another day. That is awesome. But why are we so afraid of it? Beauvoir poses an answer, hypothesizing that human existence is always an ambiguous admixture of the internal freedom to transcend the given conditions of the world and the weight of the world which imposes itself on us in a manner outside our control and not of our own choosing. In order for us to live ethically then, we must own this ambiguity rather than flee it. By not embracing the duality inherent in their quest for subjectivity (because of the seeming benefits it can bring as well as the respite from responsibility it promises), are women then not in some ways complicit in their own subjugation?

Why So Serious?

Women have had to work hard to achieve the version of equality that exists today, and the fight is unfinished. Astrid Henry writes, "there are many signs that the United States has been decentered from the world stage and that it is neither the preeminent model for women's equality nor the site of women's most urgent struggles ... the United States has fallen behind its international peers and no longer serves as a world leader when it comes to gender equality."[32] If we place Wonder Woman in context as a supernatural being who is in no way possible to emulate, then rather than demonizing her perfection, we could acknowledge her challenge—to live to our greatest potential, as women and as human beings. By calling Wonder Woman an impossibility, are we not merely acquiescing in mediocrity?

Ayn Rand, a Russian-born American novelist, philosopher, playwright, and screenwriter spoke out against such mediocrity. In her 1957 novel *Atlas Shrugged*, Rand writes:

> Do you know the hallmark of a second rater? It's resentment of another man's achievement. Those touchy mediocrities who sit trembling lest

someone's work prove greater than their own—they have no inkling of the loneliness that comes when you reach the top. The loneliness for an equal—for a mind to respect and an achievement to admire ... Of what account are praise and adulation from men whom you don't respect? Have you ever felt the longing for someone you could admire? For something, not to look down at, but to look up to.[33]

Is Wonder Woman longing for an equal—begging women to rival her achievement? Throughout her career as a superhero, Wonder Woman has fought her own battle against mediocrity—certainly from a feminist perspective—and perhaps, like feminism, she is a work in progress. She is perfect in her visual aspect (it's the nature of the comic medium) but, in fact, not so perfect in the furtherance of the ideals that brought her into being. Wonder Woman is in combat against her creators, against the culture into which she has been thrust, and even against the freedom of art and the meaning imbued by the gaze of its admirers. It thus makes total sense that in the New 52, launched by DC Comics in 2011, Wonder Woman becomes god of war after being forced to kill Ares, the original god of war and also her tutor, during a conflict with her evil half-brother, Zeus's son, the First Born.[34]

In comic book form, Wonder Woman battles intergalactic enemies, but in "real life" she's at war with man, meaning, and mediocrity. The New 52 has, however, taken on the challenge (both literal and metaphoric) faced by Wonder Woman, imbuing her with the power of a god and the skills to embrace the battle headfirst—because at heart Wonder Woman is a warrior ... but for peace. She also has a solid support crew (something new to the mythology) in the form of strong, sassy, conflicted women: Hera, Strife, and Zola.

In 2016's *Batman v Superman: Dawn of Justice*, Wonder Woman's first big-screen appearance since forever ago, Batman asks her in an email, "Who are you?" and "Where have you been?"—Questions that feminism is excited to know the answer to. Can the redemption that Wonder Woman has been afforded in the New 52 find its way into societal consciousness? Only time, plus a lot more comics and a few more flicks—*Wonder Woman* (2017) and *The Justice League Part One* (2017)—will tell.

Notes

1. Simone de Beauvoir, *The Second Sex*, edited and translated by H.M. Parshley (New York: Vintage Books, 1974), 301.

2. Ibid., xix.
3. Tim Hanley, *Wonder Woman Unbound: The Curious History of the World's Most Famous Heroine* (Chicago, IL: Chicago Review Press, 2014), xi.
4. Hanley, *Wonder Woman Unbound*, 15–16.
5. Geoffrey C. Bunn, "The Lie Detector, Wonder Woman, and Liberty: The Life and Work of William Moulton Marston," *History of the Human Sciences*, 10 (1997) 91–119.
6. Gerard Jones, *Men of Tomorrow: Geeks, Gangsters, and the Birth of the Comic Book* (New York: Basic Books, 2004), 209.
7. William Moulton Marston, *Wonder Woman* #6 (DC Comics, 1943).
8. Hanley, *Wonder Woman Unbound*, 17.
9. Ibid.
10. William Marston, "Why 100,000,000 Americans Read Comics," *The American Scholar*, 13 (1943) 35–44.
11. Paul Levitz, *The Little Book of Wonder Woman* (New York: Taschen, 2015), 22.
12. Hanley, *Wonder Woman Unbound*, 15.
13. Dorothy Sue Cobble, Linda Gordon, and Astrid Henry, *Feminism Unfinished: A Short, Surprising History of American Women's Movements* (New York: Liveright Publishing Corporation, 2014), xiii.
14. Ibid., 23.
15. Ibid., 27.
16. Ibid., 32.
17. Hanley, *Wonder Woman Unbound*, 104.
18. Ibid.
19. Robert Kanigher, *Wonder Woman* #105 (DC Comics, 1959).
20. "William Moulton Marston," http://dc.wikia.com/wiki/William_Moulton_Marston (accessed April, 2016).
21. Cobble, Gordon, and Henry, *Feminism Unfinished*, 70.
22. Denny O'Neil and Mike Sekowsky, *Wonder Woman* #179 (DC Comics, 1968).
23. Simone de Beauvoir, *The Second Sex*, translated by Constance Borde and Sheila Malovany-Chevallier (New York: Random House, 2011), 283.
24. Beauvoir, *The Second Sex*, ed./trans. Parshley, 38.
25. Beauvoir, *The Second Sex*, trans. Borde and Malovany-Chevallier, 348.
26. Cobble, Gordon, and Henry, *Feminism Unfinished*, 142.
27. Ibid., 151.
28. Ibid., 158.
29. Ibid., 193.

30. Ibid.
31. Robert Kanigher, *Wonder Woman* #167 (DC Comics, 1967).
32. Cobble, Gordon, and Henry, *Feminism Unfinished*, 213.
33. Ayn Rand, *Atlas Shrugged* (New York: Signet, 1996), 333.
34. Brian Azzarello, *Wonder Woman* #0 (DC Comics, 2012).

Feminist Symbol or Fetish?
Žižek, Wonder Woman, and *Final Crisis*
Matthew William Brake

Final Crisis was an event comic produced by DC Comics in 2008 and written by Grant Morrison. In the story, the villain Darkseid takes over the minds of a majority of the Earth's population, including many of its superheroes. The series' promo tagline was "Heroes Die. Legends Live Forever," and many of the most popular heroes in DC's history had a moment, or many moments, to shine and demonstrate their "legendary" status. Wonder Woman is a notable exception, which is odd considering her place alongside Batman and Superman among DC's top "Trinity" of heroes. In fact, Wonder Woman becomes "patient zero" for Darkseid's Anti-Life Equation, the means by which he controls the minds of others, and spends most of the remainder of the series as a thrall of Darkseid wearing a bondage-style version of her regular outfit.

In a 2009 interview, when asked about his treatment of Wonder Woman, Grant Morrison stated that he "always sensed something slightly bogus and troubling" at the heart of the Wonder Woman concept. He noted, "When I dug into the roots of the character I found an uneasy mélange of girl power, bondage and disturbed sexuality that has never been adequately dealt with or fully processed out to my mind." This being the case, his portrayal of Wonder Woman reflected his original negative feelings about the character.[1] Morrison's opinion is in opposition to the conventional wisdom that holds up Wonder

Wonder Woman and Philosophy: The Amazonian Mystique, First Edition.
Edited by Jacob M. Held.
© 2017 John Wiley & Sons, Ltd. Published 2017 by John Wiley & Sons, Ltd.

Woman as a beacon of feminism in comic books. When one digs into the history of Wonder Woman, though, it isn't difficult to see from where Morrison is coming.

The Legacy of William Moulton Marston

William Moulton Marston created Wonder Woman to be a symbol for a more loving and feminine form of justice. Mixed into this goal were elements of Marston's own unique views about human emotional make-up and sexuality. Key to Marston's understanding of the human emotional constitution were (1) "the binary emotions dominance–submission—through a close understanding of which, Marston believed, psychology could open the way for human liberation"[2] and (2) the practice of love binding, which is exactly what it sounds like. For Marston, women in particular understood how to submit and enjoy being bound, and once men learned to give up violence and oppression as a means of control and lovingly submit to women and enjoy being bound, a utopian matriarchy could lead the world peacefully. Jill Lepore describes Marston's vision as a type of "feminism as fetish."[3]

A number of different writers who have taken up the mantle of writing Wonder Woman have responded in different ways to Marston's legacy. As revealed in his comments above, Morrison's initial reception of Wonder Woman was negatively colored by the more sexually fetishistic elements of Marston's writing. Many other writers seem to have struggled with figuring out how to write and understand Wonder Woman. Is she a feminist icon? Is she a sexual fetish? Or is she something else entirely? To answer this question, let's turn to Slovenian thinker Slavoj Žižek.

On Symptoms...

If one were to speak about Wonder Woman as a fetish, what would one be saying aside from the obvious connotations of sexual idiosyncrasies? Before we can answer this question, we must first examine a term Žižek uses alongside his discussion of fetishes, the "symptom." In everyday use, it is easy to confuse what Žižek calls a symptom with a fetish. To speak of the symptom is to speak of that "exception which disturbs the surface of the false appearance," from which something that was repressed erupts.[4] In other words, there is a dirty little secret hiding underneath the surface. Symptomal readings of Wonder Woman are quite common. For instance, Woman Woman's birth is often written about symptomally. In *Wonder Woman* #1 (1942), Marston tells his readers about Wonder Woman's origins. Hippolyta, queen of the Amazons, molds a statue of a little girl, and after Hippolyta says a prayer, Aphrodite brings the statue to life. Thus, Wonder Woman was born immaculately with no help from a man. For the most part, George Pérez maintained the basics of this story in his post-*Crisis on Infinite Earths* reboot of Wonder Woman in 1987.

One example of a symptomal reading of Wonder Woman's birth narrative is found in the *Justice League Unlimited* episode, "The Balance." In this story, the villain Felix Faust usurps the throne of Hades, and Diana is ordered by Zeus through the messenger god Hermes to set things right. Wonder Woman, accompanied by Hawkwoman, enters Tartarus, and with the aid of a released Hades overcomes Faust. As the two heroines are preparing to leave, Hades thanks them and specifically refers to Wonder Woman as "my child." Hades goes on to explain that he had a hand in sculpting Wonder Woman from clay alongside Hippolyta. Though Wonder Woman has the option to use her magic lasso on Hades to ascertain the truth, she decides not to because she knows that the Amazons and the Justice League are her real family. Here, the repressed truth of Wonder Woman's actual parentage begins to make "cracks in the fabric of the ideological lie,"[5] that Wonder Woman was immaculately conceived from clay.

A much more overtly symptomal reading comes from Brian Azzarello's New 52 relaunch of Wonder Woman. In issue #2 of his run, Azzarello has Hermes recount the legend of Wonder Woman's birth: she was molded out of clay by her mother. By the end of the issue, however, the reader discovers from the goddess Strife that Wonder Woman is her half-sister, making Wonder Woman a daughter of Zeus. Issue #3 recounts Hippolyta's story of having been Zeus's lover. The symptom—the dirty, repressed truth about Wonder Woman's true parentage—emerges here in full force.

Following this, one can read Morrison's *Final Crisis* symptomally. If Morrison finds the concept of Wonder Woman to be bogus in light of the kinky sexuality associated with her origin, one could see his portrayal of Wonder Woman in *Final Crisis* as an attempt to bring to light the repressed truth underneath the surface of her image as a feminist icon. Morrison *exposes* her as the BDSM fantasy she is by having her wear a mask as Darkseid's enslaved thrall. The mask is the repressed truth about Marston's kinky sexuality coming to the surface, worn on Wonder Woman's face for all to see.

... and Fetishes

Žižek claims, though, that in today's world, one can no longer rely solely on symptomal readings of texts. We no longer live in a world defined by a naïve consciousness attempting to suppress the truth. Rather, we live in a world defined by a cynical reason that "is quite aware of the distance between the ideological mask and the social reality, but... none the less still insists upon the mask."[6] In this world, "they know very well what they are doing, but still, they are doing it."[7] Žižek describes the fetish as the "*inverse* of the symptom." Whereas the symptom involves the return of a repressed truth from under the false surface, a fetish "is the embodiment of the Lie which enables us to sustain the unbearable truth."[8] What does all this mean?

Fetishists are not naïve "dreamers lost in their private worlds, [rather] they are thoroughly 'realists,' able to accept the way things effectively are—since they have their fetish to which they can cling in order to cancel the full impact of reality."[9] Žižek uses the death of a loved one to illustrate his point about the difference between a symptom and a fetish:

> In the case of a symptom, I "repress" this death, I try not to think about it, but the repressed trauma returns in the symptom; in the case of a fetish, on the contrary, I "rationally" fully accept this death, and yet I cling to the fetish, to some feature that embodies for me the disavowal of this death.[10]

Žižek goes on to provide an example of this from Nevil Shute's World War II novel *Requiem for a Wren*. He writes:

> The heroine survives her lover's death without any visible traumas, she goes on with her life and is even able to talk rationally about the lover's death—because she still has the dog who was the lover's favored pet. When, some time later, the dog is accidentally run over by a truck, she collapses and her entire world disintegrates.[11]

A symptomal understanding of the loved one's death would involve the dog's presence constantly bringing to mind the painful death of her lover. In this case, however, the dog is the heroine's fetish through which "the dead person magically continues to live," but when it is taken away, her "'rational' acceptance of the way things are dissolves."[12] A person in the modern, cynical age may claim to reject all ideals and accept things the way they are, but Žižek responds by asking, "OK, but where is the fetish which enables you to (pretend to) accept reality 'the way it is'?"[13]

Money is a type of fetish. Žižek writes, "When individuals use money, they know very well that there is nothing magical about it—that money, in its materiality, is simply an expression of social relations."[14] Cynical human beings in the modern world "know" that money has no inherent value, but the way they act contradicts this. Žižek explains, "Contrary to the usual thesis that a belief is something interior ... belief is radically exterior, embodied in the practical, effective procedure of people."[15] It does not matter if inwardly people do not believe that money has inherent value, because they are still living and acting like it does.[16] Žižek refers to this contradiction as "fetishistic disavowal," whereby one maintains "excessive adherence to certain beliefs and practices and a simultaneous denial of any genuine belief."[17] In other words, one "knows" the reality of the situation but lives in a way that contradicts that "known" reality, thereby showing that they actually do believe that which they deny.

Wonder Woman as the Comic Industry's Fetish

Returning to *Final Crisis*, what would it mean to read Morrison's portrayal of Wonder Woman fetishistically? For all those fans and writers who proclaim that Wonder Woman is a feminist icon in comic books, one has to wonder how many of them actually believe it. The comic book industry has a very questionable history regarding how women are portrayed within its pages. After all, it was this industry that gave us the "women in refrigerators" trope in *Green Lantern* #54 (1994),[18] not to mention all of the questionably functional costumes many female superheroines wear. It seems though that as long as Wonder Woman is given equal time to shine alongside Superman and Batman in DC crossover events, those involved in the industry can fend off charges of misogyny in comic books because of their icon, or rather their fetish, which helps to draw attention away from the ghastly reality of the industry and its relationship with women.

In discussing Wonder Woman with friends, it has seemed to me like many of those who proclaim Wonder Woman to be a feminist icon do so and then let out a barely audible snicker. It is not difficult to imagine that many male comic book readers talk about Wonder Woman as a feminist symbol during the day and then watch a porn parody of her at night. Wonder Woman sometimes serves as the basis of very blatant jokes related to her as an object of sexual fantasy. Do we ourselves really believe that Wonder Woman is a feminist icon, or do we believe on the behalf of others? Žižek notes the way that many parents pretend to believe in Santa Claus for the sake of their children. Our children are supposed to believe in Santa Claus, so we try not to disappoint them.[19] In reality, however, "beyond the youngest and most naïve infants, the majority of children know that Father Christmas does not exist. In reality, the only people who truly believe in Santa Claus are the parents themselves!"[20]

Regarding Wonder Woman, the idea that she is an icon serves as a fetish in order that the mostly male writers and fans can believe that somewhere out there are potential female readers who will believe that Wonder Woman is a feminist symbol, thus ignoring the misogynistic truth about the industry while perhaps "rationally" acknowledging it. Wonder Woman is the dirty secret of the comic book industry that everyone "rationally" knows: Wonder Woman is a BDSM sex fantasy, but as long as she isn't explicitly portrayed that way, the fetish of Wonder Woman as feminist icon perpetuates.

Enter Grant Morrison. He took a character that is the object of many jokes about BDSM (hello bracelets of submission and Amazonian bondage games!) and actually portrayed her as a dominatrix. By putting her in a mask, he removed the fetishistic mask. The reaction, per the Newsrama interview, seems to have been, "Hey, hey, hey! What are you doing to this feminist icon? Why doesn't she have her moment to shine?" All Morrison had done, though, was depict Wonder Woman in a way that fits with many male fans' sexual fantasies. As such, the fetishistic nature she serves in the industry is brought to light by Morrison's story. For all the sex and dominatrix jokes one can make about Wonder Woman, it seems that there is a deep-seated belief about the role she serves in the comic book industry, that of a bogus fetish which Morrison exposes to the eyes of the reader.

Morrison and Wonder Woman: Earth One

So is that the last word from Morrison? Wonder Woman is a bogus fetish? Not necessarily. If the 2016 release of *Wonder Woman: Earth One* is any indication, he seems to have developed a much more nuanced view of the character. Here, Wonder Woman seems to still be both symptom and fetish. As Žižek acknowledges, the line between them is not always clear.[21] Wonder Woman is a symptom in Morrison's retelling. While having been told by her mother all her life that she was made from clay, Hippolyta reveals that Diana is in fact a combination of her mother's egg and Hercules's seed. This combination made Wonder Woman unbeatable, and Hippolyta's intention had been to unleash Wonder Woman on Man's World as a weapon to subdue and conquer it as revenge for Hercules's subjugation of the Amazons. The presence of Hercules's blood is what calls Diana to Man's World and away from Paradise Island. The symptom of the repressed truth that Wonder Woman was crafted by her mother to be a weapon of conquest in contradistinction to the Amazonian practice of loving submission comes to the surface.

This means that Hippolyta has knowingly lied to her daughter and the Amazons the whole time. The community of the Amazons, and Diana's birth, are both built on a lie about Hippolyta's original intentions for her daughter and her community, a lie she herself is fully aware of, like the parents who pretend to believe in Santa Claus for their children while actually believing *through* their children. So Diana is also a fetish for her own mother, the lie that sustains the unbearable truth. This reflects Žižek's comments about "the primordial lie that founds a community."[22] Likewise, Diana's mother fetishistically disavows Diana's true origin, maintaining the importance of the Amazons' separation from the violence of Man's World while knowing that her daughter contains that violence within her for the original purpose of conquering Man's World. But she maintains the fetish in order to sustain the hope of a separatist, Amazonian utopia.

This does not exhaust Morrison's rich account of Wonder Woman, however. He seems to suggest that Wonder Woman can be a type of feminist symbol when he describes her as a "counterculture, feminist heroine,"[23] but he also notes that "there's not just one type of woman and she's not representative of all women."[24] Morrison makes this point while telling how, when "Diana meets the girls of the modern world, they're all very different shapes and sizes and colors, and she starts to realize that there isn't a standardized look in the world."[25] Additionally, his opinion of Marston and his original vision for the character seems rather positive when discussing his criticism of Wonder Woman's portrayal in *Batman v Superman: Dawn of Justice*:

> The warrior woman thing is not what [Wonder Woman's creator] William Marston wanted, that's not what he wanted at all! His original concept for Wonder Woman was an answer to comics that he thought were filled with images of blood-curdling masculinity, and you see the latest shots of Gal Gadot in the costume, and it's all sword and shield and her snarling at the camera. Marston's Diana was a doctor, a healer, a scientist...[26]

It seems here that Morrison has changed his mind about whether there is something bogus at the heart of the Wonder Woman concept, even coming to the defense of Marston. That isn't to say that he doesn't still have problems with the character, noting that Marston's vision was "alternative" but "bizarre."[27] Nonetheless, Morrison seems to think that there is a feminist message at the heart of the Wonder Woman concept worth considering. In the same way that Wonder Woman isn't an exhaustive representation of all women, maybe one representation of Wonder Woman doesn't exhaust what she is. Perhaps she is a feminist symbol. And a symptom. And a fetish.

Notes

1. Matt Brady, "Grant Morrison: Final Crisis Exit Interview, Part 1," http://www.newsarama.com/2053-grant-morrison-final-crisis-exit-interview-part-1.html (accessed January 30, 2016).
2. Noah Berlatsky, *Wonder Woman: Bondage and Feminism in the Marston/Peter Comics, 1941–1945* (New Brunswick, NJ: Rutgers University Press, 2015), 8.
3. Jill Lepore, *The Secret History of Wonder Woman* (New York: Vintage Books, 2015), 236.
4. Slavoj Žižek, *On Belief* (New York: Routledge, 2001), 13.

5. Ibid.
6. Slavoj Žižek, *The Sublime Object of Ideology* (New York: Verso, 1989), 25–26.
7. Ibid., 25.
8. Žižek, *On Belief*, 13.
9. Ibid., 14.
10. Ibid., 13–14.
11. Ibid., 14.
12. Ibid., 13–14.
13. Ibid., 15.
14. Žižek, *The Sublime Object of Ideology*, 28.
15. Ibid., 31.
16. Ibid., 30.
17. Paul Taylor, "Fetish/Fetishistic Disavowal," *The Žižek Dictionary*, edited by Rex Butler (Durham: Acumen Publishing, 2014), 93.
18. In this issue, Alexandra DeWitt, girlfriend of then current Green Lantern Kyle Rayner, is killed by the villain Major Force and stuffed into a refrigerator for Kyle to find. The story is often cited as the primary example of the endemic problem in comic books whereby female characters are abused or killed as a plot device to further a male character's story arc. A website dedicated to addressing this issue was set up by Gail Simone and a group of feminists in 1999: http://lby3.com/wir/.
19. Slavoj Žižek, *The Plague of Fantasies* (New York: Verso, 2008), 138.
20. Taylor, "Fetish," 94.
21. Žižek, *On Belief*, 14.
22. Slavoj Žižek, *The Metastasies of Enjoyment: On Women and Causality* (New York: Verso, 2005), 57.
23. Melissa Leon, "Comics Legend Grant Morrison on His Queer, Kinky Wonder Woman," http://www.thedailybeast.com/articles/2016/04/06/comics-legend-grant-morrison-on-his-queer-kinky-wonder-woman.html (accessed June 9, 2016).
24. Laura Sneddon, "Grant Morrison: Why I'm Resurrecting Wonder Woman," https://www.theguardian.com/books/2013/aug/21/grant-morrison-wonder-woman (accessed June 9, 2016).
25. Leon, *The Daily Beast*.
26. Chris Agar, "'Wonder Woman': Grant Morrison Criticizes Gal Gadot Movie Version," http://screenrant.com/grant-morrison-gal-gadot-wonder-woman-movie/ (accessed June 9, 2016).
27. David Betancourt, "Grant Morrison's new Wonder Woman: 'You don't give up sex just because you gave up men,'" https://www.washingtonpost.com/news/comic-riffs/wp/2016/04/12/grant-morrisons-new-wonder-woman-you-dont-give-up-sex-just-because-you-gave-up-men/ (accessed June 9, 2016).

When Clark Met Diana
Friendship and Romance in Comics

Matthew A. Hoffman and Sara Kolmes

In the past, Wonder Woman and Superman were depicted as good friends, but as of 2016, in New 52 Wonder Woman comic books, the Amazon princess and the man of steel are in a romantic relationship. The implication seems to be that romantically compatible people cannot be *just* friends. Thankfully, philosophy can help us debunk this notion and, as we'll see, shed some light on the nature of friendship and romance as well.

Friendship in Philosophy

Aristotle's (384–322 BCE) main requirement for friendship is that it be mutual. Non-reciprocal well-wishing is goodwill for a person, but not friendship.[1] Aristotle calls a friend "another self,"[2] but this does not mean that friends are merely alike. Rather, friends influence one another, developing as individuals because of their relationship with each other.[3] In the highest form of friendship, two people will develop moral virtues in tandem, so friends will be better people for having their friendship. Since, on Aristotle's picture, being virtuous is a requirement for living a good life, people must have friends to live a truly good life. Moreover, because we are social creatures, we need friends not only for moral development, but also to have a worthwhile

Wonder Woman and Philosophy: The Amazonian Mystique, First Edition.
Edited by Jacob M. Held.

life at all.[4] Inspired by Aristotle, Immanuel Kant (1724–1804) says that true friendships are fundamentally characterized by "an exchange of welfare,"[5] in which both members are benefited and become better people by learning to truly care for another person unselfishly.

For both philosophers, true friendships are very demanding in terms of how friends treat one another, and require both members to wish one another well, to consider themselves equal in the relationship, to communicate with one another openly, and to value the friendship.[6] In order to gain the benefits of friendship, one only needs to be willing to perform the necessary actions, such as caring for one another and communicating openly, and have a friend who is willing to do the same. Prior to the New 52 reboot, Wonder Woman's relationship with Superman was like this. In a single-issue story by Greg Rucka, for example, the two spend time together not as team mates but as friends, discussing their personal lives.[7] The two call each other best friends on multiple occasions, and their friendship is clearly important to them, as they have similar powers and outlooks. They can discuss things like coming back from the dead or balancing superheroing with a personal life, because they have an unspoken understanding of each other's lives in a way Wonder Woman doesn't have with Etta Candy or Steve Trevor, or Superman with Lois Lane or Jimmy Olsen.

Friendship in Popular Fiction

As products of their time, Aristotle and Kant did not recognize women as the equal of men, but the theory of friendship they offer can be adapted and applied in a gender-neutral way. In popular culture, there are many close friendships that involve the kind of mutual caring Aristotle and Kant describe. These friendships are often a driving force in narratives about the growth of characters as people. However, the majority of close friendships in pop culture are between people of the same gender, such as Kirk and Spock of *Star Trek*, Frodo and Sam in *The Lord of the Rings*, Bayonetta and Jeanne in the *Bayonetta* video game series, and the most recent incarnations of Harley Quinn and Poison Ivy in the New 52.

In contrast, cross-gender relationships are most often romantic. Usually these relationships begin as friendships characterized by romantic and sexual tension before the characters officially become a couple, like Mulder and Scully in *The X-Files* and Oliver and Felicity in *Arrow*. Other relationships are characterized throughout by romantic/sexual tension, like Steed and Mrs. Peel in *The Avengers*. The romantic chemistry is palpable in these cases, and the relationships recognized by both the writers and fans as potentially romantic.

Wonder Woman and Superman present an interesting example of the tension inherent in depictions of close cross-gender friendships. Although they were not the most important people in each other's lives prior to the DC Comics relaunch in 2011, the characters were close friends. Despite being important to each other as friends and team mates, their relationship was not romantic, though other characters have sometimes insinuated as much. One issue of *Action Comics*, for example, includes a story of the *Daily Planet* questioning the nature of the pair's relationship, making Lois Lane jealous.[8] Now, however, Wonder Woman and Superman *are* dating in-universe. (The friendship they had belongs to the previous universe.) This literal erasure of their friendship, and its replacement with romance, indicates the value society places on cross-gender friendship: such friendship is liable to be misread as romantic, and is not accorded the value and privileges of romantic partnerships. The relationship between Wonder Woman and Superman has gotten mixed reviews, with many reviewers commenting that the romantic relationship between the two characters lacks chemistry or seems to be a bad fit.[9] Perhaps this is because the idea that close platonic friendships are precursors to romantic relationships is itself a bad fit. Superman and Wonder Woman do not require a romantic relationship to be compelling, much like cross-gender friendships do not require a romantic component to be valuable.

Popular Fiction as Action Guiding

Trends in the way friendships function in popular fiction have the potential to influence the way we build friendships in the real world. Pop culture implicitly teaches us what our lives may look like. We use fiction as a guide for how to appropriately pursue relationships, and the stories we internalize affect our view of what relationships are open to us. Cross-gender relationships in fiction thus both reflect existing social norms and help to create and sustain them. Kathy Werking calls cross-gender friendships *anomic*, because the social norms governing cross-gender relationships (as delivered by pop culture) are mainly those of romantic interaction.[10] Cross-gender friendships are relationships for which society does not provide clear guidelines, role models, or touchstones, in contrast to the normative way in which we are raised to think of romantic relationships. In consuming works of popular culture, we learn what is expected of us in our interpersonal lives: cross-gender relationships must be romantic, and friendship cannot be as important as romance. The loss of Wonder Woman and Superman as an example of a stable non-romantic cross-gender friendship therefore represents not just a change in the treatment of the characters, but a loss of support for the idea that such friendships are possible.

What we find in looking at pop culture, then, is a message that men and women cannot really be friends, symbolized by Wonder Woman and Superman's friendship becoming romantic. This message finds its most explicit form in the film *When Harry Met Sally*, where Harry says that cross-gender friendships will inevitably be ruined by sex. Pop culture's implication that close non-romantic relationships be between members of the same gender has far-reaching implications for the way that romantic and platonic relationships may be pursued.

Friendship across the Kinsey Scale

The depiction of cross-gender friendships as inherently containing sexual possibilities implicitly assumes the heterosexuality of the friends in question. If men and women cannot be close friends without becoming sexually attracted to one another, there must be a likely possibility of men being attracted to women and women being attracted to men. This contributes to the invisibility of homosexuals: if one is assumed to be straight by default, this means that being homosexual is an abnormal state, if it is considered at all. Same-gender friends, by contrast, are most often written without romantic/sexual tension except as a joke, again because the characters are straight until proven otherwise.

The heteronormativity implicit in the question "Can men and women *just* be friends?" is easily corrected for, and is not a serious problem for Wonder Woman and Superman, characters who are both explicitly attracted to the opposite gender in the comics. Although Wonder Woman's sexuality seems indeterminate given recent indications that she may be lesbian, notably in the recent *Wonder Woman: Earth One* in which Diana says that fellow Amazon Mala is her lover.[11] Even so, writer Grant Morrison still presents Diana as being interested in Steve Trevor, in some regard. In this out-of-New 52-continuity world, Wonder Woman is still attracted to men, and is also interested in building close friendships with men. What is important in the story, and to Diana's development as a hero, is not her sexual interest in any particular character, but her developing friendships with women and men outside Amazonian society.

A better version of the so-called "*When Harry Met Sally* question" might be, "Can any two people *just* be friends, if the possibility of sexual/romantic attraction exists between them?" However, this correction highlights an even more serious problem. If it is legitimate to be suspicious of the ability of people to be friends with members of the gender to which they are sexually attracted, bi- and pansexual people cannot be trusted to be friends with *anyone*. Since bi- and pansexuals have the potential to be attracted to more people than gay or straight individuals, there is a "risk" that they will become sexually involved with friends of either gender. Thus they cannot be friends with anyone outside of their exclusive romantic relationship. Given these assumptions stemming from the "*When Harry Met Sally* question," bi- and pansexuals must be treated with suspicion even by people who are straight, because they are a threat to exclusive romantic relationships. In fact, stereotypes of bi- and pansexuals as "risky" romantic partners and friends, because of the perceived likelihood of infidelity, do exist in both heterosexual and homosexual communities,[12] and authors have argued that these stereotypes present a barrier to forming romantic relationships and friendships for bi- and pansexuals.[13]

Friendship and Amatonormativity

Portrayals of cross-gender friendship in popular fiction also reflect the social assumptions and norms that contemporary philosopher Elizabeth Brake has termed *amatonormativity*, which she defines as:

> the disproportionate focus on marital and amorous love relationships as special sites of value, and the assumption that romantic love is a universal goal. Amatonormativity consists in the assumptions that a

central, exclusive, amorous relationship is normal for humans, in that it is a universally shared goal, and that such a relationship is normative, in that it should be aimed at in preference to other relationship types.[14]

Brake's views on amatonormativity have been enormously influential in the asexual community on social media websites.[15] Criticism of amatonormativity highlights the importance of friendship in people's lives. Friendship is important and beneficial between people of all genders *notwithstanding the possibility of a romantic relationship developing*.

With the norm of amatonormativity, society privileges romantic couples over other caring relationships. Being in a stable romantic relationship is the most important marker of adulthood next to having a steady job, and romantic relationships are treated as mattering uniquely. As Brake argues, this focus on romantic relationships to the exclusion of all others implies that friendships do not significantly and uniquely contribute to our lives.[16] It is assumed that all people desire romantic relationships. Under amatonormativity, any relationship that could be romantic ought to be, since it is thought this would be better for people's lives. Thus, romance in films like *When Harry Met Sally* often involves (straight) people having to take chances on turning friendship into romance, since this is thought to be preferable to cross-gender friendship. The romantic relationship is almost always considered worth risking friendship over, privileging uncertain romantic relationships over stable close friendships. Pre-New 52, Wonder Woman and Superman's friendship does not fit this mold. Although Superman loves Lois Lane, he will not sacrifice his friendship with Wonder Woman even when it risks his relationship with Lois. For example, when Lois calls Superman to save her father at the same moment that Superman thinks Wonder Woman's life is at risk, he does not hesitate in saving Wonder Woman instead.[17] This puts stress on Superman's relationship, and although he regrets not being able to save Lois's father and is devastated that she is angry, he does not doubt that the decision to try to save his friend was the right thing to do.[18]

Under amatonormativity, we are taught to view members of the opposite gender as potential romantic partners, rather than as potential friends. The continuum of cross-gender intimacy, therefore, goes from people to whom one is not close, to romantic partners. By internalizing this amatonormative framework, people are taught to read close relationships as romantic in virtue of their closeness. Thus, when cross-gender friends display affection toward one another, outsiders are likely to misread their relationship and intentions. Yet, even when Superman and Wonder Woman have been fighting the forces of evil away from Earth, and away from Lois Lane, for a thousand years and both think they are going to die, they reaffirm that they could never have a sexual relationship and instead call one another best friends.[19] Pre-New 52, Wonder Woman and Superman do not see one another as potential romantic partners even when all impediments to a relationship are swept away. Both friends explicitly reject the amatonormative assumption that they are potential romantic partners.

In privileging romantic couples over other life-structuring caring relationships, society treats romantic relationships as central to our lives merely in virtue of their being romantic. Friendship is expected to be less central to people's lives than their romantic relationships, so friendship is automatically less important. The standard reply to queries about the nature of cross-gender friends' relationship, "We're *just* friends," is as amatonormative as the assumptions behind the question. Friends are not supposed to be as close or important in one's life, so one's friends are *merely* one's friends; one's romantic partner is the person who truly matters. Yet again, however, we find a rejection of this assumption in the pre-Flashpoint comics. When Lois Lane asks Wonder Woman about her relationship with Superman, Diana repeats the question about Lois and Superman's relationship. In response to Lois's answer "We're just good friends," Wonder Woman says that the same is true about her and Superman. While Wonder Woman knows that Lois and Superman are romantically involved, her response represents an overture of friendship to the other woman. Lois's relationship with Superman is why Wonder Woman trusts her: Superman, a trusted friend, says Lois is trustworthy. The two women are on an equal footing in that they share a trusted confidant. Friendship and trust are what matter to Wonder Woman, not the potential for perceived romantic rivalry. At this point Lois begins to trust and admire Wonder Woman, seeing her primarily as a friend.[20] Pre-New 52, Wonder Woman rejects the amatonormative assumption that friendship with Superman would be "just" anything, or that the question of romance could be important to them.

Where cross-gender friends interact with family and friends whose thinking on these matters is amatonormative, they cannot pretend to be unaware of others' amatonormative viewpoint. Since the friends will be assumed to be a romantic couple, they must confront amatonormativity head-on in explaining their relationship to others, unlike romantic partners whose relationship is accepted as a matter of course. Yet cross-gender couples must often do without fictional portrayals of friends to explain and assess their lives. Similarly, cross-gender friends cannot pretend to be unaware of the expectation that both of them are straight, or that bi- or pansexuals are untrustworthy in friendships. Opting out of the norms displayed in pop culture for friendships is not simply a matter of building a successful cross-gender friendship; it is a matter of taking on board the extra work of defending such a friendship.

Despite their insistence that friendship is important in its own right, before the reboot Wonder Woman and Superman must face assumptions that because they are both straight, they therefore must be interested in developing a romantic relationship. That their relationship is romantic after the reboot legitimizes these assumptions. Because the relationship between Wonder Woman and Superman is transformed into a romantic one *without any change in the personalities of the characters*, the later romantic relationship is built on the dynamics of the earlier friendship. It therefore looks like their friendship has always had the potential for romance, and by making them romantically involved, DC editorial seems to see itself only as having taken the relationship between the two one step further along its logical track. Pre-New 52, the two characters explicitly denied this many times. The implication of the change is that close cross-gender friendships can become romantic without any change to the relationship dynamic, which means that all cross-gender friendships are the building blocks for romantic relationships.

Freeing Friendship

Pressure from a society that accepts the "*When Harry Met Sally* question" as reasonable, especially from one's family and other close friends, as well as one's own internalized standards for friendship, can serve to make cross-gender friendships unstable. To insist, in spite of social pressure, that one's friendship is real and meaningful in its own right requires a commitment on the part of cross-gender friends to each other and to their relationship, as well as more than a little stubbornness. Pre-New 52, Wonder Woman and Superman face this pressure, and resist it because their friendship brings their life value in its own right. The predominant views in pop culture that people are heterosexual until proven otherwise, that bi- and pansexuals are not trustworthy as friends for *either* gender, and that friendship is less valuable than romantic relationships, severely limit not only the friendships available but also the forms of life we can live. If friendship is a part of living well, where people think they cannot be friends with anyone to whom they could potentially be sexually attracted, there is less chance of them living well, since they rule out friendship with much of the population. As the predominant view of friendship in pop culture is unjustifiably limiting, a return to philosophical views of friendship could remove these limitations and provide models for pursuing a broader range of friendships. If, as prevailing wisdom in pop culture and philosophy agree, close friendships are valuable, this would allow people more freedom to seek such valuable relationships. We should not view friendships between the Supermen and Wonder Women of the world with suspicion, or seek to transform these friendships into romantic ones. We would be better served by noticing the good these friendships bring to both parties and ourselves, and seek friends of either gender who are willing to work with us to produce this kind of good in our lives.

Notes

1. Aristotle, *Nicomachean Ethics*, edited by Terence Irwin (Indianapolis, IN: Hackett Publishing, 1999), 1156a.
2. Ibid., 1166a.
3. Dean Cocking and Jeanette Kennett, "Friendship and the Self," *Ethics*, 108(3) (1998) 502–527.
4. Aristotle, *Nicomachean Ethics*, 1155a.
5. Immanuel Kant, *Lectures on Ethics*, edited by Peter Heath and J.B. Schneewind, translated by Peter Heath (Cambridge: Cambridge University Press, 1997), 422–423.
6. Stijn van Impe, "Kant on Friendship," *International Journal of Arts and Sciences*, 4(3) (2011) 132.

7. Greg Rucka, Cliff Richards *et al.*, *Wonder Woman* #2 (New York: DC Comics, 2006), 226.

8. John Byrne, Roger Stern, Kurt Schaffenberger *et al.*, *Action Comics* #1 (New York: DC Comics, 1988), 600.

9. Superman/Wonder Woman Reviews, http://comicbookroundup.com/comic-books/reviews/dc-comics/supermanwonder-woman (accessed December 31, 2015).

10. Kathy Werking, *We're Just Good Friends: Women and Men in Non-Romantic Relationships* (New York: Guilford Press, 1997), 38.

11. Grant Morrison, Yanick Paquette *et al.*, *Wonder Woman: Earth One* (Burbank, CA: DC Comics, 2016).

12. Patrick S. Mulick and Lester W. Wright Jr., "Examining the Existence of Biphobia in the Heterosexual and Homosexual Populations," *Journal of Bisexuality*, 2(4) (2002) 45–64.

13. Christian Klesse, "Shady Characters, Untrustworthy Partners, and Promiscuous Sluts: Creating Bisexual Intimacies in the Face of Heteronormativity and Biphobia," *Journal of Bisexuality*, 11(2&3) (2011) 227–244.

14. Elizabeth Brake, *Minimizing Marriage: Marriage, Morality, and the Law* (Oxford: Oxford University Press, 2012), 88–89.

15. Amatonormativity, https://www.tumblr.com/search/amatonormativity (accessed December 30, 2015).

16. Brake, Ibid., 94.

17. Joe Kelly, Kano *et al.*, *Action Comics* #1 (New York: DC Comics, 2001), 781.

18. Mark Schultz, Yvel Guichet *et al.*, *Superman: The Man of Steel* #1 (New York: DC Comics, 2002), 127.

19. Joe Kelly, German Garcia *et al.*, *Action Comics* #1 (New York: DC Comics, 2000), 761.

20. George Pérez, Mindy Newell, Chris Marrinan *et al.*, *Wonder Woman* #2 (New York: DC Comics, 1990), 39.

Part III

WHEN I DEAL WITH THEM, I DEAL WITH THEM

Bound to Face the Truth
The Ethics of Using Wonder Woman's Lasso

Melanie Johnson-Moxley

It's not darkness they fear ... it's the truth.[1]

Suppose that you were on a mission to make the world a better place, to combat tyrannical forces that seek to control it and to save it from outright destruction when it's threatened. Suppose that you were equipped with a unique tool that serves not only as your greatest weapon, but also as a potent instrument of healing—a golden cord created by your gods for one essential purpose: to reveal the truth. For Diana, the Amazonian princess, warrior, and diplomat of Themyscira, her "lasso of truth" is indispensable in her efforts as Wonder Woman to bring justice and peace to a world often short of both. It might not seem that there are any real ethical dilemmas to consider regarding the lasso's use. After all, a magic rope is hardly the same thing as laser vision or the power to manipulate matter, right? However, the more we consider exactly what the lasso can do and how it can do it, the more questions arise about how it *ought* to be used.

The Magic Lasso vs. the Lasso of Truth

First, we need to be clear about which version of the lasso we're discussing, because they're quite different things in the pre- and

Wonder Woman and Philosophy: The Amazonian Mystique, First Edition.
Edited by Jacob M. Held.
© 2017 John Wiley & Sons, Ltd. Published 2017 by John Wiley & Sons, Ltd.

post-*Crisis* DC universes. W.M. Marston introduced the magic lasso in Wonder Woman's origin story: created under the direction of the goddesses Aphrodite and Athena, it compelled anyone bound by it to obey whatever commands they were given. Princess Diana not only had to prove herself champion of the Amazons, but also devoted to the goddesses—to love and wisdom itself—before she was granted this "power to control others."[2] This reflected Marston's view that submission to the dominance of a loving authority figure was a beneficial thing, and it was central to Diana's mission in Man's World that she serve as a moral exemplar of this principle. This original lasso was capable of compelling action, which included, but was not limited to, truth-telling. The star-spangled heroine used it for interrogation, but also to temporarily alter the behavior of villains.

In the mid-1980s, George Pérez reimagined the Amazon's lariat as the lasso of truth, both limiting and complicating its power. This new version of the lasso is capable of compelling knowledge rather than action, that is, of making an individual bound by it *face the truth*—often a deflected, forgotten, or sublimated truth about themselves. It is still used as an instrument of interrogation, but in an expanded sense: Wonder Woman can do more than demand that someone speak the truth; she can make them confront the truth for themselves.[3] In other words, to borrow from the Greek philosopher Plato's (429–347 BCE) allegory: with the lasso, a person can be dragged from the shadowy cave of ignorance into the light of truth and knowledge, whether they want to or not. It's this version of the lasso that we'll discuss.

Four Ethical Touchstones

There are some basic approaches to ethics that make good touchstones for this conversation. First, there is *deontological* or duty ethics, as expressed by German philosopher Immanuel Kant (1724–1804), among others. A duty ethics defines "right action" as meeting universally binding obligations. One does a thing because it is the right thing to do, period, and a rational person will be able to determine this. Although, arguably, all superheroes are duty-oriented to some degree, the Green Lantern Corps are an exceptionally good example. Recruited by the Guardians of the Universe to combat evil and maintain order, the Green Lanterns are selected on the basis of their strength of will (and their non-disposition to the extreme emotions that will define other Lantern Corps) and work with a partner in an assigned sector of the universe to fulfill their oath to "shed ... light over dark evil."[4] Kantian ethics also emphasizes respect for rational beings, which dictates not interfering with their autonomy, or self-directed freedom. In this view, truth is given an unimpeachable moral status—being truthful is a *perfect duty* that we have to each other as rational, moral beings. There can be no exceptions. This forms a core element in Wonder Woman's moral framework, although it is not the only one.

Second, there are utilitarian ideas expressed by philosophers like John Stuart Mill (1806–1873) and Harriet Taylor Mill (1807–1858), which define "right action" as the thing that produces the most happiness and the least harm for everyone involved. Batman's methods are often unsentimentally utilitarian—he's not above pounding a street thug into a quivering heap to gain information that will prevent harm to Gotham's citizens, although he prefers to scare them into confessing. Australian philosopher Peter Singer is a contemporary utilitarian ethicist, whose emphasis on considering the pleasures and pains of animals as well as human beings is compatible with our vegetarian, animal-loving Amazon's moral outlook.

Third, there is virtue ethics, as discussed by Plato and his student Aristotle (384–322 BCE), by Chinese philosopher Kongzi ("Confucius," 551–479 BCE), and the Roman Stoic Marcus Aurelius (121–180 CE). These approaches emphasize the importance of becoming the kind of person who does the right kind of things by habit, as well as the presence of moral exemplars in our lives. Superman is a good example of this model, the product of Jonathan and Martha Kent's moral training, and a living symbol of what it means to be a selfless protector of the innocent and a champion of justice. Martha Nussbaum, a contemporary virtue ethicist, invites us to think about whether a society contributes to the flourishing of all its people; this is an excellent reflection of the Amazonian ideals for which Princess Diana serves as a diplomatic representative.

Finally, there is the ethics of care, expressed in traditions like Buddhism and Jainism, and by philosophers such as the French existentialist Simone de Beauvoir (1908–1986). Care ethics emphasizes the centrality of relationships and the role of compassion in our moral decision-making. "The love you carry for everything, for the entirety of creation ... it's limitless," Diana is told.[5] Some of Wonder Woman's most difficult tasks strike us as heroic precisely because she undertakes them with compassion. It is also her compassion that tempers those actions she takes from the orientation of duty or utility.

In fact, Wonder Woman is at her best when she balances two or more of these ethical bases in her actions. The pre-*Crisis* Amazon Code of Justice and Mercy includes injunctions to obey lawful authority, to be concerned with the welfare of others, to help "the innocent and distressed," and to save the lives of friends and enemies alike.[6] The post-*Crisis* Code of the Amazons affirms a mission to serve as both warriors and protectors, fostering peace by "lending reason to [man's] rages" and tempering aggression with compassion.[7] Diana views it as her personal duty to safeguard the truth through her stewardship of the lasso, as well as to serve as a moral exemplar in Patriarch's World. She emphasizes the importance of the virtues of mercy and forgiveness in her exercise of justice.

"The Truth is My Weapon"[8]

Although the Amazons have refined their combat skills over centuries, it is their core ethos to seek, whenever possible, non-violent methods of preventing harm or addressing a threat. An Amazon will defend herself and her home; she will protect those who are unable to defend themselves; but she will not act as an unprovoked aggressor. Persuasion is preferable to coercion and diplomacy to warfare. However, when these measures fail, or are clearly not an option, then the Amazons are pragmatic about using force—including violence—in as measured and precise a way as possible to eliminate the threat of more violence. In any event, the end goal is always peace.

Diana is a trained warrior, skilled at hand-to-hand combat and the use of bladed weapons. Her first mission is not a diplomatic one—she is dispatched to confront an insane god. She does not face Ares with a sword or ax, however. It would be absurd for her to do so: a mortal with a sword is no match for the god of war in a martial contest. It is by using the lasso, created for this very purpose, that she can achieve her goal, which is to end Ares's threat—not Ares himself. This action isn't even intended to hurt him if not necessary. Yet she knows, and will often state, that the truth is a formidable weapon. She knows this as she encircles the war god in her lariat, enabling him to see that the logical consequence of bringing the world to nuclear apocalypse will not be his ultimate glorification as the greatest of all gods, but the annihilation of all life on the planet. She makes him confront the irrationality of his course of action.[9]

An irrational mind is not—and perhaps cannot possibly be—truth-oriented, so it's imperative to restore reason to irrational agents whenever possible. For Ares, this is feasible; in other cases, it's not. There seems to be a correlation between vulnerability to the lasso and the capacity for reason. It's not effective when used on Bizarro, due to his inadequate intellect. ("Bizarro no like golden bugs in head."[10]) It's also not effective on the Red Panzer, whose sense of truth has been distorted irrevocably by his hatred.[11] From a deontological perspective, for Wonder Woman to respect an individual's autonomy requires that she is dealing with a rational—or at least *potentially rational*—decision-maker. If she is not, then perhaps utility is the only moral consideration that makes sense.

A utilitarian focus is evident whenever the lasso is used to neutralize or destroy an enemy's weapons. If the essential nature of a weapon is deception, it will be vulnerable to the lasso of truth. The tree on which Eris's Apples of Discord grow is incinerated when subjected to the "blazing dignity" of the lasso.[12] Phobos's fear-inducing toxin is nullified when the demi-god is subjected to the lasso's power.[13] These are objects, not persons. More ambiguous is the case when the devastating, deceit-fueled flames of the dragon Drakul Karfang are conquered by the purifying flames of truth—at great cost to the dragon, as these processes are not gentle. A critical factor in Diana's decision-making is whether she is dealing with a person or a monster. If there is neither intellect nor heart—no soul—then the ethical considerations otherwise given to creatures are suspended.

Whether the subjects are monsters or not, the use of the lasso in martial situations is rarely consensual. An enemy agent will be forced to speak the truth in the service of preventing harm to others. If it is judged that causing discomfort to a person (or, for that matter, placing them at risk of retaliation by their superiors) through interrogation will save the lives of countless others, then the choice is made to proceed. In these cases, Wonder Woman's first priority is not compelling people to confront the truth for their own good, but for the good of others. Respecting autonomy is not the first consideration.

Still, the Amazon's method of cross-examination is presented as the more merciful alternative to, say, Batman's violent and terrifying techniques.[14] For the most part, she exercises compassion during the process, which may involve entering the other's "soul"—that is, co-observing the agent's memories, including his childhood traumas, through the power of the lasso. "I tried to treat those secrets with care," she observes, "even from those who wished me harm."[15] When attaining information from an enemy who intends to destroy Themyscira, Diana states that "I can't help but feel sympathy even for him … [a]nd even for him, I follow the Amazon code when facing a vanquished foe: punishment for the adult … empathy for the child."[16] So when dealing with a *person*, even when utility trumps respect for autonomy, care—a kind of respect for an individual's wellbeing—tempers her actions.

The potential for abuse in employing the lasso is illustrated starkly when Genocide, the laboratory-created killer, forcibly wrests the lasso from Wonder Woman and has it surgically incorporated into her own body. Genocide uses the lasso's power not just to exploit and manipulate her victims, but to torture them. "I see your soul, woman. Let me clutch it. Let me wallow in it. Let me be its master … Each human soul I touch I learn a little more about cruelty." The importance of the Amazon's self-imposed code of respect and care for those in her lasso becomes even more paramount in this light. It is also revelatory, at the climax of their final battle, that Diana finds herself able to show compassion even to the monster who tortured Etta Candy into a coma. "With clarity comes … mercy."[17]

"This is my soul. Please tread carefully."[18]

The lasso is not only a weapon but also a tool for healing. It can restore those who are fragmented, who are lost because they do not remember who they are, who are trapped or paralyzed (even literally "petrified"), or whose reason has been impaired. I might use a knife as a weapon to stop a monster from attacking you, and I might use it as a surgical instrument to drain your wound of poison—both are ways of saving your life.

There are villains in the DC universe who invade the minds and bodies of others: the sorceress Circe, the demented Dr. Psycho, and a host of gods and powerful aliens who take control of ordinary and superpowered people. Diana has used her lasso to help victims of such possession, freeing gods (Hermes, trapped by his Roman counterpart) and demi-gods (Heracles, punished by Zeus) from imprisonment in stone, releasing Superman from Circe's enchantment ("This dark thing isn't you. And I won't let you betray yourself or your world this way"),[19] and so on.

These cases are pretty uncontroversial: it's a good thing to make the Man of Steel less murder-prone. Other acts of disillusionment are more ethically ambiguous, however, especially when illusion seems kinder than reality. Wonder Woman liberates teenager Vanessa from Dr. Psycho's control by unlocking a stream of the girl's actual, rather than implanted, memories. Diana is fully aware that the girl has been happier living with Dr. Psycho's fabricated memories than she had been with her own recently traumatic ones, and feels uncomfortable about the way in which she must intrude on Vanessa's privacy. Only with Vanessa's permission and great care does she proceed.

There is a moral principle expressed in the Confucian *Analects* as *shu*, or empathetic understanding. The idea is that in order to be virtuous in our treatment of each other, we need to engage our *heart-mind* in order to genuinely understand another person and care about her wellbeing in light of that knowledge. Intellect cannot be divorced from love, nor compassion from wisdom.[20] The lasso may be used to facilitate mutual understanding between two people, dissolving aggression and estrangement through a profound and total understanding of the other, described as "intimate insight." This occurs when Diana's mother Hippolyte is bound to her one-time enemy and former lover Heracles. The two are not forced together; Hippolyte voluntarily enters the communion of the lasso as an act of compassion in response to Heracles's suffering.[21]

In contrast, Wonder Woman forcibly creates such a bond between two battling warlords, although only after every opportunity has been given for them to engage in rational discussion. Diana recounts tying them up "like animals" and making them share each other's memories and secrets, so that they become "twins of pain."[22] This is not gratuitous. The aim is to make them better people and leaders, to prevent more bloodshed and improve the lives of their people as a result. It is open to question whether or not violating their autonomy is ethically permissible: is a utilitarian justification enough to trump respect for individual autonomy? The warlords are responsible for great suffering, but they are responsible as human beings—they are not, in fact, animals. However, there is a limit to how far Diana will encroach upon their autonomy. She does not force them to return to their governments urging peace, but this is an action they each take after they come to understand each other. She compels them to face the truth; what they do with their new understanding is a matter for them to choose.

Truth-Force

Nothing about Wonder Woman's use of the lasso is passive; compelling someone to face the truth involves decided *action* on Wonder Woman's part. She does not merely wrangle someone in her rope; she guides them toward memory or epiphany. She is *doing something*, not merely *letting something happen*. She is an active moral agent.

Mahatma Gandhi (1869–1948) urged members of the Indian resistance to British rule to follow a principle he termed *satyagraha*, or "truth-force." Gandhi repeatedly corrected the misimpression that the movement was one of "passive resistance." On the contrary, he said, it was an active movement, harnessing what he believed to be the irresistible power of the moral truth. "Satyagraha is pure soul force … the soul is informed with knowledge. In it burns the flame of love."[23] This language strongly echoes Wonder Woman's own.

Is the use of the lasso necessarily non-violent? Clearly not, in the case of Drakul Karfang and other entities who find being bound in the lasso torturous. Is it necessarily violent, then? Diana's decision to exercise compassion even toward her enemies suggests that it is not; if she can avoid unnecessary harm or distress, she will do so. Must the lasso's function be non-violent in order for its use on an enemy to be permissible? In Gandhi's view, there is never justification for violence. For the Amazons, the judicious use of violent force to prevent further violence is pragmatically permitted. For the most part, Wonder Woman falls closer to the pole of restraint than to unfettered use of force. Arguably, it is only when she is emotionally compromised—as when her mother is killed—that she strays to the other pole.[24]

"When we don't want it, the truth burns."[25]

Diana never wavers from her conviction that truth is an intrinsic good, that being truth-oriented is a moral duty, and that choosing to face the truth—even when it's difficult—is a virtue. In the opening pages of "A League of One," she uses the lasso on herself as a test of her own integrity. "It is no small thing she does ... being compelled to speak honestly might be uncomfortable—but facing one's true being is perilous."[26]

One troubling case of Diana's use of the lasso involves sentient apes who have lived largely unaware that their culture and religion is not ancient, but recently fabricated from human mythologies. Specialist Lukk-Nutt asks Wonder Woman to bind her in the lasso so that she might "confess," stating that she has been lying so long she can no longer trust herself to tell the truth. Lukk-Nutt sees Wonder Woman as "a pure thing. A golden mean, against which all of us must be measured." (Both Aristotle and Confucius speak of virtue as a golden mean.) There is no ambiguity in Lukk-Nutt's case. However, the priestess of the apes, Abu-Gita, does not willingly consent to be bound. The Amazon tells her point-blank that "Your entire faith is based on a lie. A fallacy which it is high time you surrender." The priestess is unable to cope with what is revealed, the "single bullet of truth" that destroys her sense of place and purpose.[27] Lukk-Nutt wanted to face the truth; the priestess did not.

The most difficult moral questions arise in cases such as these, when Wonder Woman uses her lasso to compel someone to face a truth that he does not wish to face and the consequences of blissful ignorance are not clearly dangerous to others. As often stated, the truth can be hard; it can be uncomfortable; it can be painful. Truth can burn. It can cause emotional distress, cognitive dissonance, or prompt an existential crisis. Being encircled by the lasso of truth can be invasive, even when tempered by Wonder Woman's caring intentions. Perhaps the thing most at issue is whether or not the violation of individual autonomy can be justified by framing it as a sincere act of maternalism—doing what is best for a person, even when he does not know it or desire it. This is a difficult issue to resolve. A similar issue arises in healthcare ethics: is a physician morally justified in treating a patient who does not wish to be treated? Does a perceived mission to care for the physical or psychological wellbeing of an individual warrant violating her autonomy?

Perhaps the best foundation for an answer is found in Simone de Beauvoir's *Ethics of Ambiguity*, where she addresses situations such as intervening in a drug addict's self-destructive behavior, or preventing someone from committing suicide. An existentialist holds that freedom to choose is essential to our humanity, and the results of those choices are our fundamental self-creative act. So what Beauvoir proposes is that we may justify interfering with someone's autonomy once, if an individual is not psychologically stable or rational enough to genuinely choose what she wants for herself (and the interference is not actually to serve our own ends). Removing her from whatever situation is prompting that distress and allowing her to recover her use of reason may be permissible—provided that we are then prepared to allow the individual to make her own decision and to respect whatever that may be. On this view, if someone remains steadfast in her desire to commit suicide, then we cannot justify interfering with her choice.[28]

As a rule, Wonder Woman appears to operate within this framework. If someone's self-deception is harmful to others, she will drag them toward the truth without hesitation, on utilitarian and/or deontological grounds. If a person's delusion affects only himself, then she must balance her sense of duty ("help others") and compassion ("out of love for others") with respect for autonomy ("to help themselves"). Diana once declared to the goddess Osira that forcing peace through mental manipulation is wrong.[29] If she is to remain consistent with this ethical position, then she must observe limits on encroaching on individual autonomy. Only this mindful respect, in combination with her compassion, will keep her use of the lasso in the pursuit of justice on solid moral ground.

Notes

1. Gail Simone, *Sensation Comics: Wonder Woman* #1 (2014).
2. W.M. Moulton, *Sensation Comics* #6 (June 1942).
3. Despite a recent declaration that the lasso "wasn't designed for interrogation" (Geoff Johns, *Justice League* #47, December 2015), it has without doubt been used for exactly this purpose throughout Wonder Woman's history.
4. This is the original oath made by Alan Scott. The contemporary oath used by Hal Jordan is the "In brightest day, in blackest night/No evil shall escape my sight..." version. A newer variant, recited by the Alpha Lanterns, begins "In days of peace, in nights of war/*obey the laws forevermore*" (*Green Lantern*, 4(27)) (emphasis mine).

5. Greg Rucka, *Blackest Night: Wonder Woman* #3 (2011).

6. *Wonder Woman*, 1(40) (1950).

7. *Wonder Woman Secret Files* #2.

8. Brian Azzarello, *Wonder Woman*, 4(7) (May 2012).

9. George Pérez, *Wonder Woman*, 2(6) (July 1987).

10. Matt Wagner, *Batman/Superman/Wonder Woman: Trinity* (2003).

11. Phil Jiminez, *Girl Frenzy: Donna Troy* (1998).

12. George Pérez, *Wonder Woman*, 2(30) (March 1990).

13. George Pérez, *Wonder Woman*, 2(24) (1989).

14. *Batman/Superman/Wonder Woman: Trinity*.

15. Gail Simone, *Wonder Woman*, 3(32) (2009).

16. Gail Simone, *Wonder Woman*, 3(15) (February 2008).

17. Gail Simone, "Rise of the Olympian," *Wonder Woman*, 3(28–30) (2009).

18. Gail Simone, *Wonder Woman*, 3(36) (2010).

19. Phil Jiminez, *Wonder Woman*, 2(175) (2002).

20. See Confucius, *The Analects* 4.15, 12.22, and 15.24.

21. George Pérez, *Wonder Woman*, 2(13) (1987).

22. Erik Luke, *Wonder Woman*, 2(142) (1999).

23. *The Collected Works of Mahatma Gandhi*, 13: 526 (Delhi, 1961).

24. In other rare instances, however, sheer expediency trumps mercy: the interrogation of Maxwell Lord serves as one unforgettable example. See Greg Rucka, "Sacrifice," *Wonder Woman*, 2(219) (2005).

25. Christopher Moeller, *Justice League: A League of One* (2000).

26. Ibid.

27. Doselle Young, "The Thin Gold Line," *Wonder Woman Annual*, 2(8) (1999).

28. Simone de Beauvoir, *The Ethics of Ambiguity* (Citadel Press, 1948/1976), 156 ff.

29. *Wonder Woman*, 1(232) (1977).

"What I Had to Do"

The Ethics of Wonder Woman's Execution of Maxwell Lord

Mark D. White

Killing is a topic that divides superhero fans like no other. Whether a particular superhero kills is a signature attribute of that character and one that defines who he or she is. For example, Batman never kills, even when he might have very good reason to, whereas Wolverine kills indiscriminately. Captain America and Superman have both killed on notable occasions, but are always wracked with guilt afterwards for what circumstances led them to do.

Wonder Woman is a curious case, though. Traditionally associated with compassion and love, Diana is also a fierce warrior. She has the power of Superman and the nobility of Captain America, yet when the situation calls for it—which is rare—she kills. Usually her victims are mythological creatures or demi-gods from the Greek pantheon, but on one notable occasion she killed a mortal man, and unlike her superhero brothers, she felt no remorse or regret, maintaining that her act was the right and just decision in an unfortunate circumstance. But was it? What would her fellow heroes say—or our heroes, the philosophers? And should she have felt regret for what she did?

Maxwell Lord, Check and Mate

In 2005, the DC Universe was hurtling toward "Infinite Crisis," the latest in a series of reality-altering events that started with 1985's

Wonder Woman and Philosophy: The Amazonian Mystique, First Edition.
Edited by Jacob M. Held.
© 2017 John Wiley & Sons, Ltd. Published 2017 by John Wiley & Sons, Ltd.

"Crisis on Infinite Earths." One of the storylines leading into Infinite Crisis dealt with Brother I (as in "eye"), a surveillance satellite launched by Batman after he was betrayed by his fellow members of the Justice League. Brother I was later commandeered by Maxwell Lord, one-time sponsor of the Justice League and now the leader of Checkmate, a secret spy organization.[1]

Lord had become suspicious and fearful of the world's superpowered beings and, to that end, he launched a campaign designed to discredit and destroy them, using the resources of Checkmate as well as his ability to control minds. As part of the most dramatic prong of this attack, Lord infiltrated Superman's mind, causing him to see his greatest foes, such as Luthor, Brainiac, or Doomsday, killing those he cared for, especially his beloved Lois Lane.[2] As a result, Superman lashed out with all his might at those he thought were his enemies, only to discover later that he was actually beating one of his closest friends, Batman. The timely intervention of Wonder Woman saved the Caped Crusader's life, and when Lord summoned Superman back to Checkmate headquarters, Diana followed close behind.

Once the three were together, Lord boasted of his control over Superman, which he had nurtured over several years, and made the situation crystal clear: "As long as I live, Superman's mind is mine to control."[3] Before Wonder Woman could try to talk him out of it, Lord commanded Superman to attack her, again under the delusion that she was Doomsday trying to kill Lois. After a brutal fight, Diana hurt Superman badly enough to give her a chance to wrap Lord in her magic lasso. Lord freed Superman from his control to prove to Wonder Woman that he could, and so Superman could tell her what he saw. "The next time," Lord told her while bound by the lasso of truth, "he'll kill Batman ... or Lois ... or you. You think I've lied to you but I haven't. I can't. He's mine. I'll never let him go."

Wonder Woman then demanded of Lord, "Tell me how to free him from your control," to which Lord answered, simply, "Kill me." And she did, snapping his neck and watching beside a shocked Superman as Lord's limp body fell to the ground.[4]

Killing Now to Prevent Killing Later

Let's address the immediate question: Was Wonder Woman right to kill Max Lord? Most heroes go out of their way not to kill; as we said above, Superman rarely kills and Batman flat out refuses to. Does this mean that Wonder Woman has a distinctly different ethical code than these other heroes, or was there something special about the situation with Max Lord that would have driven *any* hero to kill him?

Just to be clear, we're not talking about killing to punish a person for past crimes, but rather to prevent future ones. Superheroes usually leave responsibility for punishment to the authorities—unless their name literally *is* the Punisher, in which case not so much—but there are occasions on which, like police officers and soldiers, superheroes must decide whether to kill in order to prevent future killings. Typical cases in which killing is justified by law (justifiable homicide) include self-defense, in which a person kills to save his or her own life, and defense of another whose life is threatened. Usually, standards of proportionality and necessity have to be met: lethal force should only be used if it is the only way to stop the killer. In other words, a threat against life is not a license to kill if there are other options to save a life. (Sorry, Mr. Bond.)[5]

The case of Wonder Woman and Max Lord is not a typical case of justifiable homicide, falling more accurately under the description of pre-emptive killing, in which someone is regarded to be such a serious threat that killing him or her is considered beneficial.[6] No one's life was immediately under threat by Lord, who was incapacitated physically by Wonder Woman. So there would need to be an extraordinary circumstance to justify taking his life. As Lord made clear, though, his powers of mind control could not be restrained, and even if he were rendered unconscious, the second he awoke he would regain control of Superman and command him to kill—which he told Diana while bound in her lasso of truth. According to his word, then, Max Lord's mind was essentially a weapon that would go off with no way to stop it … except shutting it off permanently.

We can compare this situation with another proposed case of justified pre-emptive killing: Batman and the Joker. It is well known that Batman flat-out refuses to kill the Joker, despite the inability of the authorities to keep the Clown Prince of Crime imprisoned or institutionalized and the very high probability that once free he will return to his homicidal ways. Nonetheless, Batman will not end the Joker's life due to a deeply held belief in the value of life and a personal refusal to take a life himself.[7] Wonder Woman shares Batman's belief in the value of life—she is known for her compassion and love for humanity—if not his reluctance to take one. (More on this below.) But ideally, the Joker could be incapacitated and rendered harmless, unlike Lord. Also, Lord has made it clear—under the compulsion of Wonder Woman's lasso—that he would use Superman to kill once he was able. By contrast, no one knows exactly why the Joker kills, or whether there is a "method to his madness" at all, so there remains the possibility that he would stop killing even if he were not effectively incapacitated.

Would a Moral Philosopher Have Saved Max Lord?

If we look at Wonder Woman's choice through the lens of moral philosophy, it would seem that the deck is stacked against Lord in terms of one school of ethics, consequentialism. *Consequentialism* requires that we make a moral decision by choosing the option with the best (or least bad) outcomes. There are many different "flavors" of consequentialism, depending on how "best," "good," or "bad" are defined and measured. For instance, *utilitarianism* considers the total amount of happiness, pleasure, or wellbeing resulting from each option. In the case of Max Lord, however, the appropriate metric would be much simpler: human lives. If Wonder Woman kills Lord, one life is lost, and if she doesn't, he will take an untold number of lives. We don't even have to consider that the persons he would kill can be presumed to be innocent whereas he is decidedly not. The simple math dictates that Wonder Woman can guarantee the least loss of life by killing Max Lord.

This aligns with how Diana explained her decision to Batman:

> Max Lord made it very plain that he would make Superman do it again. That the next time he would surely succeed. That under his command, Superman would murder you, or his wife, or his parents, or his friends. The lasso was upon him, and with it, I asked how Kal-El could be freed. And Maxwell Lord told me. I made my decision. I stand by it as the proper one. I broke his neck. I killed him.[8]

Trusting that there was no other way to stop Lord and that he would use Superman to kill again, Wonder Woman minimized the loss of life by ending Lord's, which is consistent with consequentialist reasoning based on lives saved.[9]

Superheroes, though, are ordinarily not consequentialists in this simplistic sense. Instead, they often focus on doing the right thing, where "right" refers to some duty or principle that transcends consequences. That line of thinking is based on the school of ethics known as *deontology*, which maintains that actions should be judged by their inherent moral quality rather than their consequences. For instance, deontologists would normally maintain that taking a life is wrong based on rights, duties, or respect for life, regardless of any positive outcome that would come from a particular act of killing. This captures Batman's view on killing, and helps explain why he's never killed the Joker: in his mind, it's simply wrong.[10]

Wonder Woman is certainly sympathetic to this, and does not take killing lightly, usually killing only mythological creatures or gods. But even a deontologist must sometimes take consequences into account, lest her position follow the extreme of *fiat justitia ruat caelum*: "let justice be done though the heavens fall." For instance, many criticize Batman for refusing to consider the cost in human lives of letting the Joker live.[11] Diana can maintain a strong principle of not taking a life, but consider it overruled in particular cases if the costs of maintaining that position become too high. This way of thinking is sometimes known as *threshold deontology*, which says that deontological rules must be followed until the costs of doing so reach a certain threshold, after which consequentialist considerations take over.[12] We see this in Wonder Woman's conversation with Kate Spencer, the lawyer Diana sought out to represent her before the International Criminal Court. Kate is also known as Manhunter, a hero who occasionally kills. When Diana told Kate that it was her superhero identity that attracted her, Diana said "Your sense of justice is strong. Almost Amazonian. And you have a special understanding about what I had to do to Maxwell Lord." Kate explained, "I have killed, but never as a first choice. I have no problem with lethal force … When all other options have run out, well … sometimes safety wins," to which Diana responded, simply, "exactly."[13] This applies very well to the Max Lord case, in which the knowledge that Lord could and *would* kill again once given the chance, made the cost in terms of safety of letting him live far too high. In Wonder Woman's judgment, that level of cost crossed the threshold, and when consequentialist deliberation took over … well, we know how that ended.

No Regret, No Remorse

The decision Wonder Woman faced with respect to Max Lord closely resembles the one Superman faced when three renegade Kryptonians, each more powerful than Superman, wiped out the entire population of an Earth in an alternate dimension and threatened to do the same in his. Nearly unstoppable and determined to commit global genocide, the Kryptonians could not be incapacitated for long, so Superman chose to execute them using green kryptonite.[14]

Even though their actions were similar, the two heroes' reactions to them could not be more different. Superman was wracked with guilt and exiled himself from Earth for a time. Years later, he still regards it as one of his worst failures.[15] Wonder Woman, however, was not distraught at all. Superman thought to himself immediately after she killed Lord, "there was no rage in Diana's eyes. There was nothing. Not even remorse."[16] As Diana told Batman soon thereafter, "It was a question of doing what needs to be done. A question of doing it without hesitation ... I am not ashamed of what I have done. I did what was required to save not only Kal, but countless others."[17]

This may strike some as cold—and we can assume that both Superman and Batman heard it that way—but there is another way to look at it, as reflecting Wonder Woman's resolve and her belief that the decision she made was the right one. As we saw above, she told Batman that she had to make a decision and act on it quickly: "I made my decision. I stand by it as the proper one. I broke his neck. I killed him."[18] And it was not a difficult decision: she is a seasoned hero and warrior, who knows when the ultimate measure is called for in a battle. Perhaps with more time, she and the other heroes could have devised a way to incapacitate Lord or neutralize his mind-control powers, but she didn't have that time. She needed to act on her best judgment, and that's what she did.

This does not mean, though, that she had no regrets about the situation. As she told Batman:

> I was pained by what had happened. I regretted that there had been a need for Max Lord's death. But I was not sorry for what I had done, I shed no tears for my actions. No more than I wept when I took Medusa's head from her shoulders [referring to a recent battle which ended when Wonder Woman beheaded the Gorgon].[19]

Wonder Woman did not regret her action, but she did regret that she was in a position to have to take it. Given that she had to, however, and given that she determined it was the right thing to do, she does not regret doing it.

Another way to think about why Wonder Woman had no regrets killing Lord—while Batman would have, if he would have killed him in the first place—is that she does not have the same concerns with the way she sees herself that the Caped Crusader does. Besides the value of life and the hope of redemption, one of the most frequent reasons Batman gives for not killing is that he doesn't want to become like those he fights.[20] He's not only concerned with the consequences of his actions and the moral duties he might violate; he's also concerned with what his actions might say about himself, his moral character. This reflects a third school of ethics known as virtue ethics. *Virtue ethics* shifts the focus of moral evaluation from actions themselves to the person performing them, and asks if a virtuous person would have acted so.

Batman clearly feels he would not be the person he wants to be if he killed his enemies, even the most homicidal of them like the Joker. Wonder Woman has no such concerns, though. She is an Amazon warrior born and bred, and understands that sometimes one must take a life in order to protect lives, as she did with Max Lord.

Avoiding the Tragic Dilemma

Situations like the ones superheroes often face, in which they have to choose one person to save at the expense of another, or kill one person to save many others, are sometimes called *tragic dilemmas*, situations from which a person cannot escape "with clean hands."[21] Tragic dilemmas make for great drama, especially when the stakes are high and personal, such as when a hero's loved ones are in danger. Think of Giganta dangling Etta Candy off a skyscraper while a bomb she's placed under a school bus is about ready to blow—whom does Wonder Woman try to save?

One reason superheroes appear to us as super is that they have a way of transcending tragic dilemmas. Just when we think the villain has finally found a way to stump our hero, she refuses to choose the least bad option and the "lesser of two evils" and instead finds a way to do it all. In the situation above, Wonder Woman would defy all odds by managing to save *both* Etta and the schoolkids on the bus, *and* defeat Giganta.

While this makes for great superheroics, forcing the hero to use her powers and ingenuity to solve the villain's puzzle, it doesn't carry as much emotional weight as when a hero truly has to choose one option or another. Superman was torn between killing the three renegade Kryptonians or letting them endanger his Earth; Batman struggles with the idea of killing the Joker instead of locking him away, only to see him escape and kill again. It's terrific to see our heroes beat the odds and save the day, but we also like to see what happens when they can't save everyone or have to cross a line they never thought they'd cross.

Was the situation with Lord a tragic dilemma for Wonder Woman? Tragic dilemmas usually result when a person finds it difficult to determine what the best or right action is; both options seem uniquely bad and impossible to compare or rank, such as the choice between saving one person or another.[22] But Wonder Woman's choice was not difficult; once Lord laid out the facts of the situation, she knew immediately what she needed to do. As she later told Batman, "there was no choice." Batman argued back, "there's always a choice for people like us," to which she replied, "no, there isn't. Sometimes there is no other choice."[23] If there had been any other way out, Wonder Woman would not have killed Lord, but he made it clear that the only way to stop him was to kill him, and that removed any meaningful sense of choice she had.[24]

Would She—*Should* She—Do It Again?

Wonder Woman does not regret killing Maxwell Lord to prevent him from using Superman as a murderous weapon, but would she do the same thing again in a similar situation? There is every reason to believe she would. One thing that distinguishes a justification from an excuse in moral philosophy (as well as law) is that if an action is justified, it was the right thing to do, whereas if it is excused, it was the wrong thing to do (though the person may not be held responsible for it). It follows that if a justified action was the right thing to do once, then if a person faced the same decision again, it would be right to do the same thing again (provided there were still no viable alternative).

Wonder Woman made a deliberate decision to kill Lord, a decision she believes was right, and we can be confident she would do it again. And wouldn't we want her to? Heroes who kill may seem less heroic, but is it heroic to refuse to take necessary steps to save lives? It's nice to believe there's always another choice, but as Wonder Woman told Batman, sometimes there isn't, and then the hero has to make a decision.[25] Wonder Woman made hers. Now it's time to make yours. What would you have done?

Notes

1. For the betrayal, see *Identity Crisis* (2006); for Batman's reaction to discovering it, see *JLA: Crisis of Conscience* (2006); and on the development and corruption of Brother I, see *The OMAC Project* (2005).
2. *Superman: Sacrifice* (2006).
3. *Wonder Woman* #219 (September 2005), reprinted in *Superman: Sacrifice*.
4. The two now-classic panels showing Max Lord's death were expertly drawn by Rags Morales, who depicted Diana with a cold, dead-eyed stare while she easily twists Lord's head 180 degrees.
5. For more on the law of self-defense (of which defense-of-others is an extension), see Suzanne Uniacke, *Permissible Killing: The Self-Defence Justification of Homicide* (Cambridge: Cambridge University Press, 1994) and Fiona Leverick, *Killing in Self-Defence* (Oxford: Oxford University Press, 2007).
6. This is an increasingly serious issue given the state of modern warfare; for a fascinating discussion, see Claire Finkelstein, Jens David Ohlin, and Andrew Altman (eds), *Targeted Killings: Law and Morality in an Asymmetrical World* (Oxford: Oxford University Press, 2012).
7. For more, see my chapter "Why Doesn't Batman Kill the Joker?" in Mark D. White and Robert Arp (eds), *Batman and Philosophy: The Dark Knight of the Soul* (Hoboken, NJ: John Wiley, 2008), 5–16.
8. *Wonder Woman* #220 (October 2005), reprinted in *Superman: Sacrifice*.
9. A more complicated consequentialism would also incorporate other outcomes, such as the impact of her act on the superhero community and the public at large. Wonder Woman did not seem to anticipate that her killing of Lord would be recorded and televised around the world—part of Lord's long-term plan to discredit superheroes, even after his death—but did consider the effect on Superman of being known as a

potential threat (see *Manhunter* #29 (May 2007), reprinted in *Manhunter Vol. 4: Unleashed* (2008)).

10. Deontology can, however, incorporate justifications for killing as discussed above—such as self-defense or the defense of another, as Wonder Woman's attorney Kate Spencer told the press during the grand jury hearings at the International Criminal Court in *Manhunter* #27 (March 2007), reprinted in *Manhunter Vol. 4: Unleashed*.

11. Again, see my chapter "Why Doesn't Batman Kill the Joker?"

12. See Michael S. Moore, "Torture and the Balance of Evils," in *Placing Blame: A Theory of the Criminal Law* (Oxford: Oxford University Press, 1997), 669–736. For criticism of threshold retributivism, see Larry Alexander, "Deontology at the Threshold," *University of San Diego Law Review*, 37 (2000) 893–912 and my "*Pro Tanto* Retributivism: Judgment and Balance of Principles in Criminal Justice," in Mark D. White (ed.), *Retributivism: Essays on Theory and Policy* (Oxford: Oxford University Press, 2011), 129–145.

13. *Manhunter* #26 (February 2007), reprinted in *Manhunter Vol. 4: Unleashed*.

14. *Superman*, vol. 2, #21 (September 1988); *Adventures of Superman* #444 (September 1988); and *Superman*, vol. 2, #22 (October 1988), in which the execution occurs. Note that Superman himself justifies this killing on grounds of punishment as well as pre-emption (unlike the examples involving Wonder Woman and Batman we discussed); see *Superman*, vol. 2, #22 ("as the last representative of law and justice on this world, it falls to me to act as judge, jury … and executioner").

15. See *Superman: Exile* (1998). Captain America had the same reaction when forced to kill a terrorist who was massacring innocent civilians in a church (*Captain America*, vol. 1, #21, September 1986); see my book *The Virtues of Captain America: Modern-Day Lessons in Character from a World War II Superhero* (Malden, MA: Wiley Blackwell, 2014), 119–121.

16. *Adventures of Superman* #643 (October 2005), reprinted in *Superman: Sacrifice*.

17. *Wonder Woman* #220.

18. Ibid.

19. Ibid.

20. Once again, see my chapter "Why Doesn't Batman Kill the Joker?" (Last time, I promise!)

21. See, for instance, Rosalind Hursthouse, *On Virtue Ethics* (Oxford: Oxford University Press, 1999), chapter 3.

22. The prototypical tragic dilemma, in fact, is from the book and film *Sophie's Choice*, in which a mother is forced to choose which of her two children will live and which will die.

23. *Infinite Crisis* #1 (December 2005), reprinted in *Infinite Crisis* (2008).

24. In a sense, Lord manipulated her as effectively as he manipulated Superman, but without using his power on her (which he couldn't, as established in *Wonder Woman* #219): he made her kill him and recorded it for the world to see, furthering his plan to turn the public against the heroes.

25. Of course, ultimately it's up to the creators to decide what situations to make the hero face, and when they do this they should be respectful to the established history and moral character of the hero. This helps explain why it was not shocking to most fans when Wonder Woman, the Amazon warrior, killed Max Lord, but much more disturbing when Superman, the Big Blue Boy Scout, killed Zod at the end of the 2013 film *Man of Steel*. For more on this, see my blog post "My thoughts on *Man of Steel*" at http://www.comicsprofessor.com/2013/06/my-thoughts-on-man-of-steel.html.

Can a Warrior Care?
Wonder Woman and the Improbable Intersection of Care Ethics and Bushido

Steve Bein

In Darwyn Cooke's *DC: The New Frontier*, Wonder Woman makes her first appearance embroiled in the Korean War. Though she wears the red, white, and blue, she's not fighting for the United States. Though she's an elite Amazon warrior, she's not fighting for Themyscira. She's come to liberate abused women, and this sets her apart from other heroes in some interesting ways.

It's worth noting that Cooke's vision is more sophisticated than many other writers have envisioned for the Amazon. Wonder Woman is one of the immortals of comic-book legend, hailing back to the Golden Age when a hero didn't really need a specific moral motivation. Do-gooders fought evil-doers, and in most cases that's all there was to it. Wonder Woman was one of these generic do-gooders. She hadn't suffered some tragic injustice in her youth, as Batman and Spider-Man had. She wasn't conceived to combat a specific menace, as Captain America was born to fight the Nazis. Her creators were quite feminist in their political leanings, but she's not quite a parable about sexism either (at least not in the way that the X-Men were a parable about racism). Suffragist imagery pervades her early adventures—she's chained or imprisoned in almost every issue—but unlike the X-Men, she doesn't have to fight for her very existence. She isn't a parable, but rather a *vehicle* to address sexism. In other words,

Wonder Woman and Philosophy: The Amazonian Mystique, First Edition.
Edited by Jacob M. Held.
© 2017 John Wiley & Sons, Ltd. Published 2017 by John Wiley & Sons, Ltd.

her battle for equality has more to do with her authors' motivations than her own.[1]

Bushido and Care

Wonder Woman has evolved considerably since the Golden Age. (Thank Hera!) Different writers in different eras have tinkered with her back story and her resulting character. Yet throughout her many retellings we can point to two consistent trends: she's a warrior, and she protects the abused. As a warrior, her honor code isn't so different from bushido, the code of the samurai. She's selfless, fearless, relentless, and she even has a magic lasso to enforce the samurai virtue of honesty. On the contrary, her loyalty is not to a daimyo but rather to the downtrodden—to downtrodden women in particular—and she cares for them in a way we don't see other heroes care. (In *The New Frontier*, for example, Superman never notices that the war serves as a smokescreen for the subjugation of women. He needs Wonder Woman to point that out.) This looks a lot like a moral theory known as care ethics, born out of the feminist movement of the 1970s.

Bushido and care ethics aren't supposed to go together. In most respects they're completely at odds with one another. Bushido is as uncaring a moral philosophy as one can imagine. Care ethics is about as non–violent as a moral philosophy can get. Bushido requires a warrior to murder her own children if her lord demands it. Care ethics specifically prioritizes parental obligations above generic moral obligations. Bushido demands that a warrior divorce herself from her emotions. Care ethics demands that she embraces them. Bushido is hardly feminist. Care ethics is explicitly so.

It seems impossible that these two visions of morality could be at play in the conscience of one superhero. Could uniting them be Wonder Woman's most superhuman accomplishment? It's one that no other superhero has attempted, and as such, it makes Wonder Woman far more interesting—and far more nuanced—than many of her readers (and even some of her writers) give her credit for.

Wonder Woman and the Way of the Warrior

Since her first appearance in *All Star Comics* #8 (1941), Wonder Woman has had a number of origin stories. Two of these have reached beyond comicdom and into mainstream pop culture. The first, of course, is the iconic TV series starring Lynda Carter as Diana, the polite princess of Paradise Island who finds an American fighter pilot washed up on her shores. Though she's never seen a man before, she instantly falls for this one, and when she learns of the violent ways of the outside world she decides to leave paradise to go fight for justice.

This Wonder Woman seems torn between strength and courtesy. (In the 1975 pilot episode, "Bank Robbers," her response to being threatened at gunpoint is, "Excuse me, but that's very rude.") Just as naïve Diana struggles to figure out what's the proper place for women in this strange new world, one imagines the screenwriters struggling to figure out what they can and can't do with their new action hero, and how best to respond to the feminist movement that had swept the nation (and, no doubt, made possible the very existence of their show).

Then there's the other TV series, *Justice League*, which takes as its inspiration not the early comics of 1941–1942 (as the Lynda Carter series did), but rather the reboot launched by George Pérez in 1987. Pérez re-envisioned Wonder Woman by anchoring her deeply in her Amazon roots—that is, her roots in Greek mythology. Accidentally pierced by a feather from Hermes's winged boot, this Wonder Woman can fly. Her villains aren't merely superhuman, they're gods. Her preferred weapons are sword and shield, not the golden lasso. She's a warrior first, a princess second, and even as a princess she's tossed politeness right out the window. She has a zero-tolerance policy when it comes to bullshit, and when it comes to sheer knockdown power she can give Superman a run for his money. (In fact she nearly beats him to death on several occasions.[2])

This rougher, tougher Wonder Woman has won out as the fan favorite. She's the one we see in Frank Miller's *Dark Knight Strikes Again*, explaining to other heroes how they've compromised their morals. She's the one who saves the titular characters from certain death in Zack Snyder's *Batman v Superman*, and arguably the only one in that movie who warrants the title "superhero": of the three of them, she's the only one who never takes a civilian life. In fact, as we'll see later, she's the only one who even seems interested in the issue.

But this raises a question: *why* does she care about civilian lives? One possible answer is that it's the characteristic duty of a warrior to have that concern. The distinction between combatants and non-combatants dates back to the Code of Hammurabi and (more relevant to the bushido tradition) Sun Tzu's *Art of War*.[3] It wouldn't be fair to say the samurai always honored that distinction—their acts of civilian butchery are well known—but the best of them had no interest in non-combatants, in part because of another pillar of their honor code: the worthy warrior tested his mettle against worthy opponents. One battlefield ritual was for a samurai to step forward from the battle line, declare his name, his victories, his father's and grandfather's victories, and so on, announcing himself as a worthy opponent. A warrior of the opposing side would do the same, then they'd square off in single combat. No civilian casualties, no collateral damage, just two duelists bound by honor.

Wonder Woman comics have a similar sort of ceremony: the costume. Wouldn't the Cheetah or Silver Swan have greater success in their villainous exploits if they dressed as ordinary civilians? It's hard to blend into a crowd and make your escape when your outfit has wings or a tail. But of course the greatest villains don't *want* to blend into the crowd. They want to stand out, to be noticed, to rise above the rest. And Wonder Woman wants that too, albeit for a different reason. Her costume says by all means, focus on me, not innocent civilians. I'm your target, not them. By dressing in their outrageous fashion, comic heroes and villains mark themselves as worthy opponents.

Wonder Woman not only seeks out worthy opponents, she also lives by virtues quite similar to those of the samurai. These virtues were first codified in English by Inazo Nitobe, one of the very last samurai.[4] His book, *Bushidō: Soul of Japan*, is an overview of a martial honor code dating back hundreds of years. Bushido literally means the way (*dō*) of the warrior (*bushi*), and Nitobe sums up this way in eight virtues: honor, courage, justice, loyalty, honesty, politeness, self-control, and benevolence. It's obvious that most superheroes share a lot of these virtues in common; we don't admire characters who are cowardly, unjust, disloyal, dishonest, rude, and mean-spirited. Wonder Woman has a special relationship with these virtues, though, because she lives them as a warrior would live them—as the samurai lived them.

Take benevolence, for instance. To understand what this means in the bushido tradition we must trace this all the way back to where it comes from: Sun Tzu's *Art of War*. But what Sun Tzu calls "benevolence" is quite different from how we use it today. He'd seen the horrors of war, and from that experience he concluded that the duty of the commander-in-chief was to avoid war whenever possible. When war was unavoidable, the *benevolent* course of action was to end it quickly and decisively, using any means necessary to do so.

Compare this line of thinking to Wonder Woman's. In "The Death Card," Wonder Woman and Superman have just defeated the supervillain Despero.[5] For Superman, their work is finished:

SUPERMAN: I changed our tickets for the later show if you're still up for it.

WONDER WOMAN: I'd like that, but I don't have faith Despero's going to stay here for long, let alone the night.

SUPERMAN: When Hal shows up on earth again, we'll ask him to transfer Despero to Oa.

WONDER WOMAN: But eventually he'll escape. There's a reason I don't have a list of villains as long as Bruce's, Barry's, or even yours. When I deal with them, I deal with them.

She made big news in the comic world when she killed Maxwell Lord.[6] That's a line very few heroes are willing to cross. It's the one that makes Wolverine the outsider of the X-Men, the one that makes Rorschach a sociopathic pariah in *Watchmen*, the one that even the dark and brooding Batman has been unwilling to cross in the comics.[7] The polite princess Wonder Woman would never cross it. Only the warrior Wonder Woman will.

This is the samurai's benevolence: the willingness to kill as many as it takes—and *only* as many as it takes—to end the war swiftly and decisively. Notice how closely it's tied to the other samurai virtues. Wonder Woman must have the courage to cross this line, the self-control and sense of justice to do it only when necessary, and the honor and honesty to stand by her decision even when other heroes question it. We'd lose respect for her if she tried to cover up Maxwell Lord's death, but of course she doesn't. Whatever judgment comes her way, she accepts it.

But unlike the samurai, she's not a killing machine. They specialized in dealing death; Wonder Woman specializes in saving life. There's another important dissimilarity, too: Wonder Woman has no daimyo. The samurai swore absolute loyalty to their lords, and they were to fulfill their duty without question. But there's no one in command of Wonder Woman. Though she tends to do what her mother, Queen Hippolyte, asks of her, her obedience certainly isn't absolute. She's willing to die in defense of Themyscira, but she's willing to die in defense of John Q. Public too.

The fight against Doomsday in *Batman v Superman* is a case in point. Wonder Woman seems to be the only hero in the movie who's concerned about saving civilian lives. Batman deliberately leads Doomsday into Metropolis, where there's a shard of kryptonite he can use to kill the monster. It's Wonder Woman, not Superman, who questions his judgment, asking him why he didn't lead Doomsday away from the city. It's worth noting that Zack Snyder's interpretation of these iconic characters is radically different from what we typically see: not only do Batman and Superman kill civilians, but they do it frequently and avoidably. But this makes Wonder Woman all the more remarkable as the only one who shows a sincere interest in saving the lives of ordinary people.

So we can ask the question again: why does she care?

Wonder Woman: Samurai Feminist?

To answer this question, we must answer the one that underlies it: what does *care* mean, anyway? Philosophically speaking, it was born out of what's called *second-wave feminism*, the feminist movements of the early 1960s through the 1980s. (Wonder Woman was quite active during this period, by the way. She appears on the cover of *Ms.* magazine's very first issue, in January 1972. The headline: "Wonder Woman for President.") Feminist philosophers thought it high time to respond to the longstanding assumption that women couldn't do ethics as well as men. This assumption dates back at least as far as Aristotle (384–322 BCE), who held that women are less capable than men of controlling their emotions and making moral judgments dispassionately.[8] In the roughly 2300 years since then, the most prominent figures in western moral philosophy have consistently ruled that justice and impartiality are of the utmost importance in making ethical decisions, and that women are less capable than men of being just and impartial. Women, it was said, are simply too emotional to be fully capable moral agents.

We should add that many of these figures said little about women in any specific way, leaving the longstanding assumption untouched and untested. Others—we're looking at you, Immanuel

Kant (1724–1804)[9]—went out of their way to explain why women are intellectually unfit for moral philosophy. And then there are the (very few) exceptions, philosophers like John Stuart Mill (1806–1873), whose essay "The Subjection of Women" was probably co-authored with his wife, Harriet Taylor Mill (1807–1858).[10] The Mills treated each other as intellectual equals, and argued forcefully that men and women ought to be thought of in the same way. But for the most part, the pronouncement of the western canon over the past 2300 years has been roughly this: women are too touchy-feely to do ethics properly, since, as we all know, proper ethics requires complete emotional detachment, or in a word, impartiality.

We can point out any number of problems with this, but here's the one that launched the care ethics movement: what if, instead of saying women are bad at this brand of ethical reasoning, we were to question whether this brand of ethical reasoning really is the kind we ought to be interested in? Sure, justice and fairness are important, but are they the whole story? Are they even the most important story?

Arguably not. Nel Noddings and Carol Gilligan, the pioneers of care ethics, observed that in our most important relationships we throw impartiality out the window, and in fact we're right to do so.[11] Imagine yourself standing on a beach. Two children are drowning. You're not Wonder Woman; you're only fast enough to save one child. Both are equidistant from you, both weigh the same, both are equally likely to drown. Here's the only thing that sets the children apart: one of them is your child, the other a stranger's.

Is there any chance you'd flip a coin? That would be the fair thing to do. However, suppose justice and fairness were never to enter your mind. If you had eyes only for your own child, would you have done anything morally wrong?

Care ethics says no. It says you're *right* to ignore impersonal, dispassionate virtues like justice and fairness, because ethics itself is grounded in specific relationships. Now this isn't to say justice is immoral. Sometimes it's a good idea to step back from concrete relationships and derive independent principles. We wouldn't have a Bill of Rights without it. But the greater point is that this is an artificial project, one conceptual step removed from the very real, very human relationships that make the artificial project possible.

Moreover, these artificial, independent principles, though they're claimed to be impartial, are anything but. They classified women as inferior moral agents, and though their defenders had 2300 years to correct this injustice, either they chose not to or they didn't even notice it was there. This is the second critique from the care ethicists: your justice isn't just and your fairness isn't fair. Rather, these supposedly impartial principles have turned a blind eye to problems like rampant sexism.[12]

By contrast, look at the causes Wonder Woman takes up. Under her creator, William Moulton Marston, she founds a chain of fitness clubs, plays professional sports, founds a women's college, and leads demonstrations against unfair milk prices and unfair pay for garment workers. Under her more recent writers, she fights for oppressed women in wartime Korea and for her own infant half-brother and his mortal mother, Zola.[13] This is a far cry from Superman's truth, justice, and the American way.

Care ethics would have us re-examine the case of Maxwell Lord in a different light. Wonder Woman doesn't kill him simply because he's a supervillain. She does it because he's controlled Superman's mind, she's tried everything she can think of to incapacitate Superman, and she really doesn't want to kill her friend. Retreat isn't an option: that would allow Lord to send Superman after someone else. She catches Lord in her magic lasso and forces him to tell her how to free Superman's mind. He says the only way is for her to kill him. She knows he's telling the truth. So she crosses the line a superhero is never supposed to cross—an abstract, impartial, just and fair line, a line she's generally observed, but one she crosses in this particular case for this particular friendship.

She gets in big trouble for it, too. All the other heroes take notice. But from a care ethics perspective, this isn't so different from the case of the drowning children. Given the choice between killing Superman and killing Lord, it wasn't going to come down to a coin flip. In fact, it shouldn't.

So let's give her a harder case. Suppose Darkseid's legions are invading the Earth. Gotham City has a population of millions, while Themyscira has only a few thousand—and by the way, they're all Amazons. If ever there were an island that could defend itself, it's Themyscira. If ever there were a city that *can't* take care of itself, it's Gotham. Is Wonder Woman wrong if she wants to defend her hometown instead of Batman's?

The Caring Warrior

Maybe you think this is an easy decision. All you have to do is tally the pros and cons: how many lives can she save here versus there? How many buildings are there in both places, and how expensive are they to rebuild? (And hey, do Amazons even carry property insurance?) That would be the utilitarian approach: sum up all the positive and negative consequences, then go with whatever produces the greatest benefit and the least harm.

But as a caring warrior, Wonder Woman's going to take a different approach. For her it's not a simple numbers game. It matters that she's a sister to the Amazons, but it also matters that she's a sister in spirit to the women and girls of Gotham City. It matters that the citizens of Gotham are *not* worthy opponents—in other words, that they're non-combatants, and without a protector they don't stand a chance against the hordes of Apokolips. It matters that wherever sexism and misogyny exist, crisis tends to make them worse, not better. It matters that sexism and misogyny don't exist on Themyscira at all.

So Wonder Woman probably goes to save Gotham, but *not* because that's the way the math works out. She isn't a simple calculator of pros and cons. She doesn't just "follow the rules"—not her mother's, not the Justice League's, not anyone's. Her conscience is much more sophisticated than that.

Or at least it ought to be. As we saw earlier, Wonder Woman was originally something of a prop. Her creator, William Moulton Marston, was a die-hard supporter of the women's rights movement, and he was perfectly blunt about his new heroine's role in the cause: "Frankly, Wonder Woman is psychological propaganda for the new type of woman who, I believe, should rule the world."[14] Robert Kanigher, her first editor after Marston's death, had precisely the opposite agenda. Marston made her President of the United States; Kanigher made her a romance editor.[15] Marston created the Amazon warrior; Kanigher only wanted the polite princess.

In the hands of her best writers, Wonder Woman isn't a generic do-gooder, nor is she a milquetoast rule follower. Though her moral motivations may shift from one author to the next, what's consistent throughout her many incarnations is that Wonder Woman is uniquely placed to be the samurai feminist, the only one who can reconcile bushido and care ethics.

Notes

1. In fact, as soon as her original creators handed over creative control, she immediately gave up her fight for equality and her new editor "made clear his belief that women's political equality was a mistake—one that could be easily undone." No sooner did she join the Justice Society than she became its secretary. (Jill Lepore, *The Secret History of Wonder Woman* (New York: Alfred A. Knopf, 2014), insert 13.)
2. See, for example, the *Justice League* episode "Paradise Lost," or in the comics, "Sacrifice, pt. IV" (*Wonder Woman* #2, 219).
3. Prisoners of war were not protected by anything so robust as human rights in the Code of Hammurabi, but POW status did exist (laws 133–135), and there was a prohibition against physically abusing or attacking prisoners (law 116). Sun Tzu upholds similar principles, saying prisoners and non-combatants should be respected and cared for (*Art of War* 2.19).
4. Nitobe was born in 1862 to a samurai family; six years later the topknot and twin swords were outlawed, and his warrior caste legally came to an end. Strangely enough, he would convert to Quakerism later in life, making him a diehard samurai pacifist—a rare breed if ever there was one.
5. *Justice League*, vol. 2, 22.
6. "Sacrifice, pt. IV," *Wonder Woman* #2, 219.
7. It's worth noting that while comic writers traditionally don't allow Batman to kill, Hollywood screenwriters haven't been so observant; from Tim Burton's *Batman* (1989) onward, the Caped Crusader has racked up quite a body count on the silver screen.
8. See Aristotle's *History of Animals* 608b1–14. See also *Generation of Animals* 737a28, where he says the female is essentially a defective male; *Politics* 1259a41, where he says women are unsuited for leadership; *Politics* 1260a11, where he says they are lacking in reason; and *Politics* 1260a19, where he grants that women have their own set of virtues, albeit inferior and subservient to men's.
9. Kant is perhaps at his most egregious in *Observations on the Feeling of the Beautiful and the Sublime*, where he says women are not simply "intolerant" but "incapable" of moral principles, "they do something only because it pleases them," and even if they do manage to behave themselves morally, they "avoid the wicked not because it is unright but because it is ugly" (77).

10. Some scholars do claim that he was the sole author. A major point of contention is that the essay wasn't published until 1869, while Harriet Taylor Mill died in 1858. But John Stuart Mill himself insisted that he and his wife wrote the essay together, and in fact some of the arguments in "The Subjection of Women" mirror Harriet Taylor Mill's arguments in her own published work on women's equality.

11. Nel Noddings, *Caring: A Feminine Approach to Ethics and Moral Education* (Berkeley, CA: University of California Press, 1984). Carol Gilligan, *In A Different Voice: Psychological Theory and Women's Development* (Cambridge, MA: Harvard University Press, 1982).

12. Joy Kroeger-Mappes puts the point this way: "The ethic of rights, when it finds expression in moral theory, is typically presented as gender-neutral. In fact, what we encounter here is a male-centered morality, but it is a morality that is deceptively put forth as universal" ("The Ethic of Care vis-à-vis the Ethic of Rights" (*Hypatia*, 9(3), summer 1994), 115). This article is an excellent analysis of the troubled relationship between rights-based ethics and care ethics.

13. Darywn Cooke, *The New Frontier* and *Wonder Woman* #4(1–12), respectively.

14. Quoted in Jill Lepore, *The Secret History of Wonder Woman*, vii.

15. *Wonder Woman* #1(7) and *Wonder Woman* #1(97).

11
Wonder Woman
Saving Lives through Just Torture?

Adam Barkman and Sabina Tokbergenova

As a child, Wonder Woman stood on the beaches of Themyscira gazing out over the ocean with insuppressible curiosity, wondering what was really beyond the horizon. She wondered if the stories she had heard were true and the outside world was truly corrupt.[1] Sadly, the stories are true. We live in a corrupt world, where innocent people are vulnerable to terrorist attacks. This is why Diana left Paradise Island to spread justice on Earth. Since Wonder Woman exists only on the pages of comic books and other media, we need to find a way to fight villains in the real world. A possible lesson we might learn from Wonder Woman is that legalizing torture could protect innocent citizens.

Of course, some say that torture is wrong. After all, torture is expressly forbidden by the international Convention Against Torture (CAT). However, we think that torture can sometimes be right. Wonder Woman, arguably, not only agrees with us but uses torture in the form of her lasso of truth.

Torture and the Ticking Bomb

Before looking at how Wonder Woman uses just torture in order to save innocent people, let's get clear about what we are considering.

Wonder Woman and Philosophy: The Amazonian Mystique, First Edition.
Edited by Jacob M. Held.
© 2017 John Wiley & Sons, Ltd. Published 2017 by John Wiley & Sons, Ltd.

Article 1 of the United Nations CAT is the internationally agreed-upon definition of torture. It reads:

> Torture means any act by which severe pain or suffering, whether physical or mental, is intentionally inflicted on a person for such purposes as obtaining from him or a third person information or a confession, punishing him for an act he or a third person has committed or is suspected of having committed, or intimidating or coercing him or a third person, or for any reason based on discrimination of any kind, when such pain or suffering is inflicted by or at the instigation of or with the consent or acquiescence of a public official or other person acting in an official capacity. It does not include pain or suffering arising only from, inherent in or incidental to lawful sanctions.[2]

Henry Shue, Professor of International Relations at Oxford University, sees torture as a generally cruel assault upon the defenseless in that, for example, a terrorist, if captured, cannot defend himself, and is entirely at the torturer's mercy.[3] According to Shue, interrogational torture or more routine acts of torture to obtain information are unethical and must be avoided. However, Shue does allow for torture in extreme emergencies, such as in the case of the infamous "ticking bomb scenario."

According to this scenario, it could happen that the only way to prevent a thousand or even a million innocent people from being killed by a nuclear bomb planted by a terrorist is to torture the terrorist until he reveals the location of the bomb. In this scenario there would be no time to evacuate innocent people, and so the only hope would be to torture the perpetrator, find the device, and deactivate it. "I can see no way to deny the permissibility of torture in a case just like this. To allow the destruction of much of a great city and many of its people would be almost as wicked as purposely to destroy it," says Shue.[4] Thus, torture as interrogation is sometimes justified because it could save innocent lives.

David Luban, however, argues that if torture is considered permissible in ticking bomb scenarios, these cases may bewitch people.[5] He believes that people can be neither 100 percent certain that there is an imminent threat nor 100 percent certain that the tortured person has any information that will save lives. Luban worries that if we let torture in the door, it will lead to torture being used in many different cases. Indeed, "Why not torture in pursuit of any worthwhile goal?" asks Luban.[6]

Additionally, Luban argues that it is wrong to make the decision to torture someone based on numbers. Once people accept that only the numbers count, then anything, no matter how gruesome, becomes possible. For example, numbers could be used to justify torturing a suspect's loved ones in front of them. Luban argues, however, that it is wrong to torture a suspect's loved ones regardless of the nature of the threat or number of innocent lives potentially at risk. This type of action is beyond the pale, regardless of consequences. There are simply some things we shouldn't do.

We agree with Luban. It is important to set rules and limitations regarding the use of torture. Unless people impose some limits on the use of torture when trying to prevent terrorism, they risk going down a slippery slope into the abyss of amorality and ultimately, tyranny. Innocent children or the innocent loved ones of the terrorist must not be tortured. A willingness to torture an innocent child, for example, suggests a willingness to do anything to achieve a desired result, as Luban states.

To prevent this problem, Alan Dershowitz, a prominent American defense attorney, favors a form of legalization in which agents of the state may torture someone if they first obtain judicial permission in the form of "torture warrants."[7] According to Dershowitz, torture warrants have many benefits for both the nation and the terrorist suspect. Chief among these benefits is that there is likely to be *less* torture if it's part of the legal system. If the field officer must get judicial approval before he can torture someone, he will probably use it less often and more carefully due to red tape, transparency, and safeguards. Therefore, the rights of the suspect would be better protected because law-enforcement officials would be reluctant to seek a warrant unless they had compelling evidence that the suspect had the information needed to prevent an imminent terrorist attack.[8] The question then becomes: is torture absolutely wrong, or merely in need of stricter oversight?

The type of philosophy that argues against "anything is potentially permissible morality" is a type of philosophy that asserts some moral absolutes or morality based on universal moral principles. This universal morality, or "natural law" morality, is arguably the morality of Wonder Woman and the Justice League. Neither Wonder Woman nor any member of the Justice League would, for example, endorse torturing an innocent child, even to achieve world peace. It simply would not be right no matter how many people were to be saved. Yet, even so, Wonder Woman, at least, does endorse torture in *some* cases.

Torture and the Golden Lasso

Some people would deny that what Wonder Woman does with her golden lasso is torture. Yet, countless Wonder Woman comics and TV episodes prove that whosoever is bound by Diana's lasso experiences considerable discomfort and pain. In *Wonder Woman* #15, for example, the Princess of Themyscira mentally tortures Captain Nazi with the lasso of truth in order to save her home island from Nazi invasion. As Wonder Woman wraps the golden lasso around Captain Nazi's body, the lasso transports her mind into his and she sees the truth.[9] The magic lasso reduces Captain Nazi to tearful surrender by revealing to him the truth of his despicable actions. Shortly after, Wonder Woman captures another Nazi soldier in order to find out the location of her wounded mother. She ferociously holds her golden lasso to the Nazi's face and says, "Look at it. See the whole truth of everything you are!"[10] Looking at the lasso of truth, the Nazi expresses pure horror. "Get it away from me! For the love of God!" he screams in fright. The soldier knew that the lasso is brutal to those who try to deceive it.[11] Evidently, when Wonder Woman uses her golden lasso on captured criminals to thwart some potential harm, she is exercising a form of just or righteous torture. Yet if these cases aren't clear, then consider two cases that more closely resemble the ticking bomb scenario.

The first ticking bomb scenario is in the pilot episode of the 1970s *Wonder Woman* TV series, which was set during World War II. In this episode, Diana uses the lasso of truth on Marcia, who was a double agent for the Nazis. Wonder Woman mentally tortures Marcia, causing her significant duress while under compulsion, in order to find out where a Nazi pilot named Von Blasko is going to drop some bombs. Unable to resist the power of the lasso, Marcia reveals that Von Blasko is going to bomb the Brooklyn Navy Yard, which contains more than five miles of paved streets, four dry docks, two steel shipways, six pontoons and cylindrical floats for salvage work, barracks for marines, a power plant, a large radio station, and a railroad spur, as well as the foundries, machine shops, and warehouses. At its peak, during World War II, the yard employed 70,000 people, 24 hours a day. Thanks to the use of just torture, Wonder Woman is able to save the Brooklyn Navy Yard. By mentally torturing one Nazi agent, Wonder Woman saved 70,000 people and valuable resources.

Even if Wonder Woman's lasso hadn't given her 100 percent certainty concerning the guilt or innocence of the Nazi, torturing the Nazi would still have been the right thing to do if probable cause could be established. Reasonable doubt and probable cause are morally sufficient for many of our most serious—life and death—decisions, such as to condemn a man to jail or even go to war. Certainty is not required for most—if any—of our decisions about guilt and innocence, a point Dershowitz emphasizes.

The second ticking bomb scenario is in *Wonder Woman* #600. In this issue, Nikos Aegeus—a terrorist—demands one hundred million dollars from the government to prevent him from killing a number of innocent people.[12] When the government doesn't comply, Aegeus destroys a bridge which, in turn, threatens an approaching passenger train. While Superman stops the train, Wonder Woman captures the terrorist with her magic lasso and uses its power on him. This is appropriate because, even though the terrorist might have a general right not to be tortured, it is not an absolute right. Indeed, if Wonder Woman was, in at least one case, willing to kill a criminal to save an innocent (she breaks Maxwell Lord's neck to release Superman from his mental grip), then she should certainly be willing to torture a likely villain in order to save many innocent lives.[13] Even Superman—the Boy Scout himself, who objects to Wonder Woman's killing of Lord— has no objection to Wonder Woman torturing a villain to save an innocent life.

Yet, Wonder Woman's use of torture isn't merely about justice, but also care. In the early comics, Wonder Woman's lasso was used to bring evil-doers to submission. The submission envisioned here seems to have been the submission of the heart blinded by selfishness to the light of truth. Thus, torture, optimally, also—though secondarily— leads to the criminal's reformation. Indeed, in the world of Wonder Woman, there is a place called "Reform Island," where villains go in order to learn submission to loving authority.[14]

The Right Thing is Not the Ideal Thing

Because torture makes most of us—including the authors of this chapter—squeamish, we don't like talking about it, much less seeing it. As a result of this squeamishness, in recent years—in the real world—torture has typically been conducted in secret. The motto "out of sight, out of mind" seems to be the mantra here. But is this the way to go in conducting just torture? That is, if torture can be morally justified in some cases, such as the ticking bomb scenario, why should we hide it as if we were ashamed?

Torture is sad and unfortunate, of course, but sometimes the right thing isn't the same as the ideal thing. Thus, just as Wonder Woman tortures rarely, only when necessary, but also in the open, so we would advocate making torture official and legal. The Global Terrorism Database shows that around the world, there have been more than 140,000 terrorist attacks since 1970. In 2014 alone, a total of 13,463 terrorist attacks occurred worldwide, resulting in more than 32,700 deaths and more than 34,700 injuries. In addition, more than 9400 people were kidnapped or taken hostage.[15] And these statistics don't even take into account more recent events in Nice, France, Istanbul, or Paris. In a world with no superheroes, people must depend on themselves—and their governments—to reduce the threat of terrorist attacks, and if the torture of the suspect might help to prevent at least some terrorist acts, and decrease the number of deaths of innocent people, then torture should be legalized and used wisely.

Yet some people object that even if torture were made official, it would still be ineffective since the person being tortured is likely to say just about anything—even something false—to stop the torture. This objection was well known to the ancient Greeks, in particular, Aristotle and Wonder Woman. In *Rhetoric*, for example, Aristotle discusses judicial torture and says that those under compulsion are as likely to give false evidence as true. Some are ready to endure anything rather than tell the truth, while others are ready to make false charges against others in the hope of being released from torture.[16] To minimize this objection, we suggest the government model itself after Wonder Woman, instituting a "professional torturer," who might have more skill in reading a person who is lying. Indeed, one former CIA operative with 30 years' experience agrees, saying "A lot of people are saying we need someone at the agency who can pull fingernails out."[17] These professional torturers may not have a lasso of truth, but they could be trained to make do with techniques only minimally less effective.

Without the lasso of truth, we need to have our own way of extracting the truth from our enemies—who are always "probable enemies"—in order to save lives. Thus, the best solution is the legalization of torture, with its host of torture warrants and professional torturers, modeled, in part, on the fierce and honest Amazonian, Wonder Woman. Potentially, the fear of being tortured may reduce terrorism and other crimes, such as abduction. However, even if it doesn't, torture should be seen as permissible in a number of dire situations, as Shue, Dershowitz, and, of course, Wonder Woman make clear.

Notes

1. *The Sensational Wonder Woman* #1.
2. "Convention Against Torture," United Nations Human Rights, December 10, 1984.
3. Henry Shue, "Torture," *Philosophy and Public Affairs*, 7 (1978) 130.
4. Ibid., 141.
5. David Luban, *Liberalism, Torture, and the Ticking Bomb* (Georgetown: Georgetown Law Faculty Publications, 2005), 1441.
6. Ibid., 1443.
7. Alan M. Dershowitz, *Why Terrorism Works: Understanding the Threat, Responding to the Challenge* (New Haven, CT: Yale University Press, 2002), 457.
8. Ibid., 465.
9. *Wonder Woman* #15.
10. *Wonder Woman* #16.
11. *Wonder Woman* #20.
12. *Wonder Woman* #600.
13. Dershowitz, *Why Terrorism Works*, 457.
14. Tim Hanley, *Wonder Woman Unbound: The Curious History of the World's Most Famous Heroine* (Chicago, IL: Chicago Review Press, 2014), 50.
15. "Country Reports on Terrorism 2014," US Department of State.
16. Aristotle, *Rhetoric*, translated by J.H. Freese (Cambridge, MA: Harvard University Press, 1926), 1377a.
17. Bob Drogin, "Spy Agencies Facing Questions of Tactics," *Chicago Tribune* (October 29, 2001).

Wonder Woman Winning with Words

A Paragon of Wisdom, Disarming Threats One at a Time…

Francis Tobienne Jr.

Rhetoric is the power of persuasion, or influence, through words. And in many ways, comics exemplify, through their heroes and heroines, the power of rhetoric, of the written and spoken word to convince, persuade, and ultimately move people. But wisdom must also accompany rhetoric. In this regard, Wonder Woman exemplifies wisdom, or *sophia*, and as an ambassador and an emissary her character not only demonstrates the value of wisdom, but actively disarms threats, promoting peace through discourse. As a servant to her patron goddesses, Aphrodite and Athena, or love and wisdom, respectively, Wonder Woman is the messenger of love (*philo*) and wisdom (*sophia*), or the love of wisdom, or philosophy (*philosophia*). Wonder Woman as balanced emotion, or passionate persuasion, is an example of pathos, knowing when to use force and how to de-escalate a volatile situation.

In a World of Superheroes, She is Still a Wonder Woman

Dr. William Moulton Marston is often credited as the creative force behind Wonder Woman, but I am certain he never imagined such a character would become, according to DC Comics:

> … the most famous heroine of all time. No offense to the Lara Crofts, Buffys, or Disney princesses of the world, but none of them have been

Wonder Woman and Philosophy: The Amazonian Mystique, First Edition.
Edited by Jacob M. Held.
© 2017 John Wiley & Sons, Ltd. Published 2017 by John Wiley & Sons, Ltd.

plastered on as many magazine covers, adorned as many T-shirts, or sold the countless comics, dolls, and action figures that Wonder Woman has. The full package of beauty, brains, and brawn, she's been a feminist icon since her star-spangled intro in 1941.[1]

In a top 100 list of comic-book characters, Wonder Woman is at number five, where only Wolverine, Spider-Man, Batman, and Superman trump her status for primacy.[2] And yes, I am well aware that she remains the lone female character in the top 10, where Captain America, Hal Jordan/Green Lantern, Wally West/The Flash, The Hulk, and Daredevil reside. The closest heroines fall outside of the top 10, where Jean Grey, Barbara Gordon/Batgirl, and Catwoman round out the top 25. If this is representative of the influence of comic books and their characters, then the position of Wonder Woman as the lone female in the top 10 is impressive.

Jill Lepore notes, "The veil that has shrouded Wonder Woman's past for seven decades hides beneath it a crucial story about comic books and superheroes and censorship and feminism. As Marston once put it, 'Frankly, Wonder Woman is psychological propaganda for the new type of woman who, I believe, should rule the world.' "[3] Wonder Woman remains relevant in the twenty-first century, holding her own against her male counterparts, and arguably embodying a passionate plea of persuasion. More than any other character, beyond brute force, beyond the use of technology and battle tactics where might makes right, even if right is just, Wonder Woman often mobilizes argumentation as her greatest weapon. She is sent to Man's World as an emissary for Amazonian values, for justice and equality, not simply to physically fight. She is sent to overcome Ares, the god of war, the embodiment of irrational force, of aggression.

So how is this persuasion presented to the audience? A comic-book character steeped in Greek lore must be situated within a philosophical context. Wonder Woman cannot escape her Greek heritage, and one of its greatest thinkers, Aristotle (384–322 BCE). Aristotle defined rhetoric as effective communication that ultimately leads to persuasion. Aristotle informs us that a thing cannot be known unless the questions of *why* and *what* are answered. And to know a thing completely is to have wisdom, or *sophia*. Further, *sophia* is the ability to think well about the nature of the world, making declarations and systematically conveying why the world is the way it is.

An example of Wonder Woman's rhetoric can be found in *Wonder Woman #3: The Lies, Part 2*, written by Greg Rucka. Using uncommon pathos, or balanced emotion, she disarms problems without resorting to brute force. As the story arc unfolds, Wonder Woman is deep in the Okarango Region of Bwunda, the Urzari Jungle. Cheetah presents us with a problem; she is apparently cursed. Wonder Woman also presents us with a problem; she cannot locate Themyscira, her home. Wonder Woman thus enlists Cheetah's aid to solve her problem. Cheetah, however, blames her for being cursed, stating "... condemned to eat man-flesh to live! You were my friend!" Wonder Woman replies, "And so I remain. That has never changed." In Book VI of the *Nichomachean Ethics*, Aristotle notes that someone who has practical wisdom will recognize that she needs friends in order to be virtuous, to flourish in the long run. The exchange that follows showcases the true influence of Wonder Woman.

> CHEETAH: I HATE you.
>
> WONDER WOMAN: Love can exist with hatred, each preying on the other.
>
> CHEETAH: Hisssss ... we should move. Try to keep up. Fasterrr, princess! Fasterrr!
>
> WONDER WOMAN: No.
>
> CHEETAH: We do not have time! We must rrreach the temple!
>
> WONDER WOMAN: **Make** time. Why do we flee your worshippers?
>
> CHEETAH: Not mine! His! They hunt for him, to feed the jungle with our blood! It's too late.

Hyena-like beasts appear through the deep jungle and roar. One beast throws a spear through Cheetah's abdomen. Wonder Woman, having familiarity with Barbara Ann, now known as Cheetah, shouts to her defense, "Ann! By the gods ... haven't you beasts done enough?" The battle continues, with Ann becoming more and more feral, losing her mind in the process, and perhaps what's left of her reason. The exchange continues:

> CHEETAH: (doubled over in obvious pain) Rrrrooooooaaarrrrr...rrrr.
>
> WONDER WOMAN: GET AWAY FROM HER! Begone!
>
> CHEETAH: Snnnrrrlll (Ann devouring the beast from the mid-section amidst its screams of AAAHHHHHH).

WONDER WOMAN: Ann! STOP! STOP! (putting Ann in a familiar embrace and headlock)

CHEETAH: RRRRRR—I—Can't—I can't stop, can't control—

WONDER WOMAN: You can!

CHEETAH: Myself.

WONDER WOMAN: You're STRONGER than him!

CHEETAH: I am an animal, a beast—that must eat man's flesh to live.

WONDER WOMAN: You are no beast.

CHEETAH: He makes me—He makes me.

WONDER WOMAN: You are a WOMAN ... You are my FRIEND!

...

CHEETAH: Even without godhood and home, you keep Athena's **WISDOM**, I see. He will do to anotherrr what he has done to me. What he has done for millennia. You want my help? To find **Themyscira** again? You must do something for **me**. Help me kill Urrzkarrrtaga. **Free** me from my **currrse**. **Prrrrromise** me, Diana.

WONDER WOMAN: You have my **word**.

In the above exchange between apparent foes, Wonder Woman appeals to Cheetah's humanity, what remains of it. Wisdom trumps force and provides a return to the rational. Wonder Woman is the embodiment of wisdom and its influence toward timely resolutions. Wonder Woman needs Cheetah, to be sure. She needs her to find her home again, but Cheetah also needs Wonder Woman, to find her humanity once more. It is in this relationship that we see the power of Wonder Woman. She can bring Cheetah back from the brink of insanity, from reduction to mere animality, through persuasive argument. Through the power of her rhetoric, Wonder Woman appeals to Cheetah's humanity, controlling her emotion, and assisting Cheetah in doing the same.

Wisdom for Aristotle, "capable of being taught, and what comes within its range capable of being learned."[4] In *Wonder Woman Rebirth* #1, as a pre-launch to the "changing story" arc, Wonder Woman's thoughts appear: "Something's happening ... in my memory ... the STORY keeps changing." In search of answers, she admits: "Once a daughter was born to the Queen of the Amazons ... they loved her, taught her all they knew, sharing their KNOWLEDGE and WISDOM." The comic ends with an appeal to truth: "I will have the TRUTH." Wonder Woman's character is a clear picture of wisdom personified. This power will come to her aid time and time again to offset any and all threats; threats stemming from the irrational, from desire overcoming reason, from greed overcoming common humanity, and from aggression overcoming peace in justice.

Wonder Woman's wisdom is systematic in its influence. She is a powerful rhetor, a speaker of influence who offers fair warnings. Take, for instance, *Wonder Woman #1: The Lies, Part 1*. Wonder Woman opens by saying, "I will have the truth." Her location: above the falls overlooking the Banakane Rainforest in the Okarango Region, Bwunda. This information is immediately followed by another familiar line in the narrative: "The story keeps changing." Once in the rainforest, Wonder Woman offers the following:

> It's my preference to give three warnings. This is your first: I am only your enemy if you treat me as such [...] I give you my warning, the second: I wish to pass in peace, but I will fight if I must. If you force me to fight, you will lose [...] I know you are here. Answer me ... Your corruption is rank. It turns the stomach and it sickens the soul. I have given you two warnings. This, then, is my final: I have come to ask your goddess for aid. I will not leave until I have her answer.

Wonder Woman is addressing Barbara Ann Minerva, or Cheetah, who jumps on top of her. Pinned down, Wonder Woman delivers her message with echoes of "listen!" and "please, listen to me" until finally she states: "Themyscira! I can't find it! I can't find my way home. Barbara Ann, please ... help me find my way back home." Wonder Woman's words, her wisdom, and her pathos win Cheetah's cooperation.

Lassos, Truth, and Wisdom

Among Wonder Woman's powers are super strength, invulnerability, flight, combat skill, combat strategy, superhuman agility, and healing.[5] These powers are augmented by her accessories, such as her golden lasso, bracelets, and a tiara that can rival Batman's batarangs. As Diana Prince, she moves freely between realms and worlds, wielding diplomacy, galvanizing the strength of a Superman alongside the cerebral logistics of a Batman. She is the complete package and often a formidable opponent. Yet, Wonder Woman's influence on the world is often not about force, but persuasion, and its application at the correct moment. Wonder Woman writes books, goes on book tours, speaks to international delegations, and liaises between Paradise Island, Mt.

Olympus, the United States government, and the population of the entire Earth.

As noted above, to know a thing is to be able to answer *what* and *why*. In order to do so, one has to use good judgment. This is where Wonder Woman comes into the picture. She is the embodiment of wisdom, the rhetorical weapon of *sophia* used to influence her surroundings. She's armed with a lasso of truth for crying out loud! This is not coincidental or mere chance, but a thoughtful creation on the part of her creator(s).[6] And to further press the matter, Wonder Woman more than any other superhero is as comfortable in negotiations as she is in combat. Take, for instance, solving the problem of Power Girl, arguably one of—if not—the strongest character in terms of brute force the DCU has to offer.

Consider the fight between Wonder Woman and a misled Power Girl in *Wonder Woman: Contagion*.[7] The story arc takes place in *A Murder of Crows, Part Two*: "Throwdown." After trading blows, Wonder Woman disarms Power Girl by appealing to her disposition and reminding her of who she is. Wonder Woman is reminded of a previous conversation with Black Canary, who stated: "You know why I love to watch you fight? It's because so many of the heavy hitters, they just use their strength. That's all they need. There's no **technique**. No **style**." Drawing on this memory, Wonder Woman admits the following about Power Girl: "She's good. It's not **just** brute force. But she isn't **Amazon**. She hasn't spent every day of her life learning the sculpture of **war**. She wasn't baptized in her sister's **blood**. It's not her **fault**. She is a fierce, dedicated, and honorable warrior. But she is not **Amazon**." Finally, Power Girl is influenced by Wonder Woman's rhetoric to come to her senses:

Power Girl:	**Kill** you!
Wonder Woman:	No.
Power Girl:	Ughgn…
Wonder Woman:	You are Karen Starr, Power Girl. That's how we'll **beat** this. You are one of the stubbornest, most arrogant women I have ever known.
Power Girl:	I'll rip your **head** off.
Wonder Woman:	(Power Girl in a headlock) No. I say again. You are Power Girl. And I have one question for you. When have you **ever** … and I mean **ever** … done as you were **told**?

This disarmament brings Power Girl to her senses. She is persuaded by Wonder Woman, not physically defeated. As wisdom/*sophia*, Wonder Woman is able "to understand the emotion ... to know their causes and the way in which they are excited."[8] Wonder Woman appeals to her hearer—Power Girl in a headlock—and rhetoricizes her submission. Now it's Athena and Aphrodite we need to recall. Wonder Woman herself submits to them, to their authority, and is thus afforded her magical weaponry, because through her submission to wisdom and love she has proven herself worthy. Wonder Woman submits to *philosophia* and is thus granted her lasso of compulsion and her bracelets of submission. She is able to wield the power of absolute compulsion, pure "persuasion," while reining in her irrational, emotive, and aggressive side through her bracelets. As balanced emotion, pathos, she keeps herself in check, while wielding rhetoric in the form of a lasso. But she also assists others in reining in their irrational, emotional sides, as noted with Cheetah and Power Girl. Through her possession of wisdom and love, of *sophia* and *philia*, through her pathos, she is able to bring others to submit to her loving authority, not through force alone, but through persuasion.

Ambassador, Emissary, and Role Model

At the writing of this chapter, Wonder Woman is undergoing a rebirth. What will this new Wonder Woman be? Will she be a pathos-driven character? Will she again take on the mantle of *sophia*, persuading her audience? What can we expect from this incarnation of Wonder Woman? We are only three comics in, but all bets seem to point to a wise rhetor who just happens to be a wonder at everything! Will her mission once again be to bring the lesson of the Amazons to a corrupted Man's World, rife with war and greed? Will her mission be as ambassador, as emissary, as role model? Will she again speak to the values of the Amazons, submission to the authority of love and wisdom, the value of *philosophia*? So far we know that the story is ever changing, and perhaps Wonder Woman is the constant. She invites us to listen, to please listen; and I am reminded of the Old Testament proverb, which honors Sophia. It is not a stretch to replace the persona of wisdom with the persona of Wonder Woman:

Does not [Wonder Woman] call?
[…] To you, O men, I call,
And my cry is to the children of man.
[…] Hear for I will speak noble things,
And from my lips will come what is right,
For my mouth will utter truth;
[…] for [she] is better than jewels,
And all that you may desire cannot compare with her.[9]

Wonder Woman calls to Man's World, and brings it noble things—peace, love, and understanding—as she attempts to find answers to her own changing story. She comes armed, literally, with truth, and her lasso, which also compels. She can compel one to submit to love and wisdom; she is the ultimate argument, pure propaganda. Wonder Woman is noble and when she speaks we (should) listen, because *all that you may desire cannot compare with her.*

Notes

1. This quote is taken from the front matter of DC Comics Entertainment, at http://www.dccomics.com/characters/wonder-woman.
2. The caveat is that these lists are often subject to change, but at the time of this chapter, Wonder Woman remains number five, http://www.ign.com/top/comic-book-heroes/5.
3. Jill Lepore, "The Origin Story of Wonder Woman," *Smithsonian Magazine*, 45 (2014) 56.
4. Aristotle, *Nichomachean Ethics* (New York: Dover, 1998), 100–103.
5. See under "Character Facts," http://www.dccomics.com/characters/wonder-woman.
6. It is rumored in the new DCU *Rebirth* series that this "new" incarnation of Wonder Woman has the ability to extract the truth using the golden lasso, but that the lasso itself is merely the conduit. Hence, she may in fact be truth personified and certainly should cement her paragon status as wisdom in order to know *when* not *if* to use it.
7. Gail Simone, *Wonder Woman: Contagion* (New York: DC Comics, 2010).
8. Julian Marias, "Aristotle," in *History of Philosophy*, translated by Stanley Appelbaum and Clarence C. Strowbridge (New York: Dover, 1967), 62–63.
9. The selected passage is taken from Proverbs 8, the ESV.

Part IV
GOD(S), COUNTRY, SORORITY

Wonder Woman, Worship, and Gods Almighty
Purpose in Submission to Loving Authority

Jacob M. Held

The DC multiverse is full of beings who are immortal, eternal, or immune to the effects of time, beings who are superstrong and unimaginably smart. Some of these beings are gods. Wonder Woman and her fellow Amazons serve the full Greek pantheon, worshipping Aphrodite and Athena in particular. But Wonder Woman's realm is also home to Roman gods, African and Egyptian gods, and the new gods including Darkseid, Highfather, Orion, and Metron. The Judeo-Christian God is worshipped, but is strangely absent in a world overrun with visible deities. Yet, in *Down to Earth* (which collects *Wonder Woman* #195–200), Darrel Keyes, head of "Protect Our Children," launches a campaign against Wonder Woman and cults of Wonder Woman, such as the Myndi Mayer Foundation, who worship "false" gods. Ironically, within Wonder Woman's multiverse there is proof that her gods exist, but the same cannot be said for the God of the Bible, the God of Darrel Keyes. So, we must wonder then, what is a god? And are all gods worthy of worship, or loyalty, or obedience?

One God, Two Gods, Old Gods, New Gods

We can begin simply enough: "god" is a title that we apply to a particular entity that occupies a specific, privileged place in our universe.

Wonder Woman and Philosophy: The Amazonian Mystique, First Edition.
Edited by Jacob M. Held.
© 2017 John Wiley & Sons, Ltd. Published 2017 by John Wiley & Sons, Ltd.

We might postulate, along with James Rachels, that to be a god is to have certain qualifications, or essential attributes. A god must be "all-powerful and perfectly good in addition to being perfectly wise."[1] This is a high bar, and no gods in the DC multiverse would qualify. Sure, Zeus, Hera, Apollo, Orion, and even Wonder Woman herself are powerful, but they are not all powerful. And sure they are wise, but not perfectly so. Nor are they perfectly good, even if Wonder Woman comes close. Although they are immortal, they seem to die, or at least expire, a lot. Consider some examples that highlight these points. In *Land of the Dead* (*Wonder Woman* #214–217; *Flash* #219), Ares kills Hades, thus becoming god of the underworld, and is threatened with death by Poseidon. In *War of the Gods* (*War of the Gods* #1–4; *Wonder Woman* #58–62), Circe becomes immensely powerful, but as Wonder Woman notes, "'Supreme' is a relative term among gods…"[2] She's defeated in the end. And then in *Wonder Woman*, vol. 4: *War*, Wonder Woman kills Ares in order to defeat the First Born, thus becoming herself god of war. The list goes on, leaving the gods themselves to wonder where gods go when they die.[3] So, Rachels sets the bar quite high, maybe too high. After all, Wonder Woman does worship her gods. She pays homage to Athena, and the other Amazons engage in religious practices approximating worship of the Greek gods. Likewise, the Greeks worshipped these gods. And countless other civilizations have worshipped gods that are not absolute in the way Rachels defines a god. So, instead of adopting Rachels's definition, let's ask what the idea of a god has been historically. What common characteristics do gods have?

One possibility is to understand a god as a relational concept. That is, a god is defined as a being vastly superior to those who worship that god, as a being worthy of this worship and obedience.[4] This avoids the debate about what characteristics a god needs to have, but it still highlights a key issue. Gods are only gods insofar as they are superior to those who worship them. A contested god is no god at all, since a contested god, by definition, is not superior. Perhaps this is why the Greek pantheon is so outraged at the audacity of the Roman pantheon when they attempt a coup in *War of the Gods*. The Greeks decry the Romans as "pretenders,"[5] only to have the Romans retort with the charge of "charlatans."[6] Oddly enough, the African gods, Babylonian gods, and the rest of the divinities involved kind of sit it out for the most part, although Tiamat does make an appearance. To be a god, though, it is not enough to be the most powerful and uncontested of those known beings occupying the multiverse. In that case, Green Lantern (a.k.a. Parallax) would be a god among gods, the first among equals in *Zero Hour: Crisis in Time*.

In *Zero Hour*, Parallax harnesses entropy and is prepared to undo all of created reality and then rebuild it his way, a feat Circe attempted and failed at. This is Old Testament god power, creation *ex nihilo*, and Parallax has it. Supposedly, anyone else could have figured this out as well, so the power isn't a unique ability of Parallax. But creation is a unique power. In *War of the Gods*, the Phantom Stranger even notes that if you go back from the gods to their origins, you eventually end up at "the ultimate supreme – creation."[7] We get a similar storyline in *Second Genesis (Wonder Woman* #101–105), when Metron relates to Wonder Woman the history of her own gods, the Greek pantheon, explaining how ages ago the old gods unleashed Ragnarok, from which two worlds were born, New Genesis and Apokolips. From this act of creation, an energy wave was emitted and struck Earth, thus creating the Greek pantheon, beings Metron denigratingly refers to as "godlings." So, Wonder Woman's own gods are accidental spawn from the overflow of power that created Highfather, Darkseid, and the other gods of New Genesis and Apokolips. And, as Metron notes, her gods are mere shadows of the power he contains.[8] Yet they are still gods to her, and she behaves as such. Notice that she doesn't worship or treat Metron with the same respect, though. Maybe what made you, what created you, is owed worship. Ultimately, though, why does it matter who or what is classified as a god?

False Gods and the Cult of Wonder Woman

We ask about god(s), because we wonder about ourselves. We label an entity a god to clarify the nature of our reality, find our place within it, determine our purpose, and act accordingly. If deities play this fundamental role in our lives, then aside from what they are, what is it about what they are that legitimates them having a privileged position?

From a pragmatic point of view, it makes sense to worship gods. After all, they can reward or punish us. So self-interest, or simple prudence, would seem to dictate that we revere them at least so as not to incur their wrath, and praise them when we might be able to receive their boons. Of course, loyalties complicate matters. In the DC multi-verse you can't really worship Jupiter and Zeus. One of them is bound to find out, and then it's going to get ugly. If worship is just pragmatic, then it would make sense that Darkseid has followers. It's not because he engenders loyalty due to his love and compassion for those under his control. Desaad can attest to that. On this account, religion and worship may be motivated by our dependence and vulnerability,[9] and perhaps prayer is motivated by a desire to have our wishes fulfilled by someone powerful enough to do so.[10] But these psychological motives merely speak to our human frailty, not our ideals. They speak to our weaknesses as biological and psychological entities, not our aspirations as moral creatures. Self-interest isn't a moral motivation, it's a brute instinct.

A moral reason asks what ought to be the case, above and beyond what simply happens to be. And fear isn't a moral reason either. Although it may be "insane" to disobey or defy an almighty god, or even a kind-of-mighty one, a prudential or rational reason to obey or worship such a being is not a moral reason to do so.[11] To be morally deserving of worship is to be the kind of being that merits respect in the specific form of religious worship. Power, as mere brute force, may instill fear, may inspire awe, but it does not compel by force of reason, nor does it offer a uniquely moral ground for respect. After all, power itself is mere fact and happenstance, not a reason, nor a moral trait. Zeus happens to be powerful, but so does Darkseid. Neither deserves worship by virtue of simple strength or capacity to create/destroy.

Since one can't legitimately rule by brute force, a god needs moral authority.[12] In order for a god to be worthy of worship, it would seem that it would have to be superior in such a way as to be uniquely deserving of respect, love, or adoration. Thus, a god worthy of worship must be superior but also caring, with a focus on compassion and love for human kind. We worship a superior god, recognize our inferiority to it, adopt a stance of humility, and act accordingly in the face of a loving authority.[13] Such a god can offer us salvation, our true reward in this metaphysical reality, where our place is defined by an authority who can reward us most highly.[14] Likewise, as a moral authority seeking our ultimate good, this god has a right to command us and to demand obedience. A god is like a parent charged with the wellbeing of a child. Just as a child has an obligation to obey the parent insofar as doing so is necessary in order for the parent to discharge his duty as protector and nurturer, so we have an obligation to obey a god. Unlike a child, though, we never outgrow the need for a god's moral guidance or assistance, and so we never mature to the point where the god's authority fails to demand our respect and attention. Were such a god to exist, we'd be morally obligated to submit to its loving authority. The only remaining questions then are: does such a being exist, and is it knowable?

Whose God, Which Divinity?

Let's go back to Darrel Keyes. Mr. Keyes's objection to Vanessa Kapatelis and her peers in the Myndi Mayer Foundation is that they are cultists, that they worship either Wonder Woman herself and so are idolaters, or that they worship false gods, the Greek pantheon, to which Wonder Woman professes loyalty. Keyes is obviously a devout Christian, and insofar as he is a Christian believes he is worshipping the proper god. Some interesting problems are quickly raised by Mr. Keyes's vehement opposition to the cult, however.

First, at least we actually know Zeus and the rest of the pantheon exist. They are all over the world. Poseidon manifests in the Thames, Ares wreaks havoc worldwide, Hermes is seen gallivanting all over Boston. But where has Keyes's god been? When Parallax threatened to undo all of creation, Jesus was nowhere to be seen. Tiamat was there! In addition, we have the problem of whether or not the Christian God as traditionally defined can actually be proven to exist, or even adequately described. Any concept we'd use to try and describe or articulate the nature of a supreme being, as traditionally defined by Christian theology, would necessarily be limited; it would imply delimitation, so that we could hold the concept in our minds. You can say "infinite" or "omniscient" all you want, but try and pin down the concept and it becomes determinate, and so limited. Leave it up in the air, and it is mere sound, a vapid utterance that devolves into an incoherent mysticism. No concept can hold God, and any god held by concepts ceases to be a god worthy of worship as supreme.[15] Keyes's god is either on a par with Zeus and so gains no superiority in the debate, or is pure mystery and so can provide no firm basis for his position. We seem to be stuck in the following conundrum, "Either

God is described ... and hence not worthy of worship, or else God-talk lapses into non-sense."[16] So if it's about proof, Keyes is in a bad position.

But maybe it's not about proof, but superiority. Keyes's god is the one true God because his god is all powerful. Well, we've already noted that power alone isn't adequate. Plus, in the DC multiverse, his god wouldn't be all powerful. Circe could give him a run for his money, as could Parallax, and various others. To be worthy of worship is to be deserving of it, which demands more than power. So, this brings us to our final point. Giving Keyes the benefit of the doubt (which he doesn't deserve), maybe this is about value. Perhaps he is genuinely concerned about these young people's souls, their wellbeing. He's not worried in the sense that he thinks they'll be smote by his more powerful god. After all, Ares is a much greater threat than God, given what we've seen of both in the recent past. Keyes is concerned that following false gods, living the Amazonian way, is bad for people. It will lead to them living less praiseworthy, less fulfilling lives than they would have lived had they adopted his faith and lived according to his god's edicts. Let's assume Keyes is genuinely concerned with the children's wellbeing. Here's the rub: isn't Wonder Woman as laudable a moral exemplar as Jesus, or Keyes's god? She preaches justice, equality, fairness, care, compassion, and love. She lives it, and we see her living it daily. If we get past the dubious epistemological and metaphysical claims about what ultimate reality is and what we can know about it, we're left with an existential predicament: we want to find order and meaning in the world. And here Wonder Woman seems a viable alternative.

Not as a Princess, But as a God

In *Wonder Woman*, vol 5: *Flesh*, when Hera has lost all hope and laments to Wonder Woman that she doesn't know to whom to pray, Wonder Woman responds that you "Pray to what's going to answer your prayers. Yourself. Your own strength and character."[17] Wonder Woman is here directing Hera to seek meaning, to seek validation and strength in those sources on which she can rely, namely herself, not on ephemeral, supernatural forces. She could also have emphasized Hera's friends, her relationships. If humans are essentially social by nature, then one's character and strength are in a real sense derivative of one's community. But Wonder Woman and Hera have seen enough gods to know they aren't worthy of blind obedience, and that what they offer can be found elsewhere. Likewise, blind mysticism offers nothing, not even cold comfort, since there's nothing, literally, to offer such comfort, just hollow words and nonsensical platitudes. Perhaps we can't know the divine, and admitting that is okay. Agnosticism in the face of uncertainty is respectable.

Surely it would matter if gods existed. If Darkseid were real, we would want to know. If Zeus were real, we might want to take note. But insofar as these are mysteries, perhaps insoluble, then although we may wish, out of epistemic humility, to remain agnostic, we can't avoid the demand that humanity needs foundational values around which to orient itself, around which to craft meaning and purpose. We need to know where we fit and how we matter, and "I don't know" won't do. But if we see this as the goal of worship, the idea behind religion, then when we bring it down to earth we may find commitments here that mean as much, loyalties that speak to our purpose and our roots, and in orienting ourselves toward them we may find happiness and satisfaction in submission to the loving authority of those values. Wonder Woman speaks to loyalty, integrity, and honor. She speaks to the best in us, as we relate to each other and care for one another. These values can be enough to keep us going, this orientation is what we seek, and this is what we can know, what we understand to be true. Perhaps if we're seeking a god in order to find our place, we might look to Wonder Woman and her Amazonian virtues. We could do worse than submit to the loving authority of Princess Diana, god of war.

Notes

1. James Rachels, "God and Human Attitudes," *Religious Studies*, 7 (1971) 333.
2. George Pérez *et al.*, *Wonder Woman: War of the Gods* (Burbank, CA: DC Comics, 2016), 257.
3. Pérez, *War of the Gods*, 27.
4. James Moulder, "What is a God?" *Sophia*, 13 (1974) 5.
5. Pérez, *War of the Gods*, 28.
6. Ibid., 231.
7. Ibid., 257.

8. John Byrne *et al.*, *Wonder Woman: Second Genesis* (New York: DC Comics, 1997), 48.

9. Ludwig Feuerbach, *The Essence of Religion*, translated by Alexander Loos (Amherst, NY: Prometheus Books, 2004), 65.

10. Ludwig Feuerbach, *The Essence of Christianity*, translated by George Eliot (Amherst, NY: Prometheus Books, 1989), 122.

11. Joseph L. Lombardi, "Filial Gratitude and God's Right to Command," *Journal of Religious Ethics*, 19 (1991) 102.

12. Ibid., 93.

13. Rachels, "God and Human Attitudes," 331.

14. See Charles Lewis, "Divine Goodness and Worship Worthiness," *International Journal of Philosophy of Religion*, 14 (1983) 146.

15. This is a problem famously addressed by St. Anselm in his *Proslogion* and in Guanilo's response, "On behalf of the fool."

16. Grace M. Jantzen, "On Worshipping an Embodied God," *Canadian Journal of Philosophy*, 8 (1978) 512. She's debating corporeality vs. incorporeality, but the point is relevant here as well.

17. Brain Azzarello *et al.*, *Wonder Woman*, vol. 5: *Flesh* (New York: DC Comics, 2015).

Merciful Minerva in a Modern Metropolis

Dennis Knepp

Great Hera! Merciful Minerva! Suffering Sappho! The ancient Greek gods and goddesses live on! Ares, Hades, Hermes, and Apollo reappear today. Bridging the gap between the ancient and modern worlds, Wonder Woman wields both an ancient bronze sword and a western cowgirl lasso. She wears the red, white, and blue colors of the flag of the United States of America, while walking among classical temples with their all-white steps, columns, and triangular roofs. Art can be a visual expression of philosophy, and Wonder Woman is an artistic expression of a specific philosophy of history: the ideals of freedom first found in Ancient Greece will be spread worldwide by the United States and her allies.

"A woman with the eternal beauty of Aphrodite and the wisdom of Athena"

William Moulton Marston introduced Wonder Woman in *Sensation Comics* #1 (January 1942), with Harry G. Peter as artist. From that very first introduction, the theme was established that Wonder Woman would be using the symbolic power of Classical Greece to fight for freedom and equality in the contemporary America of World War II.

Wonder Woman and Philosophy: The Amazonian Mystique, First Edition.
Edited by Jacob M. Held.
© 2017 John Wiley & Sons, Ltd. Published 2017 by John Wiley & Sons, Ltd.

The first few sentences of the first introduction of Wonder Woman establish this theme quite clearly:

> Like the crash of Thunder from the sky comes the **Wonder Woman**, to save the world from the hatreds and wars of men in a man-made world! And what a woman! A woman with the eternal beauty of Aphrodite and the wisdom of Athena—yet whose lovely form hides the agility of Mercury and the steel sinews of a Hercules! Who is **Wonder Woman**? Why does she fight for America?[1]

Aphrodite, Athena, Mercury, and Hercules are all interesting characters from Greek Mythology, and Marston makes it clear that their powers now "fight for America" in World War II. Let's first look at the Greek mythology and return to World War II later.

Aphrodite is the goddess of love, sex, and beauty. Don't think those are trivial powers. When Hera, queen of the gods, wanted to take her husband Zeus out of the Trojan War, she turned to the powers of Aphrodite for help. Here is Homer's description of those powers in Book 14 of his *Iliad* from some 3000 years ago:

> And with that she unbound from her breast
> An ornate sash inlaid with magical charms.
> Sex is in it, and Desire, and seductive
> Sweet Talk, that fools even the wise.[2]

Wonder Woman often uses the powers of Aphrodite. Early in "Wonder Woman Comes to America," Marston has side characters commenting on this "scantily clad girl":

Old Woman 1: "The hussy! She has no clothes on!"

Old Woman 2: "The brazen thing! HMPH! HMPH!"

Young Man: "Ha! Sour grapes sister, don't you wish you looked like that!"[3]

Wonder Woman is using Aphrodite's power to fool even the wise. In the next panel, that Young Man looks like he'd do anything she asked him to do. And, when Wonder Woman cries out "Suffering Sappho!" she is referencing the ancient poet Sappho from the Greek island of Lesbos, the origin of our word "lesbian."[4]

Athena was the goddess of wisdom and skilled combat. She is depicted as a beautiful young woman in battle armor with striking gray eyes. Typically, her helmet is pushed back at a jaunty angle to show her attractive visage. But don't let that pretty face fool you: she is a powerhouse. She was born directly from the head of mighty Zeus in full battle armor and shouting a great war cry. Here is Homer's description of Athena putting on her armor and preparing for battle:

> Athena, meanwhile, Zeus' favorite daughter,
> Let her supple robe slip down to her father's floor,
> This embroidered garment her own handiwork.
> She put on one of cloudy Zeus' tunics,
> Strapped on her battle gear, and then stepped
> Into the blazing chariot cradling a spear
> Long and thick enough for heaven's daughter
> To level battalions of men in her wrath.[5]

This is the image of Wonder Woman: she's the favorite daughter who takes off the womanly tunic of housework and puts on her father's armor. And she's really good at defeating the men. Notice that when describing Athena's power, Homer specifically says that she can "level battalions of *men* in her wrath." Athena is effective in battle and can overpower the men.

By having Wonder Woman apprehend a gang of armed bank robbers early in "Wonder Woman Comes to America," Marston establishes that Wonder Woman is able to battle and defeat the opposite sex. These particular men are dressed as 1940s gangsters. First they try to shoot her, but Wonder Woman does her "bullets and bracelets" routine to deflect the shots. Then she closes in for hand-to-hand combat: she twirls one of the bank robbers in the air and then throws him onto the rest of the gang, knocking them all unconscious. When the police arrive, they respond in bewilderment: "Wha—What's goin' on around here?"[6] Wonder Woman's "Merciful Minerva!" uses the Roman name for Athena, and it is clear that her physical power and skill with weaponry is based on the ancient goddess.

Mercury is the Roman name for the Greek god Hermes: the messenger god who protects travelers as well as smooth-talking traveling salesmen and other interesting business types. Marston obviously used the name "Mercury" since that was more familiar to his 1942 audience, and he established early in "Wonder Woman Comes to America" that Wonder Woman has the twin virtues of the god's speed and the god's appreciation for the con. Continuing the story, the police arrive to find the gang of bank robbers unconscious, and Wonder Woman runs away. One of the witnesses jumps into his car and goes after her. He has to drive faster and faster to try to catch up with the sprinting Wonder Woman, until finally: "Faster and faster—until at 80 miles per hour the car draws alongside the mile-a-minute maiden!" What gets her finally to stop? "Hey—Wait—I just want to talk to you about a business proposition!"[7] Yes, just like the ancient god Hermes, Wonder Woman will stop running at 80 miles an hour to hear a business proposition.

Hercules and the Barbarian World of Men

The odd one in the list is Hercules. He's not a pleasant hero; he's a dangerous man. Hercules is a retro character: other Greek heroes like Perseus or Achilles wear armor complete with a plumed helmet, round bronze shield, and they are armed with a spear and short sword. But Hercules is more like a cave man. He doesn't wear bronze armor; he wears a lion skin and uses the lion's skull as his crude helmet. Rather than a sword and spear, Hercules uses a club like a stereotypical cave man. He is always depicted as the strongest of the heroes and frequently wins battles by sheer brute strength. Indeed, he is strong enough to hold up the entire world for Atlas. In the ancient mythology he is best known for his 12 labors, which he endured to cleanse himself of the guilt of killing his own wife and children in an insane rage. Here's a short and rather typical story about Hercules from the ancient Roman author Hyginus:

> When Hercules sought the hand of Eurytus' daughter Iole in marriage and was rejected by him, he sacked Oechalia. In order to make Iole beg for him, Hercules threatened to kill her parents right there in front of her. But she with abiding resolve allowed her parents to be killed before her very eyes. After he killed them all, Hercules took Iole captive and sent her back to Deianira ahead of him.[8]

This isn't the Disney Hercules. This is a violent and dangerous man—especially dangerous to women.

Wonder Woman: Earth One, Volume One presents Hercules as a dangerous cave man who is especially dangerous to women. This origin story starts with a scene of Hercules in his lion-skin armor (complete with lion-head helmet!) standing over a prostrate woman and holding chains that are attached to a collar around her neck and to bracelets on her arms. Hercules has the opening words: "Queen of Amazons! HAHAHAHA! To *heel*, bitch of Hercules!"[9] Hercules is the image of the oppressor—the world of barbarian men who rule by force and enslave everyone.

According to the classical tradition, Hercules's ninth labor was to steal the war belt of the Amazon queen Hippolyte. *Wonder Woman: Earth One* references this classical story in pottery fragments that adorn the edges of the page. The comic reinterprets this story for the purposes of the Amazonian origin story. Queen Hippolyte uses her Aphrodite power of whispering in his ear to get close enough to steal the war belt back from Hercules and then put him in chains. The queen orders the rest of the Amazons to kill all the men, and then they retreat to their island paradise. The Amazons must fight for their freedom and reject the men. They become free by retreating from the world of men to create their own Amazonian utopia filled with classical temples, with their white columns, white steps, and triangular roofs. They reject barbarism and embrace an idealized Greek civilization.

"Let us go back—back to that mysterious Amazon isle called Paradise Island!"

Wonder Woman's origin story is unique in its use of ancient history. Superman originates from an alien world far away spatially, and then he is raised in secrecy in Kansas, which is also far away spatially from the action. Superman must overcome distance to become a superhero on Earth. Batman's origin is more psychological: the trauma of losing his parents, and the will to continue the fight for justice. Batman must overcome his own neurosis to become a superhero. Wonder Woman's origin story is about history, and she must overcome the traditions of the past to become modern. As we'll see, the Ancient Greeks play a crucial role in a threefold dialectic of historical transformation.

Wonder Woman's origin story uses the ancient Greeks in exactly the same way the philosopher Georg Wilhelm Friedrich Hegel

(1770–1831) does in his *Philosophy of History*, which follows a threefold pattern in which the world becomes progressively more free throughout history. Hegel outlined his theory of history as a threefold progression in a series of lectures at the University of Berlin. Hegel unexpectedly died at 61 during a cholera outbreak and only left behind his lecture notes on the philosophy of history. Many of his students put together their class notes with Hegel's lecture notes, and six years later they published *Lectures on the Philosophy of History*, in 1837.[10] A philosophy of history is not the same as a regular history. A philosophy of history is an attempt to find a pattern to history, to see progress in history, to understand how history can be meaningful to us moderns. Hegel was confident that history did have a pattern. His narrative of world history has a clear beginning, middle, and end, as the idea of freedom unfolds and develops through three major stages. In the first stage, only the despot was free; in the second stage, the Greeks discovered that *some* are free; and in the third stage, the stage of the modern world, we know that *all* are free. The Wonder Woman origin story goes through the same three major stages, and uses the Greeks in that crucial second stage.

The 2001 comic "The Origin of Wonder Woman" was reprinted as the lead comic in the anthology *Wonder Woman: The Greatest Stories Ever Told*. It features the threefold Hegelian story of history as the unfolding of freedom neatly laid out over just two pages.[11] The first stage is the origin of civilization in violence, slavery, and oppression. Here is how writer Paul Dini describes this original stage: "Since the time of our creation at the hands of the gods, we Amazons have had to struggle for our place in Man's open savage world." Note that this is not a peaceful starting place. This isn't a Garden of Eden. This is a place and time of war, violence, and oppression at the hands of men. The Amazonian origin story begins in what Thomas Hobbes (1588–1679) called a war of all against all, where "the life of man [is] solitary, poore, nasty, brutish, and short."[12]

To get to the second stage of history requires denying the first stage: saying "No!" to violence and universal bondage. Dini writes: "Weary of constant warfare, we beseeched our patron goddess of a sanctuary. The will of gentle Aphrodite guided us away from the battlefields to the shores of Paradise Island." Note that they must retreat from the world of men in order to find sanctuary. They are unable to create sanctuary in the midst of violence, and so they must retreat from the world. The origin of freedom is in the negation of the world of violent men.

Dini continues: "Now free to develop our minds as well as our bodies, we created Themyscira, a refuge of spiritual and intellectual tranquility, with technological advances that far surpassed those of the mortal world." Now that the Amazons are secluded away on their Paradise Island, they have found freedom: the freedom to develop themselves physically, spiritually, intellectually, and technologically. But it is only their freedom. The boast that their advances "far surpassed those of the mortal world" emphasize that the Amazons have only found that *some* people are free. Amazons are free on their Paradise Island in their refuge of Themyscira, but the rest of the world is left in that first stage of universal bondage.

Freedom and Liberty for All

In the first stage, only the despot is free while everyone else is enslaved. But that despot must be constantly vigilant, and so isn't really free. True freedom comes from rejecting the despot and retreating into a utopian community where some are free while the rest of humanity are left in barbaric slavery. That's the second stage of history. Moving to the third stage of history requires another negation, but this time it is personal rather than communal. Queen Hippolyta creates her own child "out of the Earth itself. I named her Diana." The princess Diana is thus originally not an Amazonian girl but instead a clay child. She's originally not real. This negation of her Amazonianness happens again when she's older. The Amazons decide to have a contest to create an ambassador to the outside world. The winner of the contest is a mysterious masked figure who turns out (plot twist!) to be Princess Diana in disguise. Queen Hippolyta must agree to send her own not-real Amazonian daughter out "into the danger and uncertainty of man's world" because she was able to not be herself at the competition. Negations play a crucial role in this story of progress, development, and freedom.

Finally, Princess Diana becomes Wonder Woman in the third and final stage of history: "In her travels, she brings the sum total of Amazon courage and knowledge, guided by a compassionate heart toward all people in need." The ideals of Paradise Island are no longer just for *some* people—namely, the Amazons. No, now those ideals are for *all* people. Note that Dini writes "all people in need," for these are the values of liberating the oppressed. To celebrate this finality of history, artist Alex Ross gives us our first splash of bright color. All the other panels had been the sepia tones of old movies to give that old historical feel. But when Wonder Woman leaves Paradise Island to bring liberation to all peoples, Ross celebrates this with the bright red, white, and blue, and screaming gold eagles, of her uniform that can signal only the United States of America. This two-page "The Origin of Wonder Woman" is a perfect little illustration of the three-stage theory of world history having a beginning in universal slavery, a middle in ancient Greece where some are free, and an end in the modern world in which Americans have discovered that all are free.

World War II and the Fight for the Classical Legacy

Hegel's philosophy of history follows that same three-stage process. History starts with the first literate civilizations that are built by the despotic ruler who has enslaved everyone else and so is not truly free. The Greeks discover that some are free but have not learned yet that all are free. Hegel writes that history has come to fruition in the modern world of the 1830s because the Germans have discovered that *all* men are free: "The German nations, under the influence of Christianity, were the first to attain the consciousness, that man, as man, is free: that it is the *freedom* of Spirit which constitutes its essence."[13]

Wait … the *German* nations? Yes, German. Hegel was a German philosopher who was enamored with the French Revolution (1789–1799) and how the ideals of liberty, equality, and fraternity were further carried into existence by Napoleon Bonaparte (1769–1821). Hegel believed history showed that soon Germany would be united with the same universal ideals that inspired the French. In the town of Jena, Hegel finished his first masterpiece, *The Phenomenology of Spirit* (1807), just as Napoleon's troops were engaging Prussian troops outside the city. There was no Germany at the time—it was just a loose confederation of hundreds of territories—but the invasion by Napoleon did stir many Germans into unifying for defense. Hegel was an advocate of German unification and believed that world history was on his side. The idea of freedom from the first despotic cultures was improved in Classical Greece and would finally culminate in German unification. Hegel's philosophy of history is a long defense of the political unification of Germany. It seems funny to us now to think that the unification of Germany would be the culmination of world history, but there it is.

Hegel didn't live long enough to see the United States truly enter world history, but he did hint that it would in the future. After the failed revolutions of 1848, many Germans emigrated to the United States looking for peace and sanctuary. Some of those Germans did really well in the beer business, and their names are still familiar: Pabst, Anheuser, Busch, Schlitz, and so on. Some of those Germans brought Hegel's philosophy with them, and several Hegelian philosophical societies flourished in the decades after the American Civil War. The most famous of these societies was The St. Louis Hegelians, and the most famous of that group was William Torrey Harris (1835–1909).[14] These German–American Hegelians believed that the conflicts of the Civil War, of new waves of immigration, and of western expansion could be solved through the mediating power of a German-style education in the classics of western civilization. We still today say "Kindergarten," revealing the German origins of our K-12 education system. The Hegelians believed that the German philosophy of Ancient Greek freedom would flourish in the modern America of the 1870s and 1880s. But after World War I, prohibition, and then World War II, it was no longer cool to be German–American anything. This is why, when Wonder Woman first appeared during World War II, she represented the American triumph over Germany for control of the freedom of ancient history.

The German Psychologist Hugo Münsterberg as Dr. Psycho

Wonder Woman is more than just World War II propaganda. She represents some deeper conflicts with Germans about the nature of freedom: is it that only *some men* are free? Or is it that *all people* are free? Does freedom and liberty for all include women? William Marston was always a feminist and an advocate for women's suffrage and equality.[15] But a look at an episode of his life reveals an interesting story about rejecting German psychology on feminist grounds.

Marston worked for a while as a lab assistant at Harvard University under their first professor of psychology: Hugo Münsterberg (1863–1916). The university originally wanted to hire William James (1842–1910) as their first professor of psychology, but he was more interested in writing philosophy and encouraged them to hire a German. All the best scientific universities were German at that time, and so James thought they could import some of that to America. It worked, for a while, until Münsterberg's outspoken anti-feminist views became an embarrassment to James and Harvard. But James died in 1910 and Münsterberg stayed on for a few more years. In 1912: "… Marston began studying with Münsterberg, who found Marston so impressive that he hired him to assist him in teaching at Radcliffe, strapping girls to machines."[16] These experiments with machines would be the basis for Marston's lie detector test and for Wonder Woman's golden lasso of truth. The cowgirl lasso is an American symbol and a symbol of how Marston was able to take the search for truth away from the misogynistic German psychologist and put it into the hands of Americans fighting for freedom and equality against the despotic tyranny of Hitler and the Nazis in World War II.

Wonder Woman might have the smallest costume in the comics, but it is the richest in symbolism. Wonder Woman represents the values of freedom and equality first discovered in Ancient Greece and then spread throughout the world by the United States and her Allies in World War II and applied to everyone—even women. Merciful Minerva, indeed!

Notes

1. "Wonder Woman Comes to America," writer: William Moulton Marston, artist: Harry G. Peter, reprinted in *Wonder Woman: The Greatest Stories Ever Told* (New York: DC Comics, 2007), 8.
2. *The Essential Homer*, edited and translated by Stanley Lombardo (Indianapolis, IN: Hackett Publishing, 2000), Book 14, lines 213 to 216, page 136.
3. "Wonder Woman Comes to America," 10.
4. *Sappho: Poems and Fragments*, translated by Stanley Lombardo (Indianapolis, IN: Hackett Publishing, 2002).
5. *The Essential Homer*, Book 8, lines 389 to 399, page 86.

6. "Wonder Woman Comes to America," 11. This whole scenario is also reproduced in the pilot episode of the 1970s TV show staring the incomparable Lynda Carter.

7. Ibid., 12.

8. "Hyginus's Stories" (Fabulae), *Anthology of Classical Myth: Primary Sources in Translation*, edited and translated by Stephen M. Trzaskoma, R. Scott Smith, and Stephen Brunet (Indianapolis, IN: Hackett Publishing, 2004), 228.

9. *Wonder Woman: Earth One, Volume One*, Grant Morrison and Yanick Paquette (Burbank, CA: DC Comics, 2016).

10. Georg W.F. Hegel, *The Philosophy of History*, translated by J. Sibree (Buffalo, NY: Prometheus Books, 1991).

11. "The Origin of Wonder Woman," writer: Paul Dini, artist: Alex Ross, reprinted in *Wonder Woman: The Greatest Stories Ever Told*, 6, 7.

12. Thomas Hobbes, *Leviathan*, revised student edition, edited by Richard Tuck (Cambridge: Cambridge University Press, 1997), 89.

13. "The Origin of Wonder Woman," writer: Paul Dini, artist: Alex Ross, reprinted in *Wonder Woman: The Greatest Stories Ever Told*, 18.

14. *The American Hegelians: An Intellectual Episode in the History of Western America*, edited by William H. Goetzmann (New York: Alfred A. Knopf, 1973).

15. For a discussion of Marston's feminism, see Chapters 1 and 5 of this book.

16. Jill Lepore, *The Secret History of Wonder Woman* (New York: Alfred A. Knopf, 2014), 29.

15

Wonder Woman and Patriarchy

From Themyscira's Amazons to Wittig's Guérrillères

Mónica Cano Abadía

Golden-era Wonder Woman was a feminist icon. Indeed, William Moulton Marston and his partners Elizabeth Holloway Marston and Olive Byrne[1] intended Wonder Woman to "demonstrate to young female and male readers that female strength was not a fantastic supposition."[2] This chapter focuses on the golden era and proposes an exercise of creativity whereby we imagine Diana, the Amazon, becoming Wonder Woman in order to overthrow Man's World. With the aid of other feminist fighters, Guérrillères, she creates a new egalitarian, peaceful world.

Diana against Man's World: A Feminist Epic Tale

Diana is the only child ever born on the island of Themyscira, which is her home until she leaves with wounded solider Steve Trevor to go to Man's World. Themyscira, created 3000 years ago by five Olympian goddesses, was home to the Amazons, a race of warrior women charged with the responsibility of promoting the peaceful ways of Earth, the goddess Gaea. After Heracles and his men ransacked the first Themyscira, the Amazons were led to a remote island where they were granted immortality. There, on Paradise Island, and guarded by a

Wonder Woman and Philosophy: The Amazonian Mystique, First Edition.
Edited by Jacob M. Held.
© 2017 John Wiley & Sons, Ltd. Published 2017 by John Wiley & Sons, Ltd.

mystic invisible barrier, they rebuilt the great city-state of Themyscira, where Amazons could live in idyllic and peaceful solitude.

But this peace is disrupted by Ares' plan to destroy the world. Steve Trevor, unwitting pawn of the war god, crash lands on Themyscira. Diana is charged with the task of escorting him to Man's World, and fighting Ares. After defeating Ares, Diana embarks on a worldwide tour promoting peace and Amazonian ideals, which are very similar to the ideals of a feminist ethics of care: empathy, compassion, and strong relational bonds founded in justice, duties, and obligations toward each other.[3]

Diana becomes Wonder Woman in this fight against patriarchy. She has all the desired skills for a feminist fighter: she is one of the strongest beings on the planet; she is highly resistant to bodily harm; she is an expert in all forms of armed and unarmed combat; she is a skilled tactician and diplomat (which is one of the most important skills to bring to a feminist fight); she has a magic lasso and silver bracelets that can deflect bullets.

Through Wonder Woman's story, we can build a feminist epic that depicts women who fight patriarchy. Ana de Miguel claims that there is no feminist or feminine epic: all the great adventures and journeys have always been lived and told by men.[4] This may not be the case, however. Monique Wittig's novel *The Guérrillères*[5] is a good candidate for a feminist epic,[6] and we can imagine how Wonder Woman could be part of the story.

In *Three Guineas*, Virginia Woolf asked: Do we, women, want to be included in the public world? Under what circumstances? Is that world desirable to us? What other circumstances would we desire?[7] Themyscira's Amazons don't want to be a part of the public world if that means Man's World. They hide under an invisible protection spell; they don't want contact; and they don't want Man's World to know about their existence. However, they are forced to confront that world, and the collision between the values of their feminine world and Man's World.

Diana/Wonder Woman observes Man's World from the perspective of her otherness, her alienness, and her strangeness as an Amazon in a patriarchal world. People who have lived in Themyscira for millennia and people who have grown up in Patriarch's World have divergent life experiences that provide them with different perspectives. Wonder Woman observes Man's World with different eyes, speaks another language, and possesses a knowledge that is situated someplace else. In fact, in the recent reboot, Earth One, her origin is of Heracles, thus making her both a product of the Amazon's and Man's World. In fact, her mother even indicates that she was conceived as a weapon to be used against Man's World. The collision between Amazonian ideals and Man's World is thus envisioned to be a literal war. The collision between the two worlds is unavoidable, and uncomfortable.

Virginia Woolf took a stance against the idea that women should be assimilated into hetero-patriarchal society. Wonder Woman thus follows Woolf, in not conforming to the new society that she believes is less just than her home island. Woolf's proposal is to try and create new ways of doing things that could restructure the inherited tradition. We should dare to defy tradition by creating unexpected contexts. Woolf's idea can be linked with Elisabeth Grosz's notion of the necessity of taking quantum leaps in philosophy: we should think outside the box, we should create new concepts and ways of living with one another.[8] These experiments confront the establishment if they are made from otherness and strangeness. Woolf, in this sense, talks about a feminist utopia: the Society of the Outsiders, a secret society that cultivates the differences, that creatively experiments with otherness. These Outsiders create new political practices that re-evaluate politics. Diana would be one of these Outsiders, or at least, one of their allies.

In this exercise of feminist creation, let's imagine that Diana, after her collision with Man's World, is determined to declare war on patriarchy. Let's imagine that, in her fight, she is not alone. She meets the members of the Society of the Outsiders, who applaud her determination to destroy the old world, and approve of her politics based on Amazonian principles. Let's imagine that the news of this war arrives at Themyscira, and that Hippolyta and the other Amazons travel to Man's World in order to overthrow the old patriarchal order. They did not want to have contact with Patriarch's World, but they are eager to fight together in order to change it. Amazons and Outsiders become Guérrillères. Let's imagine that the Guérrillères win the war and, thus, a new post-patriarchal world is established. The Guérrillères now have a post-war world to reconstruct on non-patriarchal values, a Paradise Island of their own making.

How does Monique Wittig imagine such a transition? How do we arrive at a post-patriarchal world? How do we create conditions for a feminist, egalitarian world? How do we/the Amazons/the Outsiders become Guérrillères? This situates us in the broader matter of how to create the possibilities for a revolution and, of course, an answer is not easy, and we are not going to provide a definitive one here. Let's simply explore what Monique Wittig has to say about the possibilities of a revolution against Patriarch's World, and how we can imagine that the Amazons and the Outsiders may become Guérrillères.

The Guérrillères at War

In the novel *Lesbian Peoples: Material for a Dictionary*, Wittig and Zeig describe the Amazons as the warriors thanks to whom we have been able to enter the Golden Age, an age without patriarchy or sex differences.[9] Amazon names in *Lesbian Peoples* and *Les Guérrillères* include Hippolyta, Vlasta, Arete, Diana... Is this our Wonder Woman? Is Wonder Woman the one who makes both worlds collide? Is that collision the beginning of the end of patriarchy and the starting point of a new feminist utopia? In Wittig's story, the Guérrillères declare war on Man's World, which in Wittig's terms is a heterosexual social contract.[10] And how do we arrive at this age where Man's World's social contract is obsolete? Although in *Les Guérrillères* a war, in the most violent sense of the word, is narrated, Wittig proposes two other complementary ways of overthrowing patriarchy: a social revolution and a linguistic revolution. Wittig believes these two revolutions are necessary in order to subvert the heterosexual social contract, since sex discrimination is made within political and linguistic frameworks that presuppose a sexual binary.

The social revolution focuses on building new communities. The Amazons in Themyscira have established their relationships based on an ethics of care and outside the rigidity of heteronormative schemes. They, for instance, flirt with bondage games and BDSM practices that question our traditional notion of sexual consent. In Earth One, volume one, Wonder Woman is openly lesbian and comes from a homonormative society—there are no men on Themyscira. Wittig sees these relationships as revolutionary because they are lived outside heteronormative frames. If the Amazons constructed these kinds of relationships in Man's World, their novelty would have a shocking impact on Patriarch's World's categories. Their affections would be revolutionary, and they'd promote inventive ways of constructing communities, based on different affective schemes (e.g., lesbianism, BDSM relations, and polyamory), that would erode heteronormative structures.

The linguistic revolution is also fundamental to Wittig, as she considers language an important part of the heterosexual contract. Language configures realities, or as she says, "Language casts sheaves of reality upon the social body, stamping it and violently shaping it."[11] Thus, a revolution of grammar and vocabulary is needed. For the Amazons, to become Guérrillères and overthrow patriarchy, they would need to destroy the hegemonic discourses of sex by, for example, changing the use of gender pronouns, or using new concepts to talk about their revolutionary sexuality. Would Amazons have the pronoun he? Do they even know what a lesbian is? Would they care? Amazons thus force us to rearticulate and so reconceptualize sexuality and gender.

Les Guérrillères narrates two joint revolutions that socially and affectively challenge hegemonic patriarchal structures and create new languages that have no place within the social heterosexual contract. Challenge the inherited tradition, "They [the Guérrillères] say that they are starting from zero. They say that a new world is beginning."[12] The world proposed in Les Guérrillères is a radical change with regard to Patriarch's World. Thus, the Guérrillères confront us with the problem of the new.[13] The new situates us in front of an abyss, the unknown, as we cannot demand support from already known structures. A new post-patriarchal world is an abyss, an experiment of the Outsiders, the result of the revolution of Amazons.

In Les Guérrillères, Wittig creates a type of human association that doesn't exist and that is impossible in the current patriarchal social contract. Likewise, Themyscira depicts a different type of social contract, where the Amazons created affective, social, sexual, cultural, power relations outside the frame of patriarchy and within a matriarchal, idyllic framework. In their war against Patriarch's World, and by becoming Guérrillères, they brought their political practices of sorority into Man's World.

Wittig is not in favor of the feminization of the world, however. When the battle against Man's World approaches an end, certain masculine pronouns slowly join the Amazons/Guérrillères. There are men in the Guérrillères' world; there are men Guérrillères. To picture this, we can imagine that the Golden-Age Steve Trevor is with Wonder Woman in her fight against patriarchy from the beginning.

Wittig/Wonder Woman and her allies don't declare war on men, but on Man's World: on the sexual binary that locks everybody into the mandatory heterosexual social contract. So, after the war, everyone benefits from the new post-patriarchal world order. Wittig's utopian proposal leads toward a linguistic subversion of the sexual and gender binary. This subversion of the sexual binary allows Wittig to present a society in which new communities of affection and desire exist, and where new ways of social action and conviviality are possible. The use of feminine pronouns as universal in *Les Guérrillères* reflects the new type of language that has emerged in the new relational human communities of a post-patriarchal world. Elles [shes/women] are humanity, the subject that conquers the world and words.[14] We can imagine how Themyscira's Amazons could perfectly use "elles" as universal, coming from a world where, indeed, women were the universal and the only subject. Thus, in order to conquer the world and words, they refuse to speak Man's World's language.

In the Guérrillères' post-patriarchal society there are no founders, no foundational texts. There are just references to "feminaries," whose authors are unknown. The feminaries are signs of a previous feminist fight that needed to revalue some cultural, symbolic aspects of femininity that had been neglected, maligned, and made invisible by patriarchal logic. These feminaries could have been written by Wonder Woman and other of Themyscira's Amazons when first confronted with patriarchy. When she first arrived in Man's World, Diana had to learn how to deal with that misogynistic logic that was so alien to her, and thus, she had to prove to the world that she, a woman, was strong, intelligent, and powerful: she was Wonder Woman.

The feminaries emphasized female symbolism, as they lived in a world where femininity was devalued. The women from Themyscira, the women before the war, had to revalue femininity and to rely on female symbolism. In this sense, they followed the philosopher Luce Irigaray's strategy of revaluing feminine sexual difference to fight phallogocentrism. Irigaray argues that positive representation of female aspects must be restored to the western culture. For instance, myths' representations of female divinities should be encouraged to symbolically represent relationships and shared experiences of women. In this sense, we can understand Wonder Woman's references to other female figures such as Hera, especially in the New 52, as the creation of a feminist genealogy needed to fight against Patriarch's World and its misogynist, phallogocentric categories. Irigaray's strategy suggests that women talk together and learn together so that we are not caged in male language. She urges, "Let's not immobilize ourselves in these borrowed notions."[15] In the New 52, Wonder Woman, Zola, Hera, and Athena are all women committed to other women, even over and against commitments or attachments to men like Zeus, or the First Born, Hera's own first-born male child.

Perhaps the first Amazons needed these strategies to socially and linguistically fight Patriarch's World. Nonetheless, Wittig claims that the Guérrillères do not live anymore in a world like Themyscira, nor in a world like Man's World, and that these revisions of feminine myths and revaluations of feminine sexual differences are no longer needed. They belong to the past, when Man's World still existed, when femininity was the negative of two opposite poles. Diana, by becoming Wonder Woman and by fighting against heteropatriarchal injustice, leads the war toward the destruction of this dualistic division. And she does so by fighting against daily oppressions that women have to face.

From where the Guérrillères stand now, the new subject needn't be revalued through symbolism or myths: it is already universal. They have won the war against oppression, against sexual binarism, against mandatory heterosexuality, and against sex inequality. They have won: they have created a better world where these obsolete structures are absent. They have made the feminist dream a reality: they have overthrown patriarchy.

Listen to Wonder Woman: Fight Patriarch's World

Wonder Woman's original intent was to challenge patriarchy, to inspire girls and women with a heroic feminist role model and to show everybody that women could be strong, intelligent, and worthy of admiration. Sadly, we still live in Patriarch's World, so we still need to be reminded of that. Wonder Woman's mission is not at an end: the egalitarian post-patriarchal world announced by Monique Wittig in *Les Guérrillères* is yet to come. Both Amazons and Guérrillères can be viewed as feminist role models, with different strategies stemming from their different contexts.

This connection between Amazons and Guérrillères, between two generations of fighters against patriarchy, aims to inspire our sorority and union in this fight against heteronormative, oppressive structures that affect us all—especially women and other subjects with alternative sexual and gender identities. It is our responsibility to listen to Wonder Woman and the rest of the Amazons and to create new non-patriarchal ways of relating to each other, within the perspective of a global ethics of care. We have to experiment, like members of the Society of the Outsiders and allies of Wonder Woman and the Amazons, with new political, social, cultural, and linguistic relations. May Wonder Woman guide us against inequality and toward a new, better, and more equal world.

Notes

1. Les Daniels, *Wonder Woman, The Life and Times of the Amazon Princess; The Complete History* (San Francisco, CA: Chronicle Books, 2004), 31.
2. Ann Matsuuchi, "Wonder Woman Wears Pants: Wonder Woman, Feminism and the 1972 'Women's Lib' Issue," *Colloquy Text Theory Critique*, 24 (2012) 122.
3. Carol Gilligan, *In a Different Voice: Psychological Theory and Women's Development* (Cambridge, MA: Harvard University Press, 1982).
4. Ana De Miguel, *Neoliberalismo sexual. El mito de la libre elección* (Madrid: Ediciones Cátedra, 2015).
5. Monique Wittig, *Les Guérrillères* (Paris: Ubu Editions, 2007).
6. Sally Beauman, "*Les Guérrillères*: Women without Men Except to Kill for Fun and Survival," *New York Times Book Review*, 10 (1971) 5–14.
7. Virginia Woolf, *Three Guineas* (London: Hogarth Press, 1938).
8. Elizabeth Grosz, *Volatile Bodies: Toward A Corporeal Feminism* (Bloomington, IN: Indiana University Press, 1994).
9. Monique Wittig and Sande Zeig, *Lesbian People: Material for a Dictionary* (New York: Avon, 1979).
10. Monique Wittig, *The Straight Mind and Other Essays* (Boston, MA: Beacon Press, 1992).
11. Monique Wittig, "The Mark of Gender," *Feminist Issues*, 5(2) (1985) 4.

12. Monique Wittig, *Les Guérrillères* (Paris: Ubu Editions, 2007), 52.
13. Hannah Arendt, *Essays in Understanding* (New York: Harcourt Brace, 1994), 325.
14. Elvira Burgos Díaz, *Qué cuenta como una vida. La pregunta por la libertad en Judith Butler* (Madrid: Antonio Machado Libros, 2008), 83.
15. Luce Irigaray, "When Our Lips Speak Together," in Janet Prince and Margrit Shildrick (eds), *Feminist Theory and the Body. A Reader* (New York: Routledge, 1999), 90.

Part V
TYING UP LOOSE ENDS

The Lasso of Truth?

James Edwin Mahon

Six months after Wonder Woman, a.k.a. Princess Diana, the warrior princess of the Amazons, leaves Paradise Island behind in order "to help fight the forces of hate and oppression," she receives a call on the Mental Radio from Queen Hippolyte, summoning her back. She returns to the island on her silent, superfast invisible Robot Plane, and the following day she is given a gift to help her in her fight—the magic lasso of Aphrodite. Of all the weapons in Wonder Woman's arsenal, this is the most powerful and the most versatile. It is also the most misunderstood.

The Lie Detector

The comic-book superheroine Wonder Woman, who debuted in *All Star Comics* #8 in December 1941, was created by psychologist Dr. William Moulton Marston. Marston was the author and co-author of a number of scientific articles and books, as well as popular psychology books, a novel, movie screenplays, and magazine articles. Most of all, Marston was known for his work on lie detection.

While still an undergraduate psychology student, working under Hugo Münsterberg at Harvard, Marston carried out lie-detection experiments. These experiments consisted of applying blood-pressure cuffs to a subject and recording changes in his or her blood pressure

Wonder Woman and Philosophy: The Amazonian Mystique, First Edition.
Edited by Jacob M. Held.
© 2017 John Wiley & Sons, Ltd. Published 2017 by John Wiley & Sons, Ltd.

while they answered questions. When people lied, their systolic blood pressure (the pressure in the blood vessels when the heart beats) went up; when they told the truth, it did not. It was supposed to be a purely scientific way to test if a person was lying. Marston published half a dozen articles on the subject, beginning with "Systolic Blood Pressure Symptoms of Deception" in the *Journal of Experimental Psychology* in 1917. He failed, however, to get hired by the Office of Military Intelligence, the Bureau of Investigation, the New York Police Department, the Department of War, or the Department of Justice.[1] In an attempt to use a lie-detection test to exonerate a defendant on trial for murder, he succeeded only in having the results of lie-detection tests ruled inadmissible in court because of their scientific unreliability (*Frye v. United States*, 1923). However, these failures did not stop him from continuing to promote himself as an expert lie detector, or from writing a self-promoting book entitled *The Lie Detector Test* in 1938.[2]

A Magic Lie Detector?

Because of the extensive work done on lie detection by her character's creator, it is commonly believed that Wonder Woman's lasso is a magic lie detector. After all, if someone is bound by the lasso he or she is compelled to tell the truth. Geoffrey Bunn, for example, says that "Anyone caught in the lasso found it impossible to lie. And because Wonder Woman used it to extract confessions and compel obedience, the golden lasso was of course nothing less than a lie detector."[3] Les Daniels writes that "Marston created the golden lasso as Wonder Woman's version of the lie detector."[4] Even Jill Lepore implies this when she says that Marston "also used Wonder Woman to feature his long-standing work ... on the detection of deception ... In 'The Duke of Deception' ... Wonder Woman uses her magic lasso to compel a villain to tell the truth."[5] Brett Jeff gets it right when he says that "Contrary to popular belief, the Magic Lasso is not inspired by the lie detector, was not an allegory for it, and was not itself a lie detector."[6]

First of all, to state the obvious, the lasso does not detect if anyone is lying. If someone is bound by the lasso, and he or she is asked a question, then he or she must tell the truth. But to do this is not to detect that the person is lying. The only way the lasso could function as a lie detector would be if the person said something (without being bound by the lasso), the lasso holder believed that the person was lying, and the lasso holder then bound the person with the lasso and asked the person again. But this is not how the magic lasso is used.

Second, Wonder Woman already has a lie detector. That is, she already has a machine that gives readings of a person's blood pressure while the person answers questions. In her disguised civilian persona of Diana Prince, secretary and assistant to Colonel Darnell in military intelligence, Wonder Woman uses a lie detector many times, on various people. For example, in "The Rubber Barons," *Wonder Woman* #4 (April–May 1943), Diana Prince gives Elva Dove, someone she suspects is a spy, a lie-detector test. "I'll ask you questions," Diana says while strapping Elva to the lie detector. "Answer truthfully or your blood pressure curve will go up. Did you take the rubber report from the secret files?" "No, no!" Elva insists. "Well, I'll be jiggered," Steve Trevor exclaims, reading the graph. "She *is* lying." Elva, it turns out, is working for Ivar Torgson, who, along with four other wealthy industrialists, hid their rubber-extraction process from the US government in order to control the rubber market after the war. Indeed, before she ever gets the magic lasso, in "A Spy in the Office," *Sensation Comics* #3 (March 1942), Diana concludes from monitoring the blood pressure of an unsuspecting person that she is lying. Since Wonder Woman has a machine that can detect if someone is lying, there would be no point in giving her a magic lie detector.

Finally, and most important, if the magic lasso were merely a magic lie detector, it would not be a metaphor for women's power. But it is.

The Stronger Sex

Marston believed that women were stronger than men. In his *Emotions of Normal People* (1928), Marston wrote that "Women have been regarded conventionally, for thousands of years, as the weaker sex. This almost universally recognized concept of women's weakness has included not only physical inferiority, but also a weakness in emotional power in relationships with males. No concept of women's emotional status could be more completely erroneous."[7] Although women are not the stronger sex *physically*, women are the stronger sex *emotionally*. This is because women have a greater capacity for love.

Inducement and Submission

As Matthew Brown says in his article "Love Slaves and Wonder Women: Radical Feminism and Social Reform in the Psychology of William Moulton Marston," according to Marston there were four basic emotions: inducement, submission, dominance, and compliance.[8] Love is a compound emotion, built out of the basic emotions of inducement and submission. Love, summarizes Brown, "is an emotional state whose stimulus is a certain type of relationship, and moreover an asymmetric one."[9] Love requires an asymmetric relationship in which there is one party who *induces* ("The self exerts energy in order to attract an allied stimulus, e.g., infant holds out its arms to induce mother to nurse, adult attempts to seduce") and another party who *submits* ("The self adjusts itself to an allied stimulus, giving itself over to the latter, e.g., infant ceases crying when soothed, student follows instructions of trusted teacher").[10] That is, love requires a relationship in which one party is the active, captivating party, and the other party is the passive, captive party.

Both parties in this asymmetric relationship experience love: active love (the active, captivating party) and passive love (the passive, captive party). Both parties in the asymmetric relationship benefit. And both parties in the asymmetric relationship experience pleasure. As Brown summarizes, the pleasure of the active, captivating party is "The pleasure associated with charming or enticing a loved one, and seeing pleasure in the latter," and the pleasure of the passive, captive party is "The pleasure of following the lead of a trusted, loved one."[11]

Dominance and Compliance

In contrast to the asymmetric inducement/submission relationship required for love, there is another asymmetric relationship. As Brown summarizes Marston, there is the asymmetric relationship in which one party *dominates* ("The self exerts energy in order to overcome the antagonistic stimulus, e.g., baby grasps a held rod more tightly as an experimenter tries to pull it away, competitive behavior among athletes") and another party *complies* ("Adjusting oneself to an antagonistic stimulus because of the latter's superior strength, e.g., a scolded child falls in line").[12] This kind of relationship precludes love.

According to Marston, as Brown summarizes, "love is connected with traditionally and stereotypically feminine traits," whereas "appetite, domination, and force are connected with masculinity."[13] Women have a greater capacity for the compound emotion of love, because they have a greater capacity for inducement/submission relationships. Men have a lesser capacity for the compound emotion of love, because they are more prone to domination/compliance relationships. In making love primary, "Marston thus makes the feminine primary to the masculine, as traditionally understood."[14] Since love, according to Marston, is necessary for psychological and emotional health, it follows that women have a greater capacity for psychological and emotional health. Women are the stronger sex, emotionally.

Alluring and Submissive

In his article "Why 100,000,000 Americans Read Comics" (1943), published after his comic-book superheroine had become a runaway success, Marston said about the comic-book industry:

> the comics' worst offense was their blood-curdling masculinity. A male hero, at best, lacks the qualities of maternal love and tenderness which are as essential to a normal child as the breath of life. Suppose your child's ideal becomes a super*man* who uses his extraordinary power to help the weak. The most important ingredient in the human happiness recipe still is missing—*love*. It's smart to be strong. It's big to be generous. But it's sissified, according to exclusively masculine rules, to be tender, loving, affectionate, and alluring. "Aw, that's girl's stuff!" snorts our young comics reader. "Who wants to be a *girl*?" And that's the point; not even girls want to be girls so long as our feminine archetype lacks force, strength, power. Not wanting to be girls they don't want to be tender, submissive, peaceloving as good women are. Women's strong qualities have become despised because of their weak ones. The obvious remedy is to create a feminine character with all the strength of a Superman plus all the allure of a good and beautiful woman.[15]

Women—or good women—are both *alluring* and *submissive*. These qualities of women are their *strong* qualities. What was needed was a "feminine archetype"—a female superhero—who had the strong qualities of physical strength and power that were possessed by male superheroes, as well as the strong qualities of being alluring and submissive that were possessed by women. Otherwise, people would continue to believe, erroneously, that women had "a weakness in emotional power." Enter Wonder Woman.

Bracelets of Submission

As a young Amazon princess at the age of 15, the future Wonder Woman pledged, at the Altar of Aphrodite, to serve the goddess. Magic metal bracelets were duly attached to her wrists. Only then was she permitted to drink from the Fountain of Eternal Youth, which granted her immortality—at least while she stayed on Paradise Island, and away from Man's World beyond.

The history of the bracelets of submission, otherwise known as the bands of Aphrodite, or magic bracelets, is the history of the Amazons themselves. (As Lillian Robinson has said, "the stories of female superheroes make another, more transgressive use of mythological sources, borrowing from various traditions and creating new ones in order to tell different stories about gender, stories that come closer to the universe of belief than do masculine (and masculinist) adventure comics."[16]) The Amazons were originally created by Aphrodite, who was locked in a war with a man—Ares, the god of war (later referred to in the comics by his Roman name, Mars). Ares created a powerful army of men, who enslaved women. In response to the enslavement of women, Aphrodite created, out of clay, "a race of super women, stronger than men," who would also have "the power of love," and called them Amazons. The goddess gave their leader, Queen Hippolyte, her own magic girdle.

So long as the queen wore the magic girdle of Aphrodite, the Amazons as a whole were undefeatable, and could never be enslaved by men. The Amazons lived, unconquered, in their land of Amazonia. Ares was furious at Aphrodite for creating the Amazons, and sent Hercules with an army to defeat them. But Hercules was bested by Queen Hippolyte in single combat. She compassionately decided to let him go free, but then Hercules managed, by trickery, to remove the magic girdle from the queen. The Amazons were now powerless, like women beforehand. Hercules and his army put manacles on the Amazons, and chained them together, making the Amazons their slaves. Aphrodite, angry with Hippolyte for having allowed Hercules to trick her and enslave the Amazons, at first refused to help. Eventually, however, in response to the queen's pleas, Aphrodite relented. She gave them back their super strength, which allowed them to break their chains, retrieve the magic girdle, and sail on Greek ships, guided by her, to Paradise Island—and freedom from men.

Although Aphrodite gave the Amazons the strength to break their chains and escape their enslavement, she ordered them to keep their manacles on their wrists. In one version of the story, she tells the queen "You may break your chains. But you must wear these wrist bands always to teach you the folly of submitting to men's domination!" ("The Origin of Wonder Woman," *Wonder Woman* #1, Summer 1942). In another version, she tells the queen "You Amazons may break your chains. But always you must wear these chain bands— they'll make you submit to me, goddess of love and beauty—never to men!" ("Wonder Woman Syndication," syndicated newspaper strip, 1944).

Aphrodite magically endowed their manacles—now bracelets or bands—with indestructibility. (In the newspaper strip, the bracelets are said to be "heavy bronze bracelets" (1944); later, after Marston's death, it was claimed that the Amazons made their own bracelets out of indestructible "Amazonium" (1952); in the 1970s TV show, they were said to be made of "Feminum.") Because they are magically indestructible, they are able to serve as shields, protecting Amazons from all manner of weapons and projectiles, including bullets.

Aphrodite also endowed them with another kind of magic power. If an Amazon ever removes her bracelets, she loses all control, becomes consumed with rage, and goes berserk, destroying everything in her path—that is, attempting to *dominate* everything. She effectively becomes *masculine*, like Ares. As Wonder Woman says when her bracelets are removed by the villain Mavis, "I'm completely uncontrolled! I'm free to *destroy* like a man!" ("The Unbound Amazon," *Sensation Comics* #19, 1943). At another time, when one of her bracelets falls off from having a chain attached to it ("The Menace of the Rebel Manlings," *Comic Cavalcade* #18, 1946), Wonder Woman attempts to kill all of the "manlings" in the Atlantean kingdom of Venturia (she is stopped by her best friend, Etta Candy, who binds her with the magic lasso).

Aphrodite also endowed the bracelets with a final magic power. If an Amazon ever allows a man to chain her bracelets together, then she loses her super strength and becomes as weak as an ordinary woman living in Man's World. As Wonder Woman says: "It is Aphrodite's law! When an Amazon girl permits a man to chain her bracelets of submission together she becomes weak as other women in a man-ruled world!" ("The Count of Conquest," *Wonder Woman #2*, 1942).

Wonder Woman displays the strong quality of submission by wearing the bracelets of submission. She has an inducement/submission relationship with Aphrodite, which enables her to experience love. Aphrodite is the active, captivating party, who induces. Wonder Woman is the passive, captive party, who submits. The bracelets of submission are thus a metaphor for the inducement/submission relationship necessary for love.

The bracelets of submission are also a metaphor for the domination/compliance relationship that precludes love. If an Amazon ever removes her bracelets, she ceases to submit to Aphrodite. In ceasing to submit to Aphrodite, she enters into a domination/compliance relationship with others as the dominant party. Meanwhile, if a *man* chains her bracelets together, Wonder Woman loses her super strength. Here, a man is the dominating party, and Wonder Woman is the complying party. This is *slavery*. So long as Wonder Woman's bracelets are chained together by a man, she remains in a relationship of domination, as the dominated party. As Wonder Woman says in "School for Spies," *Sensation Comics #4*, April 1942, "These bracelets—they're an Amazon's greatest strength and weakness! What a fool I was to let a man weld chains upon them! It just makes a girl realize how she has to watch herself in this man's world!"

Importantly, however, a man chaining Wonder Woman's bracelets together only makes her lose her super strength. Chaining her bracelets together only makes it possible for her to be dominated by men. It does not make her *submit* to men. To be dominated, to be enslaved, is not to submit to anyone. The Amazons were enslaved by men, but they never submitted to them (the newspaper strip language of "submitting to men's domination" is imprecise here). As soon as they got their super strength back, the Amazons freed themselves from men's domination.

The Magic Lasso of Aphrodite

In the original version of her origin story, "Introducing Wonder Woman" (*All Star Comics #8*, December 1941), Princess Diana was not given any magic items after she defeated all the other Amazons in the tournament held by the queen to decide who was "strongest and wisest of the Amazons," in order to "go forth to fight for liberty and freedom and all womankind"—because, as Aphrodite and Athena tell the queen, "America, the last citadel of democracy, and of equal rights for women, needs your help." Diana already had her magic bracelets of submission from the age of 15 (indeed, she used them in the final round of the tournament, in defeating her best friend, Mala, at "Bullets and Bracelets," a dangerous competition of skill where each contestant, using only her bracelets, must deflect bullets shot from a gun by the other contestant). Queen Hippolyte simply gives her a red, white, and blue costume, saying: "And here is a costume I have designed to be used by the winner, to wear in America."

Six months later, however, Diana—now Wonder Woman—is called back ("Summons to Paradise," *Sensation Comics* #6, June 1942). Under orders from Aphrodite and Athena, the queen instructs the royal craftswoman, Metala, to take links from the queen's magnetized gold magic girdle of Aphrodite, and to make a magic magnetized golden lasso. As the queen tells Metala: "The magic girdle is made of millions of fine chain links. These are unbreakable! You will take links from the girdle and make a magic lasso, flexible as a rope, but strong enough to hold Hercules!" Metala succeeds in making a magic magnetized golden lasso. Although it is called a "lasso," and although it is said to be "flexible as a rope," it is not a rope. It is actually a *chain*. As Metala says to the queen: "This is the slenderest chain ever made, your majesty!" To which the queen replies, "Yet it cannot be broken." The lasso is a magic magnetic golden chain, made of "millions" of fine chain links, that is super flexible (because it is made of so many fine chain links), that can stretch to any length (because of the tiny spaces between the fine chain links), that can conduct and absorb electricity (because it is gold and magnetized), and that can never be broken (because each chain link is unbreakable).

The lasso is magic because it is unbreakable, but it is also magic in a much more important way. It was Aphrodite and Athena who wanted to give Wonder Woman the magic lasso, and in the original origin story, Aphrodite, speaking for both goddesses, explains why: "Having proved thyself bound by love and wisdom..." To say that Wonder Woman has proven herself *bound* by *love* and *wisdom*, is to say that she has proven herself to be one who submits to Aphrodite and Athena, the goddesses of love and wisdom, respectively. Because she has proven herself to be one who *submits* to *them* (and one who does not dominate anyone), she has earned her prize. As the goddess continues: "… we give thee power to control others! Whomsoever thy magic lasso binds must obey thee!" In the later version of the origin story in "The Origin of Wonder Woman," *Wonder Woman* #1, Summer 1942, it is the queen who gives Wonder Woman the magic lasso of Aphrodite. She tells her, "The magic lasso carries Aphrodite's power to make men and women submit to your will! Whoever you bind with that lasso must obey you!" The magic lasso, then, channels the power of the goddess Aphrodite to make men and women do whatever the lasso holder wishes them to do. To wield the magic lasso is to have the power of Aphrodite—to *become* Aphrodite, as it were.

Submission vs. Slavery

On the face of it, binding people with a chain, and making them obey you, sounds a lot like slavery. The magic lasso seems like a magic device that allows you to enslave others. But if the first and most common misunderstanding is that the magic lasso is a magic lie detector, the second misunderstanding is that it is a magic enslavement device. Brett Jett says about the lasso "It was a gift decreed by Aphrodite, not solely to extract truth, but to pacify people to obey … thus being able to turn the tables from what the Amazons suffered at the hands of Hercules & the Greeks."[17] Jett also says that people bound by the magic lasso "are like slaves to a certain degree."[18] But slavery is a dominance/compliance relationship, which is not the relationship created between the lasso wielder and the person lassoed. After all, the relationship between Aphrodite and the Amazons is not one of slavery. That was the relationship between the Greek men and the Amazons.

The proper explanation of the lasso's magic power can be found in an interview with Marston in *Family Circle*, entitled "Our Women Are Our Future" (1942). He says that,

> Her magic lasso is merely a symbol of feminine charm, allure, oomph, attraction every woman uses that power on people of both sexes whom she wants to influence or control in any way. Instead of tossing a rope, the average woman tosses words, glances, gestures, laughter, and vivacious behavior. If her aim is accurate, she snares the attention of her would-be victim, man or woman, and proceeds to bind him or her with her charm … Woman's charm is the one bond that can be made strong enough to hold a man against all logic, common sense, or counterattack.[19]

His interviewer worries that this sounds too much like slavery: "The chains that the Nazis forge on conquered people ... seem a whole lot stronger than the bonds of personal charm!" In response to this worry, Marston says "Chains of force are always broken sooner or later. No human being can put another's soul or spirit in bondage, only his body. And in the end the inner self triumphs over the outer; mind and personality win back their control over flesh."[20]

The power of the magic lasso is not the power to force someone to obey you. That is masculine power, or domination. The magic lasso is not like a loaded gun pointed at someone's head. The power of the magic lasso is the power to captivate someone. That is feminine power, or inducement (allure). The magic lasso is like a beautiful face, or an attractive perfume. It *enchants*, like a love potion. Its effect on the other person is *magnetic* (it is, after all, made of magnetic gold). That is why the lasso is always drawn as glittering or sparkling. When Diana first tests the lasso's power by commanding the royal physician, Dr. Althea, to stand on her head, the doctor says, "N-N-Yes, Princess! I wouldn't do it but something compels me!" The doctor does not want to stand on her head, but now she will do *anything* for Diana. Diana's wish is now her command. The power of the magic lasso is the power of making someone act as the lover does for the loved one. That is why one does not have to *command* that someone bound by the lasso do anything. One simply has to *ask*, and the person will do it.

This is the power that Aphrodite has over the Amazons. For Wonder Woman to wield the magic lasso of Aphrodite is for her to have the strong power of allure over others. It is for her to occupy the position that Aphrodite normally occupies. It is for her to become the captivating party in an asymmetric relationship in which the other person submits to *her*. In that sense, the magic lasso is the reverse of the bracelets of submission. For Wonder Woman to wield the magic lasso is for her to have others wear *her* bracelets of submission, as it were (which is why Etta Candy can stop Wonder Woman's rampage after she loses a magic bracelet by lassoing her with the magic lasso— wrapped around her, it functions as a bracelet of submission). The magic lasso of Aphrodite is, thus, another metaphor for the inducement/submission relationship. The difference is that in the case of the magic lasso, it is Wonder Woman who is the active, captivating party, the one who induces. The person bound—whether man or woman—is the passive, captive party, the one who submits.

The magic lasso's power is a truly incredible power to place in someone's hands. It is a much greater power than mere strength. A slave, someone who is forced to obey you, is someone who is merely dominated—someone who merely complies. A slave remains free in spirit and will always try to disobey you if possible, and will always attempt to escape and/or to overthrow you. But a lover, someone who is devoted to you, will never attempt to escape and/or overthrow you, and will always do what you ask.

Deception and Domination

Brian Cronin has said that "The lasso didn't inherently make people truthful, it just made them do whatever Wonder Woman told them to. So if she asked them a question, they had to tell her the answer."[21] The third misunderstanding of the magic lasso is that there is merely a coincidental relationship between being bound by the lasso and being truthful, because Wonder Woman just happens to wish for those bound by the lasso to be truthful. Despite the fact that the magic lasso of Aphrodite is not a magical lie detector, it is possible to find a deeper connection between not lying and being bound by the lasso.

As Brett Jett correctly says, "When people assert their own will in any way, the dominance emotion is involved. So the idea behind the Magic Lasso is that it's a fictionalized, super version of something that puts people into this submission state and nullifies any dominance emotion."[22] Someone who is bound by the lasso is someone who completely submits to the lasso wielder. She or he is in an inducement/submission relationship with the lasso wielder, as the passive, captive party. To dominate someone, by contrast, is to impose your own will on that person, so that the person complies. But the person who is bound by the lasso can never impose his or her will on the lasso wielder. Hence, the person bound by the lasso can never attempt to dominate the lasso wielder.

As Jett also correctly points out,

> Deception involves active dominance emotion ... and thus requires great psycho-neural effort and raises blood pressure. But when you're in a submissive state—especially a perfect one caused by the Magic Lasso—then you are all about submission ... and lack the active dominance to even attempt a deception of your own, so long as you're bound

by the Lasso and someone is controlling it ... So in a way, it's not so much that you're "forced" to obey and tell the truth, but that that's all you're able to do![23]

To attempt to deceive someone is to attempt to impose your own will on that person. To attempt to deceive someone is to attempt to dominate that person. As Nathan Rotenstreich has said: "in lying I am trying to dominate my fellow man."[24] That is why the person bound by the magic lasso can never attempt to deceive the lasso wielder; it would be an attempt to dominate the lasso wielder. Hence, the person bound by the magic lasso can never lie to the lasso wielder. As Jett says, "The Magic Lasso was meant to defeat all types of lies by nullifying all assertions of dominance."[25]

To be truthful with someone, by contrast, is not to impose your own will on that person. To be truthful is not an attempt to dominate that person. Hence, if someone bound by the magic lasso is asked a question, the person will tell the truth, because this is the non-will-imposing, non-dominating response. Of course, the person will only be able to tell the truth as far as it is possible to do so. When Wonder Woman uses the lasso on Serva, the twin sister of Hypnota the Great, Serva still does not tell Wonder Woman that Hypnota the Great is a woman, and her evil twin sister, because these details have been hypnotically blocked from her mind by Hypnota. But she doesn't lie to Wonder Woman, either ("The Slaves of the Evil Eye," *Wonder Woman* #11, 1944).

The fact that the magic lasso prevents people from lying to the lasso wielder does not make the magic lasso a "lasso of truth." In fact, that is a name that was never used by Marston himself. Lying is an attempt to impose one's own will on another, and so lying is necessarily an attempt to dominate, and the magic lasso prevents all assertions of dominance. So the magic lasso prevents lying.

A Final Twist

Both the bracelets of submission and the magic lasso of Aphrodite have been dropped from contemporary Wonder Woman comic books. The bracelets of submission have been replaced by the silver bracelets. The magic lasso, meanwhile, has been replaced by the "lasso of truth," which is restricted to making people tell the truth (which is all it did in the 1970s TV show). One explanation for this is that the very idea of complete submission to another—be she goddess, leader, or superheroine—is no longer morally or politically acceptable. As a blogger has said: "early Wonder Woman seemed cheerfully unconcerned with imposing her will on her adversaries through the use of her magic lasso (which was eventually de-powered down to just making people tell the truth, perhaps because everyone got the sense of just how totalitarian the original power of the magic lasso really was to begin with)."[26] The magic lasso, on this account, is fascist and anti-American.

There is another explanation for the depowering of the magic lasso, however. The lasso is a metaphor for women's power over men and women. It is hard to imagine Superman, Batman, Captain America, Thor, or The Hulk using the magic lasso of Aphrodite to captivate a villain, so that the villain will do anything whatsoever for him. To quote Marston, "it's sissified, according to exclusively masculine rules." Perhaps the lasso's captivating power was considered too feminine. If so, then the depowering of the magic lasso is part of the defeminizing of Wonder Woman, and Marston's concern about the hypermasculinity of comic books remains relevant.

Notes

1. Jill Lepore, *The Secret History of Wonder Woman* (New York: Alfred A. Knopf, 2014), 53.
2. William Moulton Marston, *The Lie Detector Test* (New York: Smith, 1938).
3. Geoffrey Bunn, "The Lie Detector, Wonder Woman and Liberty: The Life and Works of William Moulton Marston," *History of Human Sciences*, 10 (1997) 108.
4. Les Daniels, *Wonder Woman: The Complete History* (San Francisco, CA: Chronicle Books, 2000), 48.
5. Lepore, 176–177.
6. Brett Jett, "Do You Know Wonder Woman: The Magic Lasso," *World of Superheroes*, November 10, 2015, http://www.worldofsuperheroes .com/2015/11/do-you-know-wonder-woman-the-magic-lasso/.
7. William Moulton Marston, *Emotions of Normal People* (New York: Harcourt, Brace & Company, 1928), 258.

8. Matthew Brown, "Love Slaves and Wonder Women: Radical Feminism and Social Reform in the Psychology of William Moulton Marston," *Feminist Philosophical Quarterly*, 2(1) (2016) article 1.
9. Ibid.
10. Ibid.
11. Ibid.
12. Ibid.
13. Ibid.
14. Ibid.
15. William Moulton Marston, "Why 100,000,000 Americans Read Comics," *The American Scholar*, 13 (1943) 42–43.
16. Lillian S. Robinson, *Wonder Women: Feminisms and Superheroes* (New York: Routledge, 2004), xx.
17. Brett Jett, "Do You Know Wonder Woman: The Magic Lasso."
18. Ibid.
19. Olive Richard [Olive Byrne], "Our Women Are Our Future," *Family Circle*, August 14, 1942, http://www.angelfire.com/indie/jamietakot/Article3.htm.
20. Olive Richard [Olive Byrne], "Our Women Are Our Future."
21. Brian Cronin, "Comic Book Legends Revealed," *Comic Book Resources*, July 20, 2012, http://goodcomics.comicbookresources.com/2012/07/20/comic-book-legends-revealed-376/.
22. Brett Jett, "Do You Know Wonder Woman: The Magic Lasso."
23. Ibid.
24. Nathan Rotenstreich, "On Lying," *Revue International de Philosophie*, 10 (1956) 418.
25. Brett Jett, "Do You Know Wonder Woman: The Magic Lasso."
26. "Mockingbird," "Wonder Woman: Maid of Honor in a Dishonorable World," *Mockingbird*, April 5, 2016, http://www.mbird.com/2016/04/wonder-woman-maid-of-honor-in-a-dishonorable-world/.

Loving Lassos
Wonder Woman, Kink, and Care

Maria Chavez, Chris Gavaler, and

Nathaniel Goldberg

Can sexual bondage lead to a better world? Despite DC Comics' early ban on whips, chains, and other BDSM imagery, no Golden-Age superhero is bound more often than Wonder Woman. The Comics Code Authority later claimed that such images contribute to juvenile delinquency. But Wonder Woman's co-creator William Marston believed that sexual bondage was key to achieving a peaceful society. "Without a sound foundation in 'sex love,' " he wrote in 1939, "no human being of either sex can possibly submit to any social control and like it."[1]

Though Marston intended Wonder Woman to provide an alternative to the masculinity of the superheroes of his day, Marston's vision remains relevant today. The behavior and attitude of Marston's Wonder Woman anticipated contemporary feminist philosophers' contributions to the ethics of care. There is also an underlying ethics of care in Wonder Woman's role as what Marston calls a "Love Leader," and that combination of kink and care is itself reflected in contemporary BDSM.

Femdom Fantasies

William Moulton Marston was born in 1893 in Massachusetts and died in 1947 in New York. He supported women's suffrage movements in Britain and the United States, and was influenced

Wonder Woman and Philosophy: The Amazonian Mystique, First Edition.
Edited by Jacob M. Held.
© 2017 John Wiley & Sons, Ltd. Published 2017 by John Wiley & Sons, Ltd.

by nineteenth-century feminists. Elizabeth Cady Staunton, Catherine Beecher, and Charlotte Perkins Gilman in particular argued that women's roles as care-givers in the private sphere gave them a unique perspective that made them morally superior to men. Society would therefore benefit if women were included in the public sphere.

In her novel *Herland*, Gilman described a matriarchal utopia where women live peacefully and cooperatively among themselves. *Herland* and its inhabitants mirror what Marston came to create as Wonder Woman's home, Paradise Island, and its Amazons. As Wonder Woman's mother, Queen Hippolyte, explains in the premiere episode, the Amazons "have been able to far surpass the inventions of the so-called man-made civilization! We are not only stronger and wiser than men—but our weapons are better—our flying machines are further advanced!"[2]

Marston's feminist leanings also influenced his work in psychology. In his 1928 *Emotions of Normal People*,[3] Marston maintained that men are "Appetitive Leaders" with tendencies toward greed and ego-based dominance. Because a woman's body "contains twice as many love generating organs"[4] as a man's, women are naturally submissive and therefore unable to be "Appetitive Leaders." However, Marston argued, women alone can become "Love Leaders," teaching men to submit their appetites to the dominance of women. Wonder Woman muses accordingly: "Some girls love to have a man stronger than they are make them do things. Do I like it? I don't know—it's sort of thrilling. But—isn't it more fun to make the man obey?"[5] Women, Marston believed, could educate men about the happiness and freedom that come with willingly submitting to loving authority—another theme in early Wonder Woman comics. Marston also believed that women Love Leaders could educate other women about the same, which appears in the comics as well.

Related to all this, Marston supported the free-love movement of his day. Plus, he had his own kinky tendencies, which he didn't separate from his academic psychological views. That's why Marston described his psychological theories in terms of "dominance" and "submission."

Much of Marston's kinkiness was also expressed in his comics. In one adventure, Wonder Woman travels to none other than the planet Eros, guided by Desira, Queen of Venus.[6] Originally, Wonder Woman's magic lasso of truth was her magic lasso of compulsion, making anyone bound with it obey her commands: "Why you—oh!

What is this I feel—I'm compelled to obey—you've caught me with the magic lasso!"[7] Marston also had Wonder Woman's fellow Amazons engage in consensual bondage and role-playing games on Paradise Island. Wonder Woman's silver cuffs were symbols of her own voluntary submission to Aphrodite. They also reminded Wonder Woman that she should never submit to any man, as the Amazons had been forced to do to Hercules. If a man chained Wonder Woman's bracelets together, however, then he could force her submission. The Amazons' own Venus girdles, which they put on their captives, controlled the captives' appetite-driven dominance and made them submit to the Amazons. But, Marston made sure, the Amazons' dominance over their captives was loving.

Likewise, Marston's stated goal in his academic writing was to promote "a new code of conduct, based on love supremacy."[8] He wanted to re-educate women and men to willingly embrace loving submission through eroticism. Marston's comic-book creation, Wonder Woman, fit his depiction of an ideal Love Leader: a sexually alluring and powerful, yet loving, mistress whose feminine charms would make women and men submit to her authority.

Aphrodite's Law and the Ethics of Care

Like their nineteenth-century predecessors, many twentieth-century feminists regarded women's nurturing abilities as strengths. Unlike their predecessors, however, many of these later feminists also argued for creating a new morality. Instead of basing ethics on what they perceived to be masculine notions like justice, these feminists argued that ethics should be based on concrete human relationships and what they perceived to be the feminine notion of care.

Because both Marston and twentieth-century feminists had a common source in nineteenth-century feminist thinkers, some of Marston's themes can be found in twentieth-century ethics of care. In her 1983 book *In a Different Voice: Psychological Theory and Women's Development*,[9] Carol Gilligan argued that while men's emphasis on separation and autonomy leads to an ethical orientation focused on abstract ideals like justice, fairness, and rights, women's emphasis on relationships and connections leads to one focused on concrete desires, needs, and interests of other human beings. Gilligan developed this thought in her 1987 "Moral Orientation and Moral Development,"[10] where she argued for two moral perspectives, justice and care. A shift in moral perspective changes the moral question from "What is just?" to "How to respond?"[11]

This shift in perspective can be seen in the ideas of *restorative* justice, which itself incorporates ideas of how to respond. Restorative justice seeks resolution through looking at harms done by perpetrators and seeking to repair those harms by giving voice to victims. Through building on the human need for mutually supportive relationships, restorative justice in turn aims to reform—and even transform—those who do harm.

Paradise Island has its own penal colony, called "Reform Island" and later called "Transformation Island." Here Amazons reform or transform rather than punish their prisoners. When Wonder Woman and the Amazons catch Baroness von Gunther and her co-conspirators trying to sneak onto Paradise Island, they bring them to Queen Hippolyte for judgment. "This woman must not be killed—Aphrodite's Law forbids," declares Hippolyte. "We will construct a prison on Reform Island. There shall she and her poor victims be confined until their minds are completely free from evil!"[12]

Similarly, loving submission transforms the prisoner Irene's selfish appetitive-driven dominance into a dominance driven by love and care for others. This spurs Irene and the other transformed prisoners to save Wonder Woman and Queen Hippolyte from Eviless: "Without the girdle I feel dominant—invincible! But I don't feel cruel and wicked as I used to—the Amazons have transformed me! I love Wonder Woman and Queen Hippolyte! I can't bear to have them hurt—I must save them!"[13] The villainous Baroness von Gunther is herself reformed: "Wonder Woman has changed my personality. I intend to stand trial for my sins!"[14]

In addition to Gilligan, fellow feminist ethicists Nel Noddings and Joan Tronto also emphasized the importance of human relations in creating a new morality. In her 1984 *Caring: A Feminine Approach to Ethics and Moral Education*, Noddings argued that "an ethic built on caring strives to maintain the caring attitude and is thus dependent upon, and not superior to, natural caring." By affirming the needs of others, we also affirm our needs, especially the "fundamental and natural desire to be and to remain related."[15] Ethics is about particular relations: the one caring and the cared for. Combating evil isn't about punishing sinners but about minimizing pain, separation, and helplessness by strengthening human bonds.

Marston emphasized a similar ethic beginning with Wonder Woman's first appearance. Rather than traveling to the United States only to fight abstract "forces of hate and oppression," Diana is motivated by her love for the injured army officer Steve Trevor, whom she nurses herself before transporting to a US hospital: "And so Diana, the Wonder Woman, giving up her heritage, and her right to eternal life, leaves Paradise Island to take the man she loves back to America—the land she learns to love and protect, and adopts as her own!"[16]

For her part, Tronto, in her 1993 "An Ethic of Care,"[17] outlined four ethical aspects of the care process. *Attentiveness* is the recognition of others' needs required to adequately respond to them. *Responsibility* is the recognition that individuals must take it upon themselves to care. *Competence* demands that individuals be able to provide adequate care. And *Responsiveness* requires that the care-giver acknowledge the position of vulnerability that the care-receiver finds herself in. Tronto argued that good care requires that these four aspects fit together into a whole.

Like a good practitioner of the ethics of care, Wonder Woman shows concern for antagonists who are hurt. Instead of seeking retribution, the human connection that Wonder Woman makes with villains moves her to help them when their lives are threatened. At one point, Eviless accidently falls overboard and begins to drown. Even though Eviless is one of her nemeses, Wonder Woman dives into the water to rescue her. A thought bubble expresses her concerns: "Eviless cannot swim—she's drowning! I must save her—Aphrodite's Law commands us to save lives always—enemies or not!"[18] In doing so, Wonder Woman is attentive to Eviless's need for care as she falls overboard, sees herself as responsible for that care in the form of rescuing Eviless, is competent in giving Eviless that care (she is Wonder Woman, after all), and is responsive to the particular position of vulnerability—drowning—that Eviless finds herself in. But Wonder Woman's care often comes with a side of kink.

The Kinky Ties that Bind

That Marston's Wonder Woman exhibits kinky behavior didn't go unnoticed. One of her first fans, an American infantryman who wrote to DC Comics 10 months after Wonder Woman's premiere, recognized this:

> I am one of those odd, perhaps unfortunate men who derive an extreme erotic pleasure from the mere thought of a beautiful girl, chained or bound, or masked, or wearing extreme high-heels or high-laced boots … Your tales of Wonder Woman have fascinated me on account of this queer "twist" in my psychological make-up … if you have experienced the same sensation as I have from actually applying such [implements of confinement] to a beautiful girl, you'll understand exactly what I mean.[19]

Yet there's also an underlying ethics of care in Wonder Woman's role as a Love Leader who teaches loving submission. That combination of kink and care is reflected in the real-life practice of BDSM.

BDSM—short for "bondage and discipline, dominance and submission, and sadism and masochism"—is a group of sexual practices involving a power exchange between consenting adults to fulfill physical or emotional needs. The dynamic between dominant and submissive sexual partners illustrates both Noddings's idea of the one caring and the cared for and Tronto's idea of the care-giver and the care-receiver. The dominant agrees to take responsibility for her submissive. The submissive relinquishes her power to her dominant, trusting the dominant to ensure her safety and honor her limits.

BDSM is not only relationship-based but also community-based, with practitioners forming groups for support and education. Further, the BDSM community at large has developed ethical frameworks to govern their activities. These include SSC (safe, sane, and consensual), RACK (risk aware consensual kink),[20] and the 4Cs (consent, communication, caring, and caution).[21] Wonder Woman illustrates the last framework in particular.

Consent is the guiding principle of the BDSM community, "one of the most significant elements of kink. It's what separates kink from abuse."[22] More than just willingly saying "yes" or "no," consent is a process where participants express their intentions, desires, concerns, and limits to one another. Playing her part during Paradise Island's "Diana's Day" Festival, the Amazon Zoe consents to be bound: "There's a rope on the bed to tie me according to custom! […] Well, tie me up, goddess! I must pay the penalty and remain bound until morning!" Diana responds: "And then you must become a little hunted deer—you're a game girl, Zoe!"[23]

Communication (also known as "negotiation") is required for giving and receiving consent. Participants may discuss BDSM role-playing scenes, possible risks and safety precautions, safe words or signals, and limits to play. Communication continues through a scene and after. When the Amazons perform the "doe hunt," both hunters and "doe-girls" obey the game's prescribed rules. After "Wonder Woman explains the tradition to Etta Candy," her best friend, Wonder Woman "shoots a doe—the arrow carries a rope with it and fastens itself to her doe suit [...], declaring, 'I've got you, deer!' But according to the role-playing roles, the doe-girl insists, 'Not until you pull me down!,' which Wonder Woman does."[24]

Caring is the attitude that dominant and submissive should have toward one another before, during, and after a scene. The scene instantly ends if either calls out her safe word. Later, both participants administer aftercare—actions they use to process and reflect on what transpired, attend to injuries, and provide comfort and validation. Aftercare doesn't necessarily end when a scene ends either. Both dominant and submissive may experience altered emotional or mental states, moments or days later. Wonder Woman, anxious to exert caring control over the reformed Baroness, even performs an act of self-bondage with her own lasso of compulsion: "I have tied myself with the magic lasso and now I command you, Diana Prince-Wonder Woman, never to use your influence over Paula for your own selfish purposes or to make yourself feel smart. It's a tremendous responsibility to shape another girl's life and I must do it right!"[25]

Caution is essential to BDSM, because role playing can be risky. Participants must know what they're doing. For example, a dominant has to be aware of how to bind her submissive safely if she wants to avoid harming her. A lot of importance is therefore placed on education, especially sharing knowledge from seasoned members of the community. As Wonder Woman is tying up the arms of a female antagonist, she explains: "On Paradise Island where we play many binding games this is considered the safest method of tying a girl's arms!"[26] It's considered the safest by those in the know.

Being a Good Mistress

As we've seen, BDSM themes appear in Marston's Wonder Woman, and themes from the ethics of care appear in both Wonder Woman and

BDSM themselves. After witnessing the negative effects of bondage and submission under a bad mistress, Wonder Woman contemplates: "If girls want to be slaves there's no harm in that. The bad thing for them is submitting to a master or to an evil mistress like Paula! A good mistress could do wonders with them!"[27]

But what makes for a good mistress—or dominant? What makes for an evil one? In the real-life BDSM community, the ethics of care addresses the difference directly.

A good (or moral) dominant affirms the needs of her submissive, knowing that she thereby also affirms her needs as a dominant. A good dominant is also attentive to the body language and mental state of her submissive. Failing to be so shows a lack of care and might cause physical or psychological harm. Further, a good dominant is competent in providing the care that she knows her submissive needs during and after a scene. She also acknowledges the vulnerable position that her submissive is in and respects her situation and individuality when negotiating a scene. Finally, a good dominant recognizes that her submissive has entrusted her welfare to her and assumes the responsibility for her care.

So what's an evil (or immoral) dominant? As with Noddings, Wonder Woman's idea of evil is inflicting harm, isolation, or helplessness on others. Even with those who'd wish her harm, Wonder Woman takes an attitude of caring. Not doing so would make her no more moral than her enemies.

Return to Paradise Island

Popular culture views Wonder Woman as a paradox. She's a powerful feminist, but she's also frequently bound up in ropes or chains. Marston never meant to have the feminist elements of Wonder Woman separate from her kinky elements. In hindsight, we can see that both sets of elements can be connected through the ethics of care.

In her latest incarnation for DC Comics, Wonder Woman is back to both her feminist and her BDSM roots. After Wonder Woman saves Steve Trevor, she presents him with a collar. Wonder Woman explains: "To save a life is to be tied to that life. Know that I will take care of you and keep you from harm. But first—you must be willing to submit to loving authority. Kneel for we are bound."[28] The scene illustrates a ritual in the BDSM community called "collaring." A dominant gives a collar to a submissive to indicate that the submissive's wellbeing is now her responsibility.

The next panel further highlights the BDSM connection. After being rebuffed by Steve Trevor, Wonder Woman explains to Beth (formerly Etta) Candy: "I don't understand. To bow before loving authority is to show strength. On Paradise Island, we pledge our bond with collar, bracelet, and chains."

In some places, people still do pledge their bond that way. They agree with Queen Hippolyte, in one of the last scripts that Marston wrote for the series: "The only real happiness for anybody is to be found in obedience to loving authority."[29]

Notes

1. William Moulton Marston, *March On! Facing Life with Courage* (New York: Doubleday, 1939), 131.
2. Marston (writer) and Harry G. Peter (artist), *Wonder Woman Chronicles*, vol. 1 (New York: DC Comics, 2010), 7.
3. Marston, *Emotions of Normal People* (New York: Routledge, 2014, reprint).
4. Noah Berlatsky, *Wonder Woman: Bondage and Feminism in the Marston/Peter Comics, 1941—1948* (New Brunswick, NJ: Rutgers University Press, 2015), 112.
5. Marston and Peter, *Sensation Comics* #46 (New York: DC Comics, October 1945).
6. Marston and Peter, *Wonder Woman Chronicles*, vol. 2 (New York: DC Comics, 2011), 75.
7. Marston and Peter, *Wonder Woman Chronicles*, vol. 3 (New York: DC Comics, 2012), 112.
8. Marston, *Emotions of Normal People*, 393.
9. Excerpted in Rosemarie Tong (ed.), *Feminist Thought: A More Comprehensive Introduction* (Boulder, CO: Westview Press, 2009, 3rd edition), 164–167.
10. Reprinted in Elizabeth Hackett and Sally Haslanger (eds), *Theorizing Feminisms: A Reader* (New York: Oxford University Press, 2006), 200–210.
11. Reprinted in Hackett and Haslanger, *Theorizing Feminisms*, 201–203.
12. Marston and Peter, *Wonder Woman Chronicles*, vol. 2, 155.
13. Marston and Peter, "Villainy Incorporated!" reprinted in *Wonder Woman: The Greatest Stories Ever Told* (New York: DC Comics, 2007), 37.

14. Marston and Peter, *Wonder Woman Chronicles*, vol. 2, 190.

15. Reprinted in Tong, *Feminist Thought*, 169.

16. Marston and Peter, *Wonder Woman Chronicles*, vol. 1, 11, 12.

17. Reprinted in Ann E. Cudd and Robin O. Andreasen (eds), *Feminist Theory: A Philosophical Anthology* (Malden, MA: Blackwell, 2005), 251–260.

18. Marston and Peter, "Villainy Incorporated!" 35.

19. Letter to C. Moulton [W.M. Marston], September 9, 1943, reprinted in Geoffrey C. Bunn, "The Lie Detector, Wonder Woman and Liberty: The Life and Work of William Moulton Marston," *History of the Human Sciences*, 10(1) (1997) 91–119.

20. Tristan Taormino, *The Ultimate Guide to Kink: BDSM, Role Play and the Erotic Edge* (Berkeley, CA: Cleis Press, 2012), 3.

21. D.J. Williams, Jeremy N. Thomas, Emily E. Prior, and M. Candace Christensen, "From 'SSC' and 'RACK' to the '4Cs': Introducing a New Framework for Negotiating BDSM Participation," *Electronic Journal of Human Sexuality* 17 (2014), http://www.ejhs.org/volume17/BDSM.html (accessed May 2, 2016).

22. Taormino, *The Ultimate Guide to Kink*, 6.

23. Marston and Peter, *Wonder Woman Chronicles*, vol. 2, 146–147.

24. Marston and Peter, *Wonder Woman Chronicles*, vol. 2, 148–149.

25. Marston and Peter, *Wonder Woman Chronicles*, vol. 3, 192.

26. Marston and Peter, *Sensation Comics* #35 (New York: DC Comics, November 1944).

27. Marston and Peter, *Wonder Woman Chronicles*, vol. 2, 175.

28. Grant Morrison (writer) and Yanick Paquette (artist), *Wonder Woman Earth One*, vol. 1 (New York: April 2016).

29. Marston and Peter, *Wonder Woman* #28 (New York: DC Comics, April, 1948).

Golden Lassos and Logical Paradoxes

Roy T. Cook and Nathan Kellen

Wonder Woman wields a number of magical Amazonian devices: her bulletproof bracelets, her invisible plane, and most importantly for this chapter, her golden lasso of truth. According to DC Comics' mythology, anyone bound with the golden lasso is magically compelled to tell the truth. But can a shiny magical rope always compel one to tell the truth?

The Two Rules of the Golden Lasso of Truth

Before answering this question, we should get a bit clearer about what, exactly, Wonder Woman's golden lasso does. The first thing to notice about the golden lasso is that evildoers bound by it are not only compelled to tell the truth if and when they answer questions, but also compelled to answer Wonder Woman's questions in the first place. In other words, villains (and everyone else) cannot dodge the effects of the golden lasso merely by remaining silent—rather, they are forced to answer the questions that are asked, and forced to answer truthfully.

The second thing to notice is that answering truthfully does not, in this context, necessarily mean uttering a true sentence. Rather, if a person is tied up with the golden lasso, then they are compelled to answer questions with what they believe is the truth. But not even

Wonder Woman and Philosophy: The Amazonian Mystique, First Edition.
Edited by Jacob M. Held.
© 2017 John Wiley & Sons, Ltd. Published 2017 by John Wiley & Sons, Ltd.

Wonder Woman can figure out the meaning of life by just tying up some random passerby and asking them. In short, the golden lasso of truth prevents people who are tied up with it from lying—that is, it prevents them from knowingly misleading the person asking the questions—but it does not prevent the person tied up from uttering false claims so long as they believe that the claims in question are true. Thus, we have the two rules of the golden lasso of truth:

1. A person tied up with the golden lasso must answer the questions posed to them.
2. A person tied up with the golden lasso must provide answers that they believe to be true.

Interestingly—and this will be important in what follows—the golden lasso of truth is not merely a tool wielded by Wonder Woman. In addition, it is an extension of her very nature, as noted in *JLA* #54:

> The *magic lasso*, for all its legendary power, is merely a *tool*, a *conduit* … a *symbol* of what Diana *is* at her very *core*. The *spirit of truth*.

As a result, Wonder Woman herself is unable, or at the very least unwilling, to lie unless compelled to by some external force. Tie Wonder Woman up with her own lasso and she might be rendered physically helpless, but this won't have any effect on what she can or cannot say. We can now answer the question with which we began this chapter: can Wonder Woman's golden lasso always compel people to tell the truth? The answer is "no." Imagine that Wonder Woman ties you up, and then asks: "Will your answer to this question be 'no'?"

By the second law of the golden lasso, you must answer the question. Since this is a simple "yes" or "no" question, presumably you must give one of these two answers. If you answer "yes," then you answered Wonder Woman's question affirmatively, and hence are agreeing that your answer to Wonder Woman's question is "no." But then you have not told the truth, since you actually answered "yes." If you answer "no," however, then your negative answer to Wonder Woman's question implies that your answer is not "no." But your answer was "no," so once again you are not telling the truth. Thus, even if you are tied up in Wonder Woman's magical golden lasso of truth, it is *impossible* to truthfully answer this question. We'll call this puzzle the *Paradox of the Golden Lasso*. This puzzle is a variant of the Liar Paradox, a 2000-year-old puzzle that arises by considering the Liar sentence: "This sentence is false."

Since this is a straightforward, meaningful, unambiguous declarative sentence, it is presumably either true or false. But it cannot be either. If it is true, then what it says must be the case, but since it says that it is false, this implies that it must be false (and no sentence can be both true and false). Similarly, if it is false then, since it says it is false, what it says is, in fact, the case. Hence it is true (and again, no sentence can be both). Thus, this sentence cannot be either true or false, despite its seemingly being a perfectly good declarative sentence.

Bizarra and Her Lasso

Things get even more interesting when we put Bizarra into the mix. Bizarra is Wonder Woman's Bizarro World analogue. She lives on Bizarro World, a cube-shaped planet which is also known as Htrae, with a number of other Bizarro superhero doppelgängers created by Bizarro #1, an imperfect clone of Superman. Residents of Bizarro World, including both Bizarro #1 and Bizarra, routinely replace one or more words in each of their utterances with antonyms for those words. Thus, if Bizarra wants to express something like "I always speak truthfully," she might actually say "Me never speak falsely." Interestingly, the claims uttered by Bizarra are, as a result, not always the opposite of what she intends to say. Instead, the relation between what Bizarra wants to express and what she actually says is determined by the number of such substitutions and their grammatical role in the sentence (notice that in the above example the two sentences are equivalent other than the ungrammatical use of "me" in the latter). Here, however, we will assume that Bizarra always says the opposite of what she intends to express, so if she wanted to (falsely) claim that she always speaks truthfully, she would say something like "Me sometimes speak falsely."

Also, like Wonder Woman, Bizarra has a magical lasso—the Bizarro golden lasso—which compels people bound by it to say the opposite of what they otherwise would have said. Thus, anyone bound by the Bizarro golden lasso who would normally say something true will instead say something false, and anyone who would otherwise say something false will instead speak the truth. The Bizarro golden lasso—a sort of mirror image of Wonder Woman's golden lasso, also obeys two rules:

1. A person tied up with the Bizarro golden lasso must answer all questions posed to them.
2. A person tied up with the Bizarro golden lasso must provide answers that are the opposite of what they would otherwise say.

Note that the parallel is not perfect, since the Bizarro golden lasso, as we shall see, does not always require that the person who is tied up provide answers that they think are false.

To see this, consider what happens when Bizarra is tied up with her own lasso, as happens in *Action Comics* #857.[1] In this situation, Bizarra speaks truthfully: her compulsion to lie and the Bizarro golden lasso's requirement that she say the opposite of what she would say if not tied up cancel each other out. Thus, unlike Wonder Woman, Bizarra will speak truthfully no matter which lasso is used to tie her up! Note that we can easily construct a Bizarro version of the Paradox of the Golden Lasso: we need merely tie up an (honest) person with the Bizarro golden lasso and then ask them: "Will your answer to this question be 'yes'?"

If she answers "yes," then what she says is true, since she did in fact answer "yes." If she answers "no," then again what she says is true, since her answer was not "yes." Further, she can easily work through this reasoning, and come to know that either answer to this question will be a true answer. Thus, it is impossible to answer this question non-truthfully, even if tied up with Bizarra's golden lasso.

Now, Wonder Woman's golden lasso and Bizarra's golden lasso look identical, so you can only tell which is which by attending to the different effects that each lasso has on the person who is tied up. In addition, detecting differences in such effects is not always easy. For example, if you stumble upon an otherwise honest person who is tied up with one or other of the two lassos, and neither Wonder Woman nor Bizarra is nearby, you can't just ask the tied up person: "Which lasso are you tied up with?"

If they are tied up with Wonder Woman's golden lasso, then they will tell the truth and say so, but if they are tied up with the Bizarro golden lasso they will lie, and say that they are tied up with Wonder Woman's lasso. Varying this setup slightly, we come to our puzzles:[2]

Puzzle 1: Imagine Wonder Woman is tied up with one of the lassos. What question can you ask her to determine which lasso it is?

Solutions to the puzzles, or hints pointing toward such solutions, are provided at the end of this chapter. More complicated puzzles involving the lassos are not hard to construct. The following puzzle involves a bit of subtle reasoning about epistemology—that is, about knowledge and how we come to have it:

Puzzle 2: Imagine that you tie Wonder Woman up with her own lasso, but you tell her it is Bizarra's golden lasso (and she has no reason not to believe you). You then ask her "Which lasso is this?" twice. What will her answer be each time?

Here is another, more difficult puzzle:

Puzzle 3: Imagine that either Wonder Woman or Bizarra is tied up with one of the lassos and hidden behind a screen (and whoever is behind the screen knows which lasso she is tied up with). You can ask whoever it is behind the screen a question, and you can hear the answer, but you cannot tell by looking whether the person behind the screen is Bizarra or Wonder Woman, or which lasso was used to tie up the person in question. What single question can you ask to determine who is behind the screen?

Finally, for extra credit, we conclude this section with an extremely hard problem—a variant of George Boolos's "Hardest Logic Puzzle Ever" (1996):

Extra credit: Imagine that there are three screens, and behind each screen is either Wonder Woman, Bizarra, or Harley Quinn. Each of Wonder Woman and Bizarra is tied up with one of the lassos, but you don't know who is tied up with which lasso. Harley Quinn is not tied up, and since she is both a lunatic and a troublemaker she provides completely random answers to any question asked of her. Any question you ask can only be asked of one of the three women behind the screens. What three questions can you ask such that, after hearing the answers, you know which woman is behind each screen?

Revenge of the Magic Lassos

Let's return to the original Paradox of the Golden Lasso. Wonder Woman ties you up with the golden lasso and asks you: "Will your answer to this question be 'no'?"

We assumed that the only permissible way to answer this question is by uttering either "yes" or "no," and showed that neither answer will work. But perhaps this was too quick. Perhaps there are other answers that we might give. For example, perhaps we can get out of the paradox by answering "I don't know" or "my answer will be neither 'yes' nor 'no'" or "maybe."

While at first glance this approach looks promising, there are problems. If we try to answer Wonder Woman's question merely by saying that we don't know which of "yes" or "no" is the right answer, then we don't seem to get very far. The reason is simple: the reasoning of the puzzle doesn't just show that we can't *figure out* which of "yes" or "no" is the correct answer—rather, it shows that neither of these can *be* the correct answer. Further, if we give this answer (or any answer other than "yes" or "no") then we have given an answer other than "no," so it seems like the correct answer should have been "no," leading us right back into the original puzzle.

Even if we could answer Wonder Woman's question appropriately by saying something like "neither" or "maybe," we can easily construct a new paradox that we cannot solve this way. Imagine you are tied up, and when Wonder Woman asks her original question you answer by saying "maybe," and let's imagine further that this answer is okay. Then Wonder Woman can generate a new version of the puzzle—one that we'll call the *Revenge Paradox of the Golden Lasso*—by asking: "Will your answer to this question be either 'no' or 'maybe'?"

Now, even if our options have been broadened, and we are allowed to respond to yes-or-no questions with any of "yes," "no," or "maybe," none of these will work here. If we say "yes," then we are agreeing that we will say either "no" or "maybe," not "yes," so we are lying. If we say either of "no" or "maybe," however, then we did answer the question with one of these two options, so our answer should have actually been "yes." Thus, the puzzle arises anew even if we allow ourselves more options. This is a version of a phenomenon known as the Revenge Problem, which originally arose with respect to purported solutions to the Liar Paradox. When faced with the Liar sentence: "This sentence is false," many theorists decided that the right way to proceed was to deny that it was either true or false, and claim that it had some third status instead—call this third status "other." On this sort of view, every sentence is either true, false, or other, and no sentence falls into more than one of these categories. Most everyday sentences remain either true or false, but problematic sentences such as the Liar sentence receive the value "other" instead. The problem then arises when we consider the Revenge Liar sentence: "This sentence is either false or other."

By following reasoning similar to that given for the Revenge Paradox of the Golden Lasso, it is easy to see that this sentence cannot be true, and cannot be false, and cannot be other.

Other Topics in Lasso Logic

These examples show that contemplating Wonder Woman's golden lasso, and Bizarra's golden lasso, can provide us with a wealth of interesting and entertaining paradoxes and puzzles. But these are not *merely* puzzles that can entertain us for a few moments. On the contrary, the study of the nature of truth is one of the most important sub-disciplines of philosophy. This is not surprising, of course, since figuring out what truth is and how we are to determine which claims are true and which claims are not is critical to successfully navigating the world and achieving our goals, whatever they might be. The Paradox of the Golden Lasso, like the Liar Paradox before it, shows that there is something wrong with our intuitive notion of truth, and thus we need to examine that intuitive conception in order to correct it and arrive at an understanding of truth that is not subject to paradoxes and contradictions. Further, one of the most fruitful ways to collect data for this project is via consideration of additional paradoxes and puzzles such as the ones outlined above. Thus, the study of such logical enigmas is not only entertaining, but can also provide insights into how truth works, and how things go wrong in cases like the Liar Paradox and the Paradox of the Golden Lasso.

Paradoxes based on or related to the Liar Paradox are not the only way that Wonder Woman's golden lasso can be used to illustrate philosophical issues pertaining to truth, however. We will conclude by mentioning two.

The first is addressed in Matt Wagner's Batman/Superman/Wonder Woman tale titled *Trinity*.[3] In this comic, Wonder Woman attempts to subdue Bizarro #1 by binding him with the golden lasso. Instead of remaining a captive of the magical, unbreakable rope, Bizarro #1 does the unthinkable—he *breaks* the golden lasso. The narration that accompanies this scene is telling:

> Confused. Its fractured brain is bombarded by an overwhelming urge … something of which it can make no sense. The awful, unthinkable concept of … **truth.** (p. 102, emphasis in original)

In this comic, Bizarro #1's habit of substituting antonyms into his speech is explained in terms of his having no understanding of what truth is—that is, his having no conception of an objective sense of getting things right or wrong. Of course, philosophers have often questioned whether there is an objective, absolute notion of truth—that is, a sense in which we can get things right in an unbiased, definitive, universal sense. Thus, the shattering of the supposedly unbreakable golden lasso vividly illustrates the idea of imposing a view of truth as objective and independent of our own opinions and actions onto a portion of the world—in this case, Bizarro #1—to which such notions utterly fail to apply.

Even more interesting is an episode that occurs in *JLA* #49, written by Mark Waid.[4] In this issue the JLA, including Wonder Woman, battle the Queen of Fables, a fictional character who has been magically brought to life and who is terrorizing Earth due to the mistaken belief that Wonder Woman is a princess of fairy tales. Nothing is literally true of fictional characters, since they do not exist. Thus, since the Queen of Fables and her minions are fictional, and not real, truth does not apply to them. As a result, the queen's huntsman is able to snap the golden lasso easily.

This story, in effect, addresses philosophical issues at the heart of the philosophy of fiction, since it delves into the difference between what is correct to say about fictional characters—that is, what is fictionally true (e.g., Sherlock Holmes lives on Baker Street)—versus what is literally true of the actual world (e.g., Sherlock Holmes does not live on Baker Street, since there is no such person). Understanding this distinction, and explaining why it is permissible, and even desirable, to make claims about fictional characters that are, taken literally, quite false, is one of the central projects of contemporary philosophy of fiction.

Of course, we have barely scratched the surface with regard to the various aspects of truth that can be, and have been, explored via the use of Wonder Woman's golden lasso of truth (and, to a lesser extent, via Bizarra's golden lasso). There are no doubt more to be discovered in the 75 years of Wonder Woman comics, many more puzzles and paradoxes to be studied. As Bizarra would say, so long as she isn't tied up with a lasso: "You no learn about truth by not read comics."

Solutions

Puzzle 1. Just ask her whether $1 + 1 = 2$. If she says "yes," it is the golden lasso, since the golden lasso compels her to speak truthfully, and if she says "no," then it is the Bizarro golden lasso, since the Bizarro golden lasso compels her to speak falsely.

Puzzle 2. When you ask the first question, Wonder Woman believes that she is tied up with Bizarra's golden lasso. Since she always intends to speak truthfully, she will intend to say something like "I am tied up with Bizarra's lasso," but because she believes that she is tied up with the Bizarro golden lasso she will expect to actually hear herself say something like "I am tied up with my own lasso." Given that she is tied up with her own lasso, however, she will in fact say something like "I am tied up with Bizarra's lasso," as this is what she believes. This mismatch between what she expects and what actually happens will clue her in to the fact that she is actually tied up with her own lasso, so when you ask her the second time she will say something like "I am tied up with my own lasso."

Puzzle 3. Ask: "If you were tied up in the other lasso (i.e., not the one you are tied up with now) and someone pointed to Wonder Woman and asked "Is that Wonder Woman?" what would you say?" There are four possible cases to consider:

1. The woman behind the screen is Wonder Woman and she is tied up with the golden lasso. If Wonder Woman were instead tied up with the Bizarro golden lasso and we pointed to Wonder Woman and asked "Is that Wonder Woman?" she would say "no." Since Wonder Woman is actually tied up with the golden lasso, she will tell the truth and say "no."

2. The woman behind the screen is Wonder Woman and she is tied up with the Bizarro golden lasso. If Wonder Woman were instead tied up with the golden lasso and we pointed to Wonder Woman and asked "Is that Wonder Woman?" she would say "yes." Since Wonder Woman is actually tied up with the Bizarro golden lasso, she will lie and say "no."

3. The woman behind the screen is Bizarra and she is tied up with the golden lasso. If Bizarra were instead tied up with the Bizarro golden lasso and we pointed to Wonder Woman and asked "Is that Wonder Woman?" she would say "yes." Since Bizarra is actually tied up with the Bizarro golden lasso, she will tell the truth and say "yes."

4. The woman behind the screen is Bizarra and she is tied up with the Bizarro golden lasso. If Bizarra were instead tied up with the golden lasso and we pointed to Wonder Woman and asked "Is that Wonder Woman?" she would say "yes." Since Bizarra is actually tied up with the Bizarro golden lasso, she will tell the truth and say "yes."

Thus, if the answer to this question is "no," then it is Wonder Woman behind the screen: Wonder Woman will either tell the truth about the fact that she would lie in the hypothetical situation described in the question (case i), or she will lie about the fact that she would tell the truth in the hypothetical situation (case ii). If the answer is "yes," then it is Bizarra. Since either lasso compels her to tell the truth, she will tell the truth about the fact that she would tell the truth in the hypothetical situation described, regardless of which lasso was actually used to tie her up.

Note that this question allows you to determine whether it is Wonder Woman or Bizarra behind the screen, but does not allow you to know which lasso she is tied up with. (You would need a second question to learn that!)

Extra credit. The solution to this puzzle is too complicated to include here, but we will provide two hints for the ambitious reader. First, what you ask for your second and third questions might depend on the answer you receive for previous questions. Second, at the end of the three questions you will know which of the three women hidden behind the screens is Wonder Woman, which is Bizarra, and which is Harley Quinn, but you still might not know which lasso each of the first two women is bound with (compare **Puzzle 3**). This puzzle is a variation on George Boolos's "World's Hardest Logic Puzzle," which the reader is encouraged to look up for further information and clues.[5]

Notes

1. Geoff Johns, Richard Donner, and Eric Powell, *Superman: Escape from Bizarro World* (New York: DC Comics, 2008).
2. These puzzles are variations on Raymond Smullyan's knights and knaves puzzles—e.g., *What is the Name of this Book?* (Upper Saddle River, NJ: Prentice Hall, 1978). In Smullyan's original puzzles (as well as in many other puzzles based on his setup), knights are a group of people who always tell the truth, and knaves always lie. In our examples, Wonder Woman plays the role of a knight, and Bizarra the role of a knave, although these roles can switch depending on whether they are tied up with one or another of the two lassos.
3. Matt Wagner *et al.*, *Trinity* (New York: DC Comics, 2004).
4. Mark Waid, Bryan Hitch, *et al.*, *JLA:* #5 (New York: DC Comics, 2014).
5. George Boolos, "The Hardest Logic Puzzle Ever," *The Harvard Review of Philosophy*, 6 (1996) 62–65.

Index

Wonder Woman and Philosophy: The Amazonian Mystique, First Edition.
Edited by Jacob M. Held.
© 2017 John Wiley & Sons, Ltd. Published 2017 by John Wiley & Sons, Ltd.